TOLERATING STRANGERS IN INTOLERANT TIMES

Psychoanalytic, Political and Philosophical Perspectives

Roger Kennedy

LONDON AND NEW YORK

First published 2019
by Routledge
2 Park Square, Milton Park, Abingdon, Oxon OX14 4RN

and by Routledge
711 Third Avenue, New York, NY 10017

Routledge is an imprint of the Taylor & Francis Group, an informa business

© 2019 Roger Kennedy

The right of Roger Kennedy to be identified as author of this work has been asserted by him in accordance with sections 77 and 78 of the Copyright, Designs and Patents Act 1988.

All rights reserved. No part of this book may be reprinted or reproduced or utilised in any form or by any electronic, mechanical, or other means, now known or hereafter invented, including photocopying and recording, or in any information storage or retrieval system, without permission in writing from the publishers.

Trademark notice: Product or corporate names may be trademarks or registered trademarks, and are used only for identification and explanation without intent to infringe.

British Library Cataloguing in Publication Data
A catalogue record for this book is available from the British Library

Library of Congress Cataloging in Publication Data
A catalog record for this title has been requested

ISBN: 978-1-138-36024-2 (hbk)
ISBN: 978-1-138-36025-9 (pbk)
ISBN: 978-0-429-43247-7 (ebk)

Typeset in Bembo
by Taylor & Francis Books

Printed and bound in Great Britain by
TJ International Ltd, Padstow, Cornwall

CONTENTS

1	Fear of strangers: Whose home is it?	1
2	Strangers to ourselves	16
3	Home and identity	32
4	The early history of tolerance	46
5	Spinoza, Locke, and Bayle	57
6	Later Enlightenment: From Voltaire to the American Revolution	77
7	John Stuart Mill, liberty, and the harm principle: Towards modern liberal tolerance	95
8	Plurality and tolerance: Some key modern views on tolerance	108
9	Tolerance and the arts	132
10	Conclusions: The tolerance process	142

References   *146*
Index   *152*

1

FEAR OF STRANGERS

Whose home is it?

The tolerance issue

Zygmunt Bauman has said that 'Modern living means living with strangers, and living with strangers is at all times a precarious, unnerving and testing life',[1] challenging us to understand the strains of how we may come to live alongside those who appear to us as strange and who may enter our social space and cause us all sorts of anxieties about our sense of identity. Such a challenge inevitably means looking at ourselves and the basis of that sense of identity.

The sense of *home* as the basis of our sense of self, the place we need in order to feel secure, is fundamental. Yet we often feel within ourselves, to a greater or lesser extent, incomplete, divided, and lacking a sense of unity. There is a yearning for wholeness, for a home where we can feel truly ourselves, but this yearning can also cause us considerable unhappiness. Some carry a firm sense of home within; they know where they belong. Others need something external, such as an ideology or a political movement to give them security; yet others need a being that transcends daily life such as a God in order to feel complete. Whatever the nature of the home we seek, the fear of *homelessness* is never far from that of the sense of being at home.

I would suggest that a fear of a loss of home, or more fundamentally a fear of a loss of a psychic structure which provides a central core of our identity—a *'psychic home'*[2]—accounts for a considerable amount of prejudiced and intolerant attitudes to strangers; that basic fears about being displaced by strangers from our precious and precarious sense of a psychic home can tear communities apart, as well as lead to discrimination against those who appear to be different and, with this, a lack of openness and hospitality towards foreigners; that this fear of the loss of home accounts for a certain amount of fear of otherness and of 'foreignness'. This intolerant attitude makes peaceful coexistence between groups of people with different histories, cultures, and identities, which is the basis of tolerance[3] very difficult at times. Yet one of the major political issues today is how to manage or *accommodate* all the different communities within society with the least amount of turmoil, both managing perceptions and beliefs between different groups, but also within groups where intolerance of difference can be just as problematic.

In order to make sense of these kinds of problem, I shall explore in detail issues of *tolerance* and *intolerance*, as well as the role of the *stranger* and *strangeness* in provoking basic fears about our identity. The aim of this exploration is to attempt to answer the question—is a respectful and human world possible in intolerant times? I will be following a three-pronged approach—looking at intolerant states of mind, the social and political history of tolerance, and what kind of structures would be necessary for managing intolerance and encouraging tolerant thinking. It is proposed that any consideration of tolerance has to be proactive in facing intolerance, and how intolerant states of mind and practices can undermine open public debate.

A main preoccupation of much liberal thinking, exemplified in the work of John Rawls, is how to find a way of managing a 'diversity of opposing and irreconcilable religious, philosophical, and moral doctrines'[4] and how 'reasonable' citizens might live together peacefully in a just world.[5] The notion of tolerance is often embedded in these approaches to managing differences. However, while I will look at general political theory and practice from time to time, the main intention throughout the book will be to focus on just the tolerance element and the tolerance/intolerance dynamic, which is often embedded in liberal political theories and only occasionally explored in detail. I will also aim to look at *different kinds of tolerance*, of which there are several, and what kind of tolerance is most likely to lead to the most effective way of managing conflicting views and values within and between communities.

I hardly think it is an exaggeration to maintain that currently fears about the stability of society, the threat of 'foreign' invasion, and a tendency for societies and majorities in whole nations to turn inwards, predominates many Western countries, at times creating an ugly atmosphere of suspicion and prejudice towards those perceived as different and hence dangerous, whether they be minorities within society or those wishing to enter our society. The new intolerance includes fears about the 'hordes' of immigrants—a fear which is often confused with realistic fears about terrorist attacks—populist fears about loss of cultural integrity and with it a sense of powerlessness, and fearful debates about such basics as truth, the so-called 'post truth' issue. Such fears, as I shall explore, mirror old arguments going back centuries to the early enlightenment thinkers and even before, when the parameters of discussion about tolerance were mainly around religious tolerance. There is an urgent need to address these kinds of issue once more at a time when the 'ground rules' of what makes for a civilized society seem to be under threat.

It may be the case that the so-called liberal consensus has been responsible for some of the alienation of many people towards government due to an excessive focus on the rights of minorities over the needs of the so-called majority, rather than looking at the fears and anxieties of both positions. If that is so, that gap needs to be addressed, but not by intemperately sweeping aside the foundations of a decent society. Hence, looking at the origins of liberal thinking in the early Enlightenment may help to clarify current confused positions, as can looking at how the notion of tolerance developed around issues concerning religious intolerance. While the freedom to practice different faiths may not be the most pressing of contemporary concerns, nonetheless how religious intolerance was managed in the past, when religion played a key role in society, can have considerable relevance to how intolerance towards different contemporary beliefs, opinions, and assumptions is managed.

But management of such differences can be a complex and at times almost impossible task, however necessary for social stability. As Bernard Williams pointed out, if there is to be a question of tolerance, then something needs to be tolerated, some belief or practice or way of life of one group of people that another group of people may disapprove of. There is an essential ambivalence at work when one considers tolerance. If one group hates another group, then what is needed is to lose that hatred, but this imposes a difficult task, involving fundamental *tensions*. It can be very challenging for one group to shift in their views and perceptions of another group. Inclusiveness is not an easy undertaking.

> If we are asking people to be tolerant, we are asking something more complicated than this. They will indeed have to lose something, their desire to suppress or drive out the rival belief; but they will also keep something, their commitment to their own beliefs, which is what gave them their desire in the first place. There is a tension here between one's commitments and the acceptance that other people may have other and perhaps quite distasteful commitments. This is the tension that is typical of toleration, and the tension which makes it so difficult.[6]

Of course an attention to tolerance and intolerance does not provide a full answer to how to manage these kinds of social tensions. As Michael Walzer[7] has written, intolerance is commonly most virulent when differences of culture, ethnicity or race coincide with class differences. The latter issues will also have to be tackled, but that is not my theme in this study.

Tolerance is a notion with elusive and multiple meanings, moving away from and towards the use of the term in social and political contexts, and any consideration of tolerance invariably means bringing in issues of intolerance. One can just tolerate something, or only tolerate it, or barely tolerate it. Tolerance has certain limits, depending on the context. For example, there may come a point in any group where someone's behaviour goes too far and they test the tolerance of other group members; they may be too drunk, they may be too insulting, increasingly bizarre or mad, or too aggressive to be tolerated within the group and so may be expelled. But equally a group can become too easily intolerant of minor differences, through ignorance or prejudice. Being tolerated can feel like an attack if it is skin deep, so mere tolerance can be wounding. There is so-called zero-tolerance, an ironic use of the word to mask intolerance in one context or just to indicate a strong boundary in another. One can be too tolerant, for example as a parent, or not tolerant enough. No one would want to tolerate incompetence, except the incompetent. There is organ tolerance, when transplanted organs are accepted from a donor, and engineering tolerance, where a design has enough extra capacity to withstand damage or loss of some of the structure. An addict can become tolerant to a drug and need more and more of it to have the same effect.

The notion of tolerance has natural links to a number of other notions such as freedom, autonomy, and respect, and so tends to merge with these sorts of ways of understanding individual and social realities. However, tolerance usually implies some kind of managing of conflicts between different beliefs and values in a variety of different circumstances, from questions about limitations on the sales of alcohol to whether or not female genital mutilation should be banned, from whether or not use of cannabis should be legalized to whether or not there should be a limitation on the public display of religious clothing, how far immigrant communities should integrate into their host country, and how differences between and within communities are managed.

It comes into contentious issues such as the question whether or not cartoons of the Prophet Mohammed should be published. Those who believe in absolute free speech and expression of opinion might well say they should be published. Those who consider this would be sacrilegious would be for censorship of such images. These first two options are absolute opinions. But others could argue that one cannot ignore the feelings and views of minorities, whatever one's own viewpoint, nor can one ignore current social and political realities, for example that such publication would be bound to be an incendiary act, and that thus a 'reasoned discretion' might be wiser, while encouraging debate and airing of opposing views before coming out with a definitive answer. For the latter process to be possible, a tolerant default position would seem to be essential. Whatever the final outcome, at least a process of inquiry with a chance to bring to light opposing views might be therapeutic, or at least give both sides of the debate pause to consider their position. Of course this is probably an optimistic vision of how to manage oppositional attitudes. For tolerance to have a crucial place in managing conflict, it would need to be integrated at various levels—at the level of top down or vertical structures at the state level, at the horizontal level between people, and at the level of organizations involving different group structures.

There is a minimalist view of tolerance as a useful way of organizing thoughts about how to manage different ways of life with the minimum of conflict in a good enough way; or, as I would favour, a wider view of tolerance as being necessary to develop human individuality, independence and well-being, enlarging the range of human options and possibilities, and involving a process of inquiry and reasoned debate. But, whatever one's notion of tolerance, it does require the presence of quite a complex attitude of mind. As Preston King[8] pointed out, there is the logical aspect, where a double negative is often in play; that is there is both an objection to something and then *not* acting on the objection. And there is the psychological aspect involving restraint, despite the urge to act. He describes two elements, the *objection* component, the initial element that enters into every case of tolerance and which, hopefully, involves some form of assessment of the situation, and the *acceptance* component, an act which follows from the initial assessment. Of course without any act of assessment or judgment, there might well be plain intolerance. The act of acceptance has various degrees, ranging from minimal to maximal acceptance. Tolerance could then be seen as a special form of liberty, a socially generated power either to remove an obstacle or to rescue a benefit. It also has certain risks or side-effects about which one must be wary—it can become an excuse for being paternalistic, for example by justifying the use of power arbitrarily and then perpetuating inequalities in the name of liberty, and hence I would add, there is the need to add some modifying or 'safeguarding' principles, into tolerance thinking in order to reduce this danger.

Tolerance[9] as a central concept arose in the Enlightenment period in the context of the religious and political conflicts throughout Europe following the Reformation; those conflicts reached a peak with the Thirty Years War (1618–1648) and were brought to an uneasy end by the Treaty of Westphalia, with the hope of a lasting European peace. In the course of time tolerance became a significant political issue, rather than just one requiring some sort of permissive or benevolent attitude to religious differences, with the formation of the modern state, the separation of governmental and religious powers, and the emerging concept of the individual citizen's entitlement to rights. The favouring of tolerance but within limits as a way of managing intense differences in beliefs still holds today.

An ability to manage conflict is very much involved in the day to day work of psychoanalysis, and so it would seem reasonable for a psychoanalyst to make a contribution, however limited, to the wider issues of the role of tolerance in both human relations and political life.

As I shall discuss in detail later, one can adopt **two basic limiting principles** to be applied on the part of both sides of a potential conflict; these limits may act in accord or be taken separately in any situation under consideration. **The first limiting principle** is the '*harm principle*', borrowed from J. S. Mill,[10] my version of which states that one needs to tolerate people's practices, beliefs or values provided they do not significantly harm the current society and offend the basic rights of its citizens. The **second principle** limiting prejudice and based on Rainer Forst's thinking[11] and that of John Rawls[12] is the '*respect principle*', that is, any action towards others starts with the assumption of the right for people to receive *mutual* respect for different ways of life, based on a reasoned and empathic or at least sympathetic judgment of the other's behaviour, ideas, and values.

With these two principles in action, I will suggest that one can develop a notion of '***Subject Tolerance***'. By this I mean that one *respects* the other and others as subjects *of* their experience, with agency and capacity for independent judgment. This contrasts with '***Object Tolerance***', when the other and others are put up with as mere objects, to be treated as subject *to* those in power. Subject tolerance requires a

tolerant internal space as much as a capacity to respect the right of others to hold different beliefs. This allows for the individual to hold in their imagination the possibility that their own views may be incorrect, only partially true, or open to debate. That is, one has to assume that one is capable of intolerant ways of thinking in order to find a way through to tolerance of the other. The degree to which others are treated as subjects will of course vary, providing a complex interplay between subject and object tolerance. In a clinical setting, one could imagine a patient moving from a position of object tolerance to subject tolerance as their capacity to 'become a subject', with increased agency, develops.[13]

Subject tolerance also begins with an attitude of being open towards the unknown, the strange and unfamiliar. This is a wide view of tolerance, not one limited to managing differences of views and opinions, but rather a fundamental way of managing interpersonal relations at the individual and group level by an opening out towards the strange and unfamiliar. The two limiting principles have the role of enhancing or protecting subject tolerance.

To give just a brief example illustrating the two limiting principles at work, it would be incorrect to tolerate someone who showed no mercy, who considered beheading hostages and displaying their action on the internet as acceptable, as it would be inconsistent with both the harm and respect principle. Such active intolerance in these and similar circumstances can be accorded the label of 'evil' as it goes beyond what is generally accepted as human or legal.

However, even the harm and respect principles in ordinary life are open to interpretation and each may conflict with the other. For example, controversially, in 2004, the French decided to ban Muslim girls wearing conspicuous religious symbols, including the Hijab or headscarf, at school or in any other public space. The ban on the wearing of religious symbols included the wearing of Jewish skullcaps and large Christian crosses. The justification for this law was that the wearing of these religious symbols went against the principle of the French principle of 'laicity', that France was a secular state. The argument was that what people did in private was their own business but when they went into public spaces such as schools, then the wider issue of what was compatible with the values of the state had to be primary. In 2011 it became illegal to wear any face covering but not the headscarf. For those opposed to the ban, it was argued that the banning of the veil went against the values of the Muslim families and hence did not respect their way of life and traditions. A counter argument was that the veil represented female oppression or servitude—a view strongly denied by many Muslim women who feel their veil is a free reflection of their faith.

The harm principle, to which I shall return when considering the work of Mill, is also open to interpretation and its application depends upon context and values. For example, when considering the issue of gay marriage, fundamentalist Christians have argued that this offends the 'integrity' of marriage, as based upon God's law. Thus opening up marriage to gay people would cause harm to fundamentalists by causing emotional and spiritual discomfort. However, disenfranchised gay people would argue strongly that this harm is not equivalent to theirs when their own bodily and mental integrity is undermined by not being allowed to marry.[14] Hence the powerful argument here in favour of gay marriage is that preventing access to it for millions of people greatly harms their well-being, and that this harm is not equivalent to the mental discomfort felt by those who dislike the idea of gay marriage.

The point here is that there are no absolutes in this field where differences in values, beliefs, and attitudes towards other human beings are in play. We can only provide a structure for thinking about these matters, and they certainly do need to be thought about very seriously. Using a tolerance framework can be helpful in this regard as a way of facilitating shifts in attitudes between groups in conflict. It is not irrational for people to hold different values, beliefs, and attitudes, but irrationality may well come into play, particularly when people's long-held views about life are challenged or come up against equally strongly held views.

The fact that tolerance has to be seen in a social and political context, has limits or boundaries that may have to be defined but can be difficult and ambiguous to define, and yet offers a complex and rich way of thinking, makes it very suitable for addressing modern issues in a diverse, complex, and at times divided society. The results of this way of thinking are not always clear, and one may end up with a number of incompatible alternatives, but sometimes experiencing the 'journey' itself is more instructive or therapeutic than arriving at a destination.

While there is a strong case for considering that intolerance is generally a bad thing, ultimately not good for social cohesion, harms the victims of intolerance in unacceptable ways and can even be morally wrong, it is far from easy to make the case for tolerance. It is also an unfortunate fact that intolerance can sustain group identity, giving people a target to aim at, a sense of coherence and even meaning; combatting intolerance can then require considerable personal and social resources. Defining the boundaries of what can be tolerated or not tolerated requires *hard work*.[15] Such work is necessary given the hard reality that intolerance tends to come and go, is rarely absent and just when you think that its excesses have been defeated, it is just as likely to burst through some weak point in a society's structure.

The two examples I mentioned above also bring into focus the so-called 'paradox' of tolerance. Put simply, one could argue that if you believe in tolerance, then that could mean even accepting the intolerant person's right to express and promote their intolerant views. Thus there could be a tolerant racist, whose extreme racist views could be described as tolerant if he or she just showed reasonable restraint in his or her actions. Apart from the unlikely situation that such a racist could be so restrained, the point is that other considerations need to come into play around making judgments about the boundaries of tolerance. For example, anything, which makes it virtually, or actually, impossible to have a tolerant society or situation, needs to be checked in some way or neutralized. So intolerant attitudes such as racism poison society and make it difficult or impossible for different races and religions and ways of life to coexist. Therefore the principle of toleration is denied or even destroyed by certain kinds of strongly held and menacing beliefs and also in certain kinds of political regimes, such as totalitarian states, where different views cannot anyway be openly expressed. Violent fascist parties simply do not accept the basic values that go into making a tolerant society; for such people tolerance is a dangerous concept, as it requires judgment, openness to thinking, and the acceptance of uncertainty. It would be reasonable then not to tolerate, or anyway to put some kind of restrictive boundaries around, a political party that promoted intolerance as their organizing principle. The same applies to those who hold beliefs where there is a refusal to ever enter into an open debate about different views. This would include those such as terrorists who often have a fixed fantasy that it is only through destruction that a new purified world can be achieved. The appropriate, and effective, way, of dealing with these kinds of challenge to political and social stability would be to find ways of managing them, not trying to create a setting where their views and practices can be facilitated.

Therefore, reasonable measures need to be put into place to maintain freedom of expression embedded in the notion of tolerance; neutrality in this area is, I would maintain, not possible. Certain basic values are bound to come into play in these sorts of considerations, values such as respect for others, and the right to debate issues in a way where there is a wish to understand the other's viewpoint. And all kinds of *judgment* will have to be made about what may or may not be tolerable in the thought and behaviour of individuals and groups. Tolerance in one sense has been described[16] as being non-judgmental; it implies, for example, accepting a situation or a person's different views and customs. On the other hand, because of the many and conflicting issues involved in any situation where differences between people interact, judgment about values and arguments for and against tolerating a practice or an attitude or a policy, and therefore debate, have to come into the picture. A reluctance to judge may be a symptom of disinterest or moral cowardice, a reluctance to confront difficult and embarrassing questions.

There may be a temptation or even a need to tolerate one aspect of a situation for the gain of another more advantageous position, or even a view that indulgence of, or indifference to, an objectionable situation is better than nothing. This form of tolerance implies that live and let live is the most we can expect from being with strangers in a complex world and that having an open dialogue and listening to what the other has to say may just be too much to expect. This would be a minimum form of tolerance, but I suspect not one that provides for social stability, because it would be too precarious. Genuine tolerance depends on human subjects understanding, or at least trying to understand, where each comes from, and this means an *acceptance of otherness*. This is what I mean by 'Subject Tolerance'. This is a wider view of tolerance than just seeing it as managing a difference of opinion or conflicting views.

However, merely using political or philosophical arguments in favour of, or against, the value of tolerance misses out the *emotional* context driving intolerant states of mind and attitudes, which more often than not overrides or ignores rational argument. There are times when no amount of enlightened thinking, however radical and progressive, can sway those influenced by prejudice and fear.

Unless such fears and prejudices are addressed, both by understanding their basis, and, if necessary, confronting the fantasies accompanying them, no amount of rational argument will be effective in reducing intolerance. There is a need to explore tolerant and intolerant states of mind and their relation with different kinds of fantasy, teasing out the different 'narratives of intolerance'.

Realistic threats of terrorism, the creation of the notion of a '*homeland*' that needs to be *defended* against those aiming to destabilize society both from abroad and from within, spilling over into irrational 'populist' movements which focus on fears about being swamped by millions of immigrants and such like, all echo many of the preoccupations of the times when religious wars and fears of society being plunged into chaos by heresies or by radical thinkers abounded, putting societies, as now, into considerable conflict. Hence the relevance of reexamining the thought of those such as Pierre Bayle, John Locke, Benedict Spinoza, and others, who considered the nature and boundaries of tolerance and the dire consequences of intolerance in those equally dark times.

But tolerance is not an easy topic and is full of pitfalls. One person's or community's tolerance may be another's intolerance and vice versa. Total tolerance of the other is naïve and may even be dangerous. Nor is tolerance a one-way process; it requires some sort of *mutual* understanding, based upon a willingness to at least understand the other point of view. It is an *inter-subjective* process. And there are boundaries to draw or frontiers to define, based on public *debate*, however difficult this may be. Yet without some degree of tolerance and without an examination of the issues raised in the tolerance debate, I maintain that we will be lost in an ever-increasing cycle of violence and prejudice. Even thinking about tolerance opens up dangerous and controversial areas of thought and practice, yet without some such notion we would not be human.

Voltaire[17] wrote that, 'If one religion only were allowed in England, the government would very possibly become arbitrary; if there were but two, the people would cut one another's throats, but as there are such a multitude, they all live happy and in peace.' Though of course this may now seem a rather idealized view of English society, it does point to the value of a pluralistic society, where differences, far from being merely the source of conflict, are also the basis of mutual benefit. Maintaining the 'peace' in such a society is a complex business, but what is often missing in looking at these difficult issues is psychological understanding of what motivates intolerant attitudes. That does not justify intolerance or provide easy solutions to a complex social and political situation, but can help to focus thinking and inform actions. Contemporary dilemmas are often focused around the ever-shifting boundary between state power and interference and individual liberty of action, belief, and opinion. In a dangerous world, with terrorist threats, as well as the threat of climate change, governments must act; but we still need to question how far they can do so. Can the 'soul', our private inner world, be kept free from government interference as Locke maintained was necessary, when there is so much minute intrusion into our lives?

Incidentally, there is another strange contemporary resonance with the times of religious conflicts—the underlying role of severe climate change in creating global instability and uncertainty. Geoffrey Parker in his book *Global Crisis*, points out that the world in the seventeenth century was rarely without war of some kind; more wars took place around the world than at any other era before the Second World War. As well as interstate conflicts, the mid-seventeenth century also witnessed more civil wars than any previous or subsequent period, ranging from the conflicts between Ming and Qing dynasties for the control of China, the English civil war, the 30 years' war between the German states, five years of civil war in France, and the two years' succession war in the Mughal Empire. There were also conflicts in the Dutch republic and Swiss Confederation that nearly tipped over into civil war.

Simultaneously there was throughout much of the seventeenth century an intense episode of global cooling—the so-called 'Little Ice Age', a phenomenon without parallel in the previous 12,000 years. Parker makes the point, with a mass of illustrative detail, that a fatal synergy developed between the natural factors linked to global climate change and the human factors in the way that populations responded to the consequences of this change to create a series of demographic, social, economic, and political catastrophes that lasted for two generations and convinced contemporaries that they faced unprecedented hardships.[18] There was not a simple causal relationship between climate change and war, but the global cooling produced poor harvests, food shortages, and urban squalor, leading to political instability, rebellion, and a lack of resilience in many populations.

However, by the turn of the century, there was a shift in attitudes, coinciding with Enlightenment thought and the delineation of toleration.

> In most parts of the globe, the experience of state breakdown and the continual fear of danger and violent death cooled the ardour of many advocates of economic, political and religious change, leading to greater political stability, economic innovation and religious toleration.[19]

Not the least change was a more welcoming attitude to immigrants, needed to fill the considerable gap in heavily depleted populations.

Would it be too fanciful to see similar direct links between the current global climate change and global instability and the frequent fear of strangers, trespassing on our homes? While the globe is warming not cooling, the potentially destructive effects are even more serious for the world's populations. Could one say that the fact that our 'global home' is under threat creates massive uncertainties about our ongoing sense of being and security, creating elemental anxieties about survival, which in part impel irrational attacks on anyone who seems to represent a threat to our national homes?

There are of course other factors that contribute to the way that irrational opinions quickly seem to dominate everyday life—the way that information flows between people as a result of the global information networks being perhaps the most obvious and problematical, creating a sort of 'rapid' if unstable democracy of view, an unstable 'general will' of the people. As exciting as these latter developments are, and as vital now for regulating and marking all aspects of our lives, there is a mismatch between people and technology. The old checks and balances, with time to think and to moderate extreme opinions, have been eroded. The Internet can give the web user a powerful fantasy of control due to an ability to switch on line or off line at will. The proliferation of information technology abolishes physical distances between people and blurs national boundaries, but it has not necessarily led to greater tolerance between people, nor reduced mutual incomprehension. The era of the referendum of popular opinion, the instant twitter statement, while appearing to be more democratic, in fact bypasses the ordinary democratic structures. In the name of complete tolerance of expression of views, the 'democratic' nature of the Internet, extreme views are given a voice and, more than that, a route for their expression in the real not the virtual world. While there is a strong argument for letting any person have their say on the Internet, we do see how powerfully a group of followers for any bizarre or threatening views can be created. We have yet to find ways of effectively and responsibly managing the bombardment of hazardous digital information.

There is also[20] a current and powerful trend for a kind of mindless intolerance of risk, with many organizations so risk-averse, through a lack of proper judgment, that they become focused on over-regulating our behaviour. Of course as a result this often creates more rather than less risky situations. Risk is a necessary accompaniment of any human endeavour. Tolerance is risky. But too much obsession with the risks of an action, often these under the cover of a so-called 'risk assessment' can become anti-development. At the same time, there has developed a pervasive victim culture, making people readily unable to tolerate relatively minor slights.

> The assumption that people lack the resilience to deal with harmful language offers a dreary and pessimistic account of personhood, as critics of free speech often communicate the belief that the recipients of hurtful or insulting speech are too powerless to respond effectively.[21]

Such an expectation can become self-fulfilling, helping to create a culture of excessive vulnerability.

Slavoj Zizek[22] puts the blame for current dark times squarely on global capitalism for creating a 'violent' world, sustaining contemporary violence rather than mitigating it. It is the 'metaphysical dance of capital that runs the show, that provides the key to real life developments and catastrophes. Therein resides the fundamental systemic violence of capitalism.' He sees the 'liberal' attitude (the basis of tolerance thinking) as misguided and even dangerous.

Thus, he states that,

> Opposing all forms of violence, from direct physical violence (mass murder, terror) to ideological violence (racism, incitement, sexual discrimination),

seems to be the main preoccupation of the tolerant liberal attitude that predominates today ... Is there not something suspicious, indeed symptomatic, about this focus on subjective violence—that violence which is enacted by social agents, evil individuals, disciplined repressive apparatuses, fanatical crowds? Doesn't it desperately try to distract our attention from the true locus of trouble, by obliterating from view other forms of violence and thus actively participating in them?[23]

While I would certainly agree that one cannot ignore the dark underbelly of global capitalism, equally one cannot ignore the dark side of any alternative way of regulating economic and political life, be it Marxist or Anarchist in persuasion. I would also maintain that a full account of the complexities of liberal tolerance needs to keep these Zizekian warnings in mind, without conceding that all liberal thought is an illusion or collusive with the forces of darkness.

With this latter point in mind, I will be looking at tolerance and what I call the '**tolerance process**' as a way of creating a public **tolerant space** for tolerant thinking and practice, with the aid of a number of disciplines such as philosophy, history, sociology, politics, and psychoanalysis, in the hope of contributing to the amelioration of some current intolerant attitudes. I would see the tolerance process as providing a neutral 'third position' outside conflicting parties, a space where there is the possibility for changing perceptions and misperceptions about other people. It would involve naming intolerant practices and defining what makes them intolerant. When I talk of such a process, I mean that we need to have a constant debate about the limits of the tolerable. To have such debates is emblematic of tolerance, but it also requires tolerant forbearance for such a debate to occur at all. This debate will also have to include the contributions of those such as Wendy Brown[24] who criticizes existing tolerance discourses for downplaying issues of power. She has argued that tolerance can be a way of marginalizing people, and that it can be used as a way of justifying the misuse of power, a valid point I mentioned previously as a possible side-effect of tolerant thinking, that stands as a warning for those who see managing social tensions in a simplistic way. Herbert Marcuse[25] argued that tolerance only masks and cements social exclusion. He urged for the suppression of objectionable views, not their toleration. This surely must be correct when it comes to extremist views, such as those promoting genocide or random killings, but not for a good deal of less destructive viewpoints.

One of the main points of the book is that there are many political traditions, each with something important to offer in trying to understand personal, social and political life. But I would suggest that rather than favour one approach over another, I am offering a model where the main purpose of a strand of political thought is seen as providing a framework for trying to think about the complex issues facing everyday living. A framework then provides the structure for a tolerance process, a detailed working out of different positions in regard to a particular practice, whether that is, for example, the wearing of religious items of clothing or whether or not to maintain immigration controls.

The two limiting principles, the harm and the respect principle, provide the basic boundaries around this process of working out a reasonable way forward. Of course the answer to a dilemma about a practice will depend how a question is posed, and that will in turn depend upon the starting framework. Each political tradition will have a different answer, although there may well be an 'overlapping consensus'[26] and if not, the different answers in themselves may well be significant pointers to the best way forward.

Such an approach could be seen as essentially liberal in the widest sense, and as I think will gradually become clear, owes much to the pioneers of early liberal thought, but I will argue that this **pluralistic approach** matches our current complex needs. It can be compared to the work of a jury. The 12 different people, all with different backgrounds and ways of thinking, have to come to a conclusion about the evidence presented to them, as a result of deliberation and comparing and contrasting different views and perspectives, and guided by the judge's interpretation of the law.

After the more political arguments, I will also put forward my wider than usual view of tolerance, based on a reading of the arts. I shall argue that the arts in general are in the main tolerant activities, requiring mutual understanding and communication on the part of artists, performers, and audiences in order for the artist's vision to be fully realized. This may stretch the meaning of the term tolerance further than usual and there is thereby a risk of diluting its relevance, but I hope that what I propose will be convincing or 'good enough' as a way of looking at old ideas through a different perspective.

I shall use a commentary on Shakespeare's *Comedy of Errors*, with the confusion between two sets of twins, two 'doubles', as a way of showing a world where different and apparently alien cultures can be tolerated in a situation of conflicting desires and confusions about identity and the meaning of home. I shall argue how Shakespeare demonstrates in this and other texts a remarkable ability to tolerate conflicting, strange, and ambiguous elements, which offer us a vision of a *respectful* and *human world*, where *otherness is to be wondered at*, not disavowed, a vision which still stands as a beacon of humanity in dark times. I shall also explore how Shakespeare challenges comfortable notions of identity and difference, strangeness and familiarity, and that pervading his dramas there is often a question of where is one's true home?

I shall also examine how music can facilitate toleration. For example, Daniel Barenboim[27] describes how in musical performance, 'two voices are in dialogue simultaneously, each one expressing itself to the fullest, whilst at the same time listening to the other.' This kind of communication, close to early intersubjective communication between mothers and infants, as I shall later describe, is not only about music but is a life-long process. For Barenboim this capacity of music for engaged conversation, its dialogic quality, can help in mutual understanding between people who might otherwise be deaf to what they have in common. His West-Eastern Divan orchestra, formed from Israelis, Palestinians, and other Arabs is a concrete manifestation of this hopeful principle. One can see here the power of music's ability to bring people together in a mutually satisfying endeavour, breaking down barriers to understanding and facilitating and heightening mutual communication.

The processes of emotional and musical 'entrainment', with music's power to synchronise emotions and actions, seem to have their origins not only in early communicative musicality but go back some way in evolution. Ian Cross[28] has argued that the very fact that music does not convey specific and singular meanings makes it much more suitable for conveying the ambiguity of actual human interactions; it involves a form of communication more adept than language at conveying shared and cooperative interactions. From this follows his argument that the faculty for music is as a result likely to have had strong evolutionary advantages for humans in their interactions.

Gary Tomlinson[29] provides a magisterial overview of the gradual evolution in parallel of language and music through interpretation of data from tool making and settlements over a million years or so. Crucial to this evolutionary process was the increasing organization of hominin tool making or 'taskscaping', the source of increasing cognitive and social complexity, which finally resulted in language and music production as separate but interconnected developments. My reading of this account, in summary, is that the gradual building up of a *home base* through a process of what one could call '*homescaping*' became one crucial element of this evolution. One can see in the data how tool making became slowly but increasingly sophisticated as loose gatherings of hominins began to form settlements, where skills could be passed on rather than created ad hoc. Music may have evolved as a powerful means of enhancing early intersubjective communication as early humans began to gather into loose and then more organised communities and early homes. This in part accounts for how music reaches powerfully and universally into the depths of our psychic rootedness, into the interior of our souls or the 'other world' of our unconscious. Hence also music's potential to facilitate powerful intersubjective communications.

Notes

1. Bauman, 1993, p. 161.
2. Kennedy, 2014.
3. Walzer, 1997, p. 2.
4. Rawls, 1993, pp. 3–4.
5. Rawls, 1999, p. vi.
6. Williams, 1999, p. 127.
7. Walzer, 1997, p. 56.
8. King, 1976, p. 37.
9. I do not make a distinction between tolerance and toleration. Definitions of both nouns are virtually synonymous in the OED, though toleration is more linked to the legal process of accepting different beliefs. I also prefer the term tolerance as its opposite intolerance follows naturally—the word intoleration does not make sense.
10. Mill, 1859, p. 135ff.
11. Forst, 2003.
12. Rawls, 1993.

13 Kennedy, 2007.
14 Creppell, 2008, p. 348.
15 Forst, 2003, p. 505.
16 Furedi, 2011, p. 80.
17 Voltaire, 1734, p. 30.
18 Parker, 2013, p. xxii.
19 Parker, 2013, p. xxix.
20 Furedi, 2011, p. 119.
21 Furedi, 2011, p. 120.
22 Zizek, 2009, p. 11.
23 Zizek, 2009, p. 9.
24 Brown, 2008.
25 Marcuse, 1969.
26 Rawls, 1993, p. 133.
27 Barenboim, 2008, p. 20.
28 Cross, 2009.
29 Tomlinson, 2015.

2

STRANGERS TO OURSELVES

The sense of home and the need for roots is so basic that there is a danger that we can take it for granted, unless the continuity provided by a stable home is undermined. I often see the way that a lack of a clear home can drastically affect a child's stability while doing assessments for social services and the courts. Children often have to be placed in foster care when their own family has become unsafe. While they may settle well into the foster placement, it is rare not to see how confused and troubled the child becomes, if only beneath the surface, until a final decision is made about their future. Some young children in these circumstances will draw two houses, with little connection. Others may be unable to represent the confusion symbolically and just remain confused and behaviourally challenging.

One's original home consisted not only of the bricks and mortar of the building, its physical surroundings, and interior structures, but also the memories of relationships. Renos Papadopoulos,[1] psychoanalytically exploring issues raised by the treatment of refugees, also emphasizes how the notion of home is one of the most fundamental for humans; it is both the place of origin and the destination we try to reach. Thus home and homecoming are basic to many human experiences and much of literature. Already this is clear in Homer, when, for example, Odysseus near the beginning of the Odyssey yearns to see the smoke from his homeland and then die, setting the theme and the tone for the poem.

One could add that there are a number of famous examples in Homer's Odyssey where one can see the resonances of the place of home and homecoming, for example, when Odysseus has finally returned home to Ithaca after nearly twenty years away, disguised as a beggar but also of course greatly changed physically. As he approaches his home in order to confront the pack of suitors who have intruded disrespectfully into his palace and are vying for the attentions of his wife, Penelope, a friendly swineherd who is unaware of his royal identity accompanies him. Nearing the palace they come across an old dog left abandoned on a pile of mule and cattle dung, hardly able to move. But as Odysseus passes, the dog pricks up his ears and raises his head, recognizing the master who trained him and went hunting with him. Odysseus is unable to reciprocate as he wishes to keep his identity secret but carefully wipes a tear away. As the master passes on, the dog finally gives up his struggle and dies.

Later in the palace and still disguised, Odysseus is offered hospitality by his wife who still does not recognize him. She asks his old nurse to wash his feet as a token of hospitality. This nurse at first finds him strangely familiar, very much like her old master. But he manages to fob her off. However as she prepares to wash him, he has to reveal his thigh on which is engraved an old scar he received from the tusk of a boar, while hunting. When the old woman passes her hand over the scar she at once recognizes who he is and lets the basin fall onto the floor. With tears in her eyes, she wishes to let her mistress know his identity, but Penelope is distracted and the moment passes. Indeed, it is only later, and after he has slaughtered the suitors, that Penelope is convinced of her husband's identity, when he reveals the intimate secrets of the marital bed, which he himself had built out of a thick olive tree.

Thus we have here, in Homer's homecoming scenes, so many of the basic issues surrounding that of identity and home, for example how much a person remains the same over time, how much they change beyond recognition, yet are still capable of being recognized, given the right conditions; what kind of evidence we require to confirm a person's unique identity; what marks out the subject as having that unique identity, how the identity of the subject and recognition by the other are intimately linked; how one's identity is marked forever by one's home, the psychic home one carries around in exile, during various adventures in foreign climes, as well as when at last one returns to the family hearth. As Papadopoulos[2] describes it, 'The fundamental sense of home forms part of the substratum of identity which is structured as a mosaic and consists of a great number of smaller elements which together form a coherent whole.' This mosaic substratum provides us with the primary sense of our humanity, continuity, and belonging—hence the degree of trauma when a refugee loses their home.

If one is to understand the place of homelessness in the human psyche or soul, then Freud's paper on *The Uncanny*—*das Unheimliche*, in German, literally, the 'unhomely'—is fundamental. Uncanny experiences include those that are frightening and arouse a sense of horror and dread. Freud traces such experiences back to what is previously known and familiar, and yet which erupt in unexpected ways. The word *das Heimliche* in German can be traced back to what is homelike, what belongs to the house, but also something that becomes concealed, withdrawn from the eyes of strangers.[3] Typical uncanny experiences include inanimate objects apparently coming to life, a sudden appearance of a double, the appearance of ghosts and spirits and other hauntings. Something becomes uncanny when the distinction between imagination (*Phantasie*) and reality is effaced. Ultimately, the uncanny is something which is secretly familiar and has undergone repression and then returned from it—hence the double feeling of the strange and the unfamiliar that is indicative of an uncanny experience. (Such an uncanny atmosphere is soon built up in *The Comedy of Errors*, as I shall describe.)

Stanley Cavell[4] writes of an uncanny experience like horror as a human response to the 'perception of the precariousness of human identity, to the perception that it may be lost or invaded, that we may be, or become, something other than we are, or take ourselves for; that our origins as human beings need accounting for, are unaccountable.'

Heidegger in his early *Being and Time* [5] describes anxiety as a basic state of mind where one feels uncanny, or not at home. We can flee from this primordial sense of anxiety into the state of being 'at home' as an escape, rather than face the reality of not being at home. That is, for him the 'not-at-home' is the more primordial phenomenon. This perhaps contrasts with a different emphasis he makes in his late thought[6] where dwelling becomes the basic character of being. Dwelling is different from being housed. Man may inhabit a house, but dwelling has a different and more elemental quality, which for him involves some kind of safeguarding of freedom; the house is not just a shelter, but also a place where man dwells at peace and, I think, connected with the world around him in a primordial and open way.

Anthony Vidler in his book, *The Architectural Uncanny*, influenced by Freud and Heidegger, explores the uncanny as a metaphor for a 'fundamentally unlivable modern condition.'[7] With an architectural emphasis, he traces the history of the spatial uncanny through the numerous 'haunted houses' of the romantic period, as well as how it can become a way of understanding a number of contemporary architectural and urban projects. The unease felt in the uncanny experience had as a favourite motif the 'contrast between a secure or homely interior and the fearful invasion of an alien presence; on a psychological level, its play was one of doubling, where the other is, strangely enough, experienced as a replica of the self, all the more fearsome because apparently the same'.[8]

At the heart of this anxiety of an alien presence, Vidler suggests was a fundamental insecurity—that of the newly established bourgeois, not quite at home in its own home. Since then, estrangement and unhomeliness have emerged as the intellectual watchwords of the modern, given periodic material and political force by the resurgence of actual homelessness generated by war and/or poverty.[9]

There is thus an uneasy tension in the modern soul between feeling at home and feeling estranged. This tension is revealed in uncanny experiences I have described, which one might say remind us of the precariousness of our hard-won sense of psychic organization. Michel de M'Uzan[10] emphasizes how uncanny experiences commemorate a crucial phase in the development of psychic functioning, a moment which brings to the fore the indeterminate nature of identity, when the self becomes 'strange' to itself.

The latter point resonates with Julia Kristeva's meditation on the stranger— *Strangers to Ourselves.* [11] She writes that with Freud, an uncanny foreignness creeps into the tranquillity of reason. 'Henceforth, we know that we are foreigners to ourselves, and it is with the help of that sole support that we can attempt to live with others.'[12] That is, *we are our own foreigners*, strangers to ourselves, divided and estranged. Psychoanalysis is a 'journey into the strangeness of the other and of oneself, towards an ethics of respect for the irreconcilable. How could one tolerate a foreigner if one did not know one was a stranger to oneself.'[13] One could indeed say that in order to listen psychoanalytically at all requires one to abandon the familiar so as to be receptive to the strange and unfamiliar.

Yet is only with the greatest of efforts at times that we can learn to tolerate both the strange within and the stranger without, providing what one could call a '*home for otherness*'.

Developmental considerations also need to be taken into account here. 'Stranger anxiety' is a developmental phase, which usually shows itself fully around 8 months, when the baby begins to have a sense of others as whole people. Infants are already learning to recognize their caretakers from early on, while also being interested in other figures, to whom they are less attached. But from around 6 months they begin to show unhappiness around strangers, and by 8 months they may burst into tears if a stranger approaches or gets too close physically. This fear of strangers can last until around the age of 2 to a greater or lesser extent, but by then it also begins to reduce as children build up more of a sense of reality and learn to trust based on awareness of the other's trustworthiness rather than the blind trust of early infancy. This kind of developmental picture assumes a normal attachment pattern, with the child making a primary and secure attachment to their caregivers. If they become secure with their parents, they feel during this period anxious when separated from them. In time, from about 18 months, they learn that the parent who goes will return; they symbolize presence and absence. However, children who have been traumatized or severely deprived may not develop secure attachments. Some of them, with attachment disorders, may show no fear of strangers and may go up to strangers, as if seeking some sort of lost primary parental object. A test for attachment difficulties is called the 'Strange Situation', in which children are put in a room with their caretaker, the latter the suddenly leaves, and the child is then observed, both when the caretaker leaves and when they return. Secure infants are distressed when their caretaker leaves but are easily comforted when they return. Children with insecure attachments show a variety of abnormal responses, and may show various kinds of disorganized behaviours, which may lead on to attachment disorders and behavioural and emotional difficulties.

It is difficult to know how much adult attitudes to strangers are affected by some of these early developmental considerations. But the latter do show that the fear of the stranger goes deep into our developmental histories, making it difficult at some deep level to accept others who appear to be different. Stranger anxiety may have had an evolutionary protective factor; being wary of strangers would be appropriate in a potentially dangerous world. But we need to relearn how to trust the other if we are to have workable interpersonal relationships. As we learn to trust others outside our home circle, so we may also need to learn to trust the unfamiliar stranger by overcoming our elemental fears, but also having the possibility in mind that the stranger may be trustworthy, putting aside the tendency to view the stranger by nature as a suspicious figure.

Otto Fenichel's 1940 paper on anti-Semitism resonates with Kristeva's thought, and remains relevant for understanding contemporary intolerance to strangers, such as minorities within communities or migrants and refugees from other cultures. Of course Fenichel had mostly in mind East European Jews in Czarist Russia or the Jews in the Middle Ages, while he was battling to understand the prejudice against Jews in a Germany where they were much more integrated. Yet his notions still have a contemporary resonance in trying to look at issues of projection and displacement, as well as paying attention to how psychoanalysis and social theory can enrich one another.

For Fenichel, the anti-Semite arrives at his hatred of the Jews by a process of displacement or projection, seeing the Jew as everything that brings him misery, not only from his external oppressor but also misery from his internal world, his unconscious instincts.[14] The Jew, as with other persecuted groups, can be a vehicle for such projections because of the difference in Jewish life and practices, their apparent difference in appearance, their 'foreignness' and their long history of retaining their identity. There are of course also social factors, such as their role as moneylenders at a time when usury was a sin for Christians, which perpetuated their long-standing outsider role. A racial minority can become suitable as a carrier of projections because 'One's own unconscious is also foreign. Foreignness is that which the Jews and one's own instincts have in common.'[15] The foreigner can become 'uncanny', a reminder of archaic and repressed desires. Thus,

> The Jew with his unintelligible language and ununderstandable God appears uncanny to the non-Jews, not only because they cannot understand him and therefore can imagine all sorts of sins in him, but still more so because they can understand him very well somewhere in the depths, because his customs are archaic, that is contain elements which they once had themselves, but later lost.[16]

Perhaps the archaic history of the Jews, who were enslaved, gained their freedom from servitude and then found their homeland, only to be expelled from it and forced to wander into foreign homes in order to settle, has a particular resonance, stirring up primitive fears about the loss of home and a threat to identity. It may also be possible to extend Fenichel's explanations about attitudes to Jews to prejudiced attitudes towards refugees from Syria and other parts of the world, many of whom are also fleeing from a form of servitude.

Another factor making it difficult for the newcomer to be accepted into a host community concerns fears about what the newcomer may bring with them, particularly if the stranger is deeply *traumatized* as a result of what they have experienced in their own country of origin. They may be seen as 'carriers' of trauma, as if infected with some virulent virus, and so needing to be either excluded from entering in the first place, or else 'quarantined' on arrival.

An alternative and equally unhelpful attitude to the traumatized stranger is to ignore their suffering, or as Pope Francis recently put it: 'In this globalized world, we have fallen into global indifference: we have learned to become used to the suffering of others—"It doesn't affect me; it doesn't concern me; it's none of my business!"'[17]

Thus one can see how the myth of the stranger as different, strange, weird, uncanny, can make people feel not 'at home' with the stranger, seeing them as potential threats rather than as potential allies. They may just about be tolerated, but *living with* them can be a step too far. They bring their own ways of life, their habits and customs, or their 'habitus',[18] that is, their durable, transportable, dispositions, their feel for their own fields of cultural practice, which may or may not overlap with the fields of practice of the indigenous population. Equally those already at home in their country can forget that the history of many European countries involves waves of mass migration, going back thousands of years. This history reveals how identity is not a fixed entity, but fluid, hybrid, and complex.

The identity issue

Of course, identity matters in immediate and indeed practical ways. For example, if you wish to renew your UK passport, you now have to apply to the 'Identity and Passport Service', which will authenticate your personal details and confirm your identity as a UK citizen, or not. Having a home is vital to this. Without an address, you cannot really be a citizen. This dilemma was especially poignant after the Second World War. Tony Judt[19] has charted, in his ground-breaking book *Postwar*, how there took place then a massive movement of millions of people, due to the aftermath of the fighting and displacement of communities, the opening up of the concentration camps and also the civil wars that soon took place in what became communist Europe. Not only had there been, as a result of Stalin and Hitler, the uprooting, transplanting, and deportation of some 30 million people between 1939 and 1944, but after the war Europe had to deal with an unprecedented exercise in ethnic cleansing and population transfer. Untold millions were displaced or were refugees. The distinction between displaced persons, assumed to have somewhere, a home to go to, and refugees, who were classified as homeless, was one of the many nuances that were introduced by the authorities trying to deal with this trauma, whose legacy remains to this day, marking the European identity. Yet there are places in Europe where this history has either been forgotten or just erased, so that all those wishing to enter European space are lumped together as one threatening entity.

Incidentally, one of the motivating factors for Germany's relative openness to the current wave of refugees is the resonance with their own post war history, where many millions of displaced German speakers were given shelter in Germany, forming an essential element of the so-called German economic 'miracle'.

Those fleeing wars, such as the current wave of Syrian refugees, are of course hoping for a safe haven, a place where they can rebuild their lives. One of my main points is that it is not only that such people require practical help, but that there are some fundamental issues concerned with the nature of identity that need to be faced by both the refugee populations and the potential host countries if there is to be a hope for reasonable integration. In particular, there is a complex interaction between, as it were, the psychic homes of refugee and host. The refugee feels a stranger in a new environment, carrying within their own sense of psychic home (however ravaged by trauma) and the host may feel a fear of a loss of their secure sense of a psychic home as a result of being 'invaded' and 'enveloped' by all these strangers, 'diluting' and 'contaminating' their own culture and sense of community.

In order to understand the place of the stranger in communities, one can look at some key sociological texts, which already point the way towards some resolution of some of these basic tensions. There is a substantial literature on the nature of the stranger, mainly from the last century. The stranger can be defined as a person who tries to be permanently accepted or at least tolerated by the group which he approaches.[20] For George Simmel,[21] the stranger is not the wanderer who comes today and leaves tomorrow, but the man who comes today and stays tomorrow; he is a potential wanderer, who has not quite got over the freedom of coming and going. In the case of the stranger, the union of closeness and remoteness involved in every human relationship is patterned in a particular way—'the distance within the relation indicates that one who is close by is remote, but his strangeness indicates that one who is remote is near.[22] A trace of this strangeness, the elements of closeness and remoteness, enters into even the most intimate relationships. Because of their strange intermediate position, neither owning a home within the community nor being totally outside, the stranger can be more objective about attitudes, freer from local prejudices, and thereby, like the psychoanalyst, can be the receiver of confidences.

The stranger can thus be a potentially creative force, a catalyst for change and for challenging the 'thinking as usual' approach of the home group. Of course the stranger may also be a significant threat to the home community and even destabilizing, and, as I have indicated, this matches current fears about being 'swamped' by those wishing to escape wars from outside Europe.

The theme of the stranger as potentially destructive reaches far back into history. One has only to recall the catastrophic effect of the god Dionysus in Euripides' play *The Bacchae*, who, coming as a stranger to Thebes, unleashes daemonic forces, tearing apart the city and literally its King, Pentheus. In more recent times, we have the image of Clint Eastwood as 'the stranger' who rides into a corrupt town to become an avenging figure in 'High Plains Drifter', leaving mayhem and destruction in his wake as revenge for the death of a US Marshall—the stranger may have been a relative or the Marshall's ghost. And Eastwood plays the 'man with no name' in Leone's Spaghetti westerns, as a stranger who ends up pitting good against evil in small communities, for the sake of justice.

The stranger is thus imbued with a good deal of ambivalence, and may or may not be integrated into the home culture. They may remain in a transitional position, neither in nor out, but for that reason a potential force for change.

Margaret May Wood[23] made the point that the way that a stranger may or may not be integrated into the home culture will depend upon the social relationships already within that culture. Thus factors which tend to allow integration of the stranger will include similarity of language or the stranger learning the new language, shared values, a lack of affection from the stranger to their own country of origin (though that could potentially cause more difficulty if they bring with them too many resentments), gratitude to the host community if they make available a new home, owning property and land, and intermarriage. Conversely, a stranger may fail to integrate if these sorts of elements are not present.

Bauman emphasizes that strangerhood has become a permanent condition of modern life. The problem of modern society is not how to eliminate strangers, but how to live in their constant company, in a situation of constant uncertainty as to their responses. After all, to live in a modern city, at least in a democratic society, is to be faced by millions of strangers. There need to be spaces, such as cinemas, theatres, and parks, 'managed playgrounds', where strangers can meet or pass by without fear of being challenged. This would contrast with totalitarian regimes that demand absolute conformity; any stranger, any strange behaviour can be seen as a challenge to absolute authority.

Issues around attitudes to strangers also come into play when tackling how to handle *immigration*, one of contemporary society's most pressing and controversial areas of concern. Michael Walzer[24] provided one of the first reasoned arguments for limiting immigration, putting forward the case that sovereign states had the right to choose an admission policy, as there was a need to consider the shape of a community. But he also argues that once admitted the immigrant should be given full rights of citizenship. One should add that he does also consider the very difficult situations of those who need asylum, particularly when they have come from situations created by the state they wish to enter; the example of Iraq or Syria of course comes to mind, with the US and UK in particular having some collective liability for producing the refugee crisis. Walzer does not have an obvious solution to how to justify taking in large numbers of such people; there would seem to be a basic conflict between his theory of justice and that of community membership.

In contrast, Joseph Carens[25] argues comprehensively for an ethics of immigration, putting forward the view that basic democratic principles imply a commitment of states to their citizens, including those who are born there, and those who arrive later as children or adults, including migrants, asylum seekers, and refugees.

The notions of belonging and of home are central to his argument about those who are born in or are admitted into a community. Democratic states usually confer citizenship on those born there; it becomes their natural home country. The international system accepts that everyone is supposed to be assigned to a state that then becomes responsible for its citizens though there is an absence of general guidelines for how states ought to assign citizenship at birth. Being stateless is a precarious and vulnerable condition, and Carens argues that there is a moral requirement established by having the close connections that are inevitably established by a child being born in a particular community. The state where a child lives, their home territory, inevitably structures, secures, and promotes their relationships with other human beings, including his or her family. He emphasizes then the importance of '*belonging*', not merely human rights in the abstract.

To justify his claims he puts forward a theory of 'social membership'. This is that 'living within the territorial boundaries of a state makes one a member of society, that this social membership gives rise to moral claims in relation to the political community, and that these claims deepen over time ... (S)ocial membership matters morally.'[26] Thus social membership comes from residence over time. Time in this context matters morally.

Residence and length of stay are the two basic elements of social membership, which is why he argues for the acceptance for citizenship of even those who have arrived in a state by illegal means, or what he names 'irregular migrants', years after they have entered, when attachments to their new home have become established.

Carens further argues that freedom of movement between countries is a basic freedom to which people are morally entitled, even though he recognizes that this is an ideal to which many states would not sign up. The EU of course has such an open policy for its own citizens, but a less clear policy for those outside the EU. Carens considers that richer countries do have a moral obligation to poorer countries, and that granting people the right to move and settle wherever they want would contribute greatly to human freedom and equality, that this open policy would be ultimately in the interests of the whole world community. He realizes of course that this is a controversial view and one opposed to most state policies. But he argues that restricting entry fails to recognize why in the first place most people have to leave their poor countries—indeed as revealed many times in the media, when journalists interview those who have risked their lives by placing themselves and their children in crowded boats to come to the EU, the vast majority have harrowing stories of trauma, extreme poverty and degradation in their home countries.

Thus though Carens recognizes that the conventional view is that states are morally entitled to exercise discretionary control over immigration, he argues that this view is wrong in principle and that our deepest moral principles require a commitment to open borders, even if in practice there may have to be some compromises. Once here, of course, from his earlier arguments, such migrants should be entitled to have full access to citizenship; there needs to be a 'political culture of inclusion and respect for migrants',[27] that is a basic tolerance to strangers.

Intolerant states of mind

Even in democratic societies there can be periods when intolerance of strangers becomes an acute problem, the period of McCarthyism in the US in the 1950s being one typical such period. This was revealed in cinemas at the time in horror films like Don Siegel's 1956 film Invasion of the Body Snatchers. Alien pods arrive in a small town in the US and take over individuals. The film could be seen as a commentary on the fear of loss of identity during the cold war, fears about a communist takeover, or about fear of an alien invasion from within.

There were a number of similar films made at that time. There were, for example, War of the Worlds (1953) based upon H.G. Wells' story of Martian invaders, Invaders from Mars (1953) where aliens take over the minds of small town citizens, as in the Invaders of the Body Snatchers (1956), and I Married a monster from Outer Space (1958), when a wife realizes an alien has taken over her husband—a common fantasy!

Current Islamophobic utterances reveal that intolerance can always find someone eager to blame strangers for the ills of the world. Indeed, *fear* and intolerance go hand in hand.

Martha Nussbaum has tackled the role of fear in underpinning much of intolerant attitudes to strangers in her book *The New Religious Intolerance*.[28] On the one hand, fear is a basic emotion with has evolutionary survival value, enabling a person to react to perceived danger. Indeed the fear response is necessary for being able to perceive otherness; psychopaths seem unable to have a normal fear response and this makes them dangerous to others. However fear can be irrational and can also produce unreliable and unpredictable behaviour, which can be exploited by politicians eager to whip up aggression against minority groups. This kind of fear tends to be narcissistic, with a narrow focus around self-preservation. It may start from some real problem such as economic insecurity, but it can be easily displaced, or projected, onto something that has little to do with the underlying problems. It is also nourished by the idea of the 'disguised enemy', who may do harm,[29] as in the film Invasion of the Body Snatchers. Fear can also spread quickly and easily like a forest fire; fear encourages further fear; it may need considerable resources to quench the fires of hate. Thus, though fear is valuable and essential in a genuinely dangerous world (we are, for example right to be fearful of North Korean aggression), it can be of itself one of life's great dangers.

Fearful and paranoid attitudes to strangers contrast with the reality of the necessity for close and creative contact with foreign cultures in order for societies to be enriched. One has only to think of how Picasso and Braque appropriated forms and motifs from African art, which brought to its climax a long interest which nineteenth century France had shown in the exotic, the distant, and the primitive.[30]

Appiah in his book, *Cosmopolitanism, Ethics in a World of Strangers,*[31] explores the vital importance for the health of societies that they foster a notion of decent living with strangers. He defines cosmopolitanism as involving having obligations to others, that stretch beyond those we have to our family and to our own culture; and that we take seriously the values of others who do not have our beliefs or take part in our practices. We can live with one another without having to agree on religious and/or secular values. Such an attitude, which is of course a value in itself, contrasts with the *intolerant* totalitarian position, which involves loyalty to only one portion of humanity, often excluding others. It is no coincidence that people in such regimes have a constant and realistic fear that their homes will be invaded. In between there are many other variations, or what Appiah calls a 'partial cosmopolitanism', that is a certain amount of openness to other cultures, with *degrees of tolerance*, while retaining one's own strong tendency to stick to one's own psychic home as a refuge and shelter. Having such a strong sense of one's own psychic home as a strong and stabilising structure does not imply one should have only a single affiliation.

Such texts then point on the one hand to the universal ambivalence towards strangers, and yet also to the need to recognize and overcome such ambivalence if societies are to grow. There would need to be a basic 'Psychological' tolerance towards the stranger. But one can add that for that process of growth to be achievable, there needs to be attention to the nature of tolerance and intolerance and their impact on issues of identity and fears about loss of identity.

Linked to this is the complex question of what kind of psychological attitude is most effective in fostering decent living together of different communities. One might think that an empathic approach, requiring some tuning into or replicating the emotions of others is best suited to bring people together. *Empathy* is, however, a complex emotional response, with a variety of types. There is a basic kind of 'low-level' empathy, something like 'emotional contagion', where one can easily and quickly pick up the emotions of those around. For example, one can easily feel sorrow for an unknown person at a funeral or happy in a laughing audience even without having heard a joke.

Then there is a 'higher-level' kind of empathy, linked with thought and imagination; it may or may not involve putting oneself in the other's shoes, for just being receptive to the other's feelings is often enough to be perceived as empathic. There is some overlap here with compassion or sympathy.

But one may ask how close does one want to feel with a neighbour? Would one be happy for them to come into one's garden (if that is one had a garden)? The usual response to a stranger in one's garden would be to phone the police. Empathy for strangers thus has obvious limits. Furthermore, empathy can be a tricky emotional response. Not everyone wants to be understood intimately. A safe, discrete and respectful distance may be enough to promote peaceful coexistence. Zizek[32] even suggests that a shared sense of alienation, even disrespectful laughter, is more likely to foster good relations, with neighbours keeping their distance and definitely not sharing their inner world. While he may be playing ironically with the reader here, Zizek points towards an important point about the dangers of empathy, of imagining we can truly understand the other's inner world. Otherness may remain essentially unknowable, yet we can still respect the stranger's different way of life. At some point then they may no longer be strangers, but good neighbours. Nonetheless, I would think that empathy joined with some form of judgment plays an essential part in overcoming intolerant attitudes to strangers.

Using empathy alone as a way of managing potentially caring relationships carries certain risks. For example, the Nazi doctors who practised in the concentration camps were often caring family fathers, with a good deal of empathy for their children, while at the same time they took part in horrific degradation of the camp inmates. Robert Jay Lifton in his extensive study of Nazi doctors describes a psychology of 'doubling', with the 'division of the self into two functioning wholes, so that a part self acts an entire self.'[33] The 'Auschwitz' self became psychically numb to the reality of death and destruction all around them, even finding euphemisms for the act of killing. Doubling is the psychological means by which one invokes the evil potential of the self. That evil is neither inherent in the self nor foreign to it. To live out the doubling and call forth the evil is a moral choice for which one is responsible, whatever the level of consciousness involved. By means of doubling, Nazi doctors made a Faustian choice for evil.[34]

So not only does empathy need to be joined with some kind of generalizing principle, such as the harm or respect principle, for its target to remain humane, but there also needs to be attention to intolerant states of mind, which are anti-empathy.

In his recent work, Lifton[35] has described how the Nazi excesses were indicative of a particular kind of '*Apocalyptic violence*', now visible in terrorists and even at times in the West's reactions to terrorist risks. Apocalyptic violence, whatever its origins in feelings of past humiliation or social disadvantage, involves extreme fantasies of spiritual renewal through killing. Hitler's followers

> sought to destroy much of what they saw as a racially polluted world by means of a vast biological purification program. Despite being murderously anti-Jewish and significantly anti-Christian as well, the Nazis drew upon what was most apocalyptic in both of those traditions. The Nazis came to epitomize the apocalyptic principle of *killing to heal*, of destroying vast numbers of human beings as therapy for the world.[36]

The idea of apocalyptic martyrdom, now so visible in ISIS and other terrorist developments,

> intensifies the ordeal of the killer as well as his claim to spiritual renewal, while dramatizing his death as transcending those of his victims. The martyr brings his own being—the sacrifice of his own life—into the dynamic of world destruction and recreation, thus exemplifying that death-and-rebirth process.[37]

Unfortunately the West, at least in the years immediately following the 9/11 slaughter, also responded with apocalyptic logic, maintaining that the forces of evil would be wiped out by the forces of democracy, cleaning the world of the extremists. In the name of destroying evil, each side sought to destroy the other. This kind of potentially very dangerous thinking continues to be visible today, for example in current relations with the North Korean dictatorship.

Christopher Bollas[38] describes in detail what he calls the 'fascist state of mind', visible not only in genocidal acts but potentially in all of us. Whatever the social factors that might lead to genocide, the core element in the fascist state of mind is 'the presence of an ideology that maintains its certainty through the operation of specific mental mechanisms aimed at eliminating all opposition'. In this frame of mind, doubt, uncertainty, and self-inquiry are considered to be weaknesses and must be expelled. Language also becomes distorted in its uses, in ways already described vividly by George Orwell, for example in his essay 'Politics and the English language' (1946), where he shows how language can corrupt thought through 'making lies sound truthful and murder respectable, and to give an appearance of solidity to pure wind.'[39]

Bollas gives a detailed picture of the dynamics of how the fascist ideology becomes so destructive, as the intolerance of uncertainty and destruction of opposition create a moral void.

> At this point the subject must find a victim to contain that void, and now a state of mind becomes an act of violence. On the verge of its own moral vacuum, the mind splits off this dead core self and projects it into a victim henceforth identified with the moral void ... As contact with the moral void is lost through projective identification into a victim, and the victim now exterminated, the profoundly destructive processes involved are further denied by a form of delusional narcissism ... As the qualities of the other are destroyed via the annihilation of the other, a delusional grandiosity forms in the Fascistically stated mind.[40]

Michael Burleigh gives multiple examples of on-the-spot behaviour of soldiers and civilians in his book *Moral Combat*, which gives some support to the descriptions of both Lifton and Bollas. Burleigh reveals how the Nazis and their allies

> tried fundamentally to alter the moral understanding of humanity, in ways that deviated from the moral norms of Western civilization. They did this by locating their murderous depredations beyond law, but also in a warped moral framework that defined their purifying violence as necessary and righteous.[41]

Burleigh had already in his book *Sacred Causes* described in detail how the Nazis and the Bolsheviks used a pseudo-religious pathology to justify their abuses, 'ranging from the Nazi's skillful manipulation of such notions as "rebirth" and "awakening" to the Bolsheviks' bizarre resort to perpetual confession and remorseless search for heretics.'[42]

One can thus see in the accounts from Lifton, Bollas, and Burleigh how apocalyptic thinking in its various guises creates extreme forms of intolerance, offering a perverse moral universe, where the awareness of difference is destroyed. While intolerance may not reach the extremes perpetrated by the Nazi and communist regimes, the way that intolerant states of mind can arise and be sustained in groups, particularly when encouraged by a populist leader, is similar.

One cannot of course underestimate the *trauma* of being on the receiving end of such persistent intolerant regimes. The Czech psychoanalyst Michael Sebek, having experienced at first hand living through the traumas of a communist regime, has written about the nature of the psychological processes involved in totalitarian regimes, emphasizing the place of what he calls the *'totalitarian object'* that can come to dominate individuals in a repressive society, but may also function in post-totalitarian regimes as well as at times in more democratic societies. This is a repressive and intrusive form of psychic structure that becomes internalized in a society that demands compliance and obedience, where there is *low tolerance* for the difference of others, stressing unity and sameness. In addition,

> Totalitarian objects (external and internal) may also bring some safety to immature persons who like to merge with a strong authority in order to get a feeling of importance and wholeness. The idealization of totalitarian objects may be an important device for saving objects from destruction and using the process of splitting to attain some psychic balance.[43]

There is always a risk that the totalitarian object may take over the individual and the group's functioning, creating a rigid intolerance towards anything outside the narrow functioning prescribed as acceptable. This is visible not only in a totalitarian society but also in pockets of other forms of society, such as with radicalized youth, or any extreme political organization that demands compliance, obedience coupled with an identification with charismatic leadership.

Hannah Arendt in her book *The Origins of Totalitarianism*[44] provides a detailed examination of the nature of totalitarian regimes, using Nazi Germany and Soviet Russia as exemplars, which provide uncomfortable parallels with the current rise of 'populist' movements in the West. Indeed sales of her book have escalated since the Brexit vote and the election of Donald Trump as US President.

Arendt describes a form of social pathology developed in modern times, emphasizing the way these totalitarian regimes were mass movements of a particular kind. They recruited their members in Europe after 1930,

> from the mass of apparently indifferent people whom all other parties had given as too apathetic or too stupid for their attention. The result was that the majority of their membership consisted of people who never before had appeared on the political scene. This permitted the introduction of entirely new methods into political propaganda, and indifference to the arguments of political opponents.[45]

The mass of generally dissatisfied and desperate people increased rapidly in Germany and Austria after the First World War, with inflation and unemployment adding to the disruptive effects of military defeat, and this mass also increased after the Second World War, supporting extremist movements in France and Italy, and one can now add that there has been another increase globally since recent worldwide economic crises.

Arendt describes how social atomization or fragmentation had preceded the mass movements, creating a large number of socially alienated, lonely individuals, ready to be organized into a movement. 'The totalitarian movements depended less on the structurelessness of a mass society than on the specific conditions of an atomized and individualized mass.'[46] These mass organizations demand total, unconditional, and unalterable loyalty of the individual member, essentially making individual human beings 'superfluous', and thus expendable.

Vaclav Havel in his essay *The Power of the Powerless* pointed out how in the modern totalitarian state the centre of power is identical with the centre of truth; only the centralized state has the truth, which the individual cannot question. The way that power is structured then affects every individual; by insisting that truth is in the centre, the individual lives within a lie rather than the truth. He points out that this is a situation that is possible in part because humans are capable of being easily seduced by the offer of clear answers and certainty.

Havel describes how this occurs with the manager of a fruit and vegetable shop, when he places a communist slogan in his window, in order to ingratiate himself with the authorities, whether or not he agrees with the slogan's content. Havel describes in detail how multiple similar acts bolster up and bind together the entire totalitarian power structure, with the 'glue' of a lying ideology focused around the notion of some central site, often personified in the single dictator and/or their party machine, where truth can be found. However, Havel also, and prophetically, imagined what could happen one day if the greengrocer were to snap and stop putting up those slogans. If that act were to be repeated all over, then he suggested that the 'entire pyramid of totalitarian power, deprived of the element that binds it together, would collapse in itself, as it were, in a kind of material implosion.'[47] This would be a revolution of the powerless, as of course occurred in central and east Europe in 1989. At that moment, there was a mass refusal to tolerate the intolerable.

Notes

1. Papadopoulos, 2002
2. Papadopoulos, 2002, p. 17.
3. Freud, 1919, p. 225.
4. Cavell, 1979, pp. 418–19.
5. Heidegger, 1926, p. 223.
6. Heidegger, 1971, pp. 145–61.
7. Vidler, 1992, p. x.
8. Vidler, 1992, p. 3.
9. Vidler, 1992, p. 9.
10. De M'Uzan, 2005.
11. Kristeva, 1991.
12. Kristeva, 1991, p. 170.
13. Kristeva, 1991, p. 182.
14. Fenichel, 1940, p. 37.
15. Fenichel, 1940, p. 31.
16. Fenichel, 1940, pp. 31–2.
17. Quoted in Bauman, 2016, p. 22.
18. Bourdieu, 1990, p. 53.
19. Judt, 2005.
20. Schutz, 1944, p. 499.
21. Simmel, 1971, p. 143.
22. Simmel, 1971, p. 143.

23 Wood, 1934.
24 Walzer, 1983, pp. 31ff.
25 Carens, 2013.
26 Carens, 2013, p. 158.
27 Carens, 2013, p. 288.
28 Nussbaum, 2012.
29 Nussbaum, 2012, pp. 23–4.
30 Hughes, 1991, p. 20.
31 Appiah, 2006.
32 Zizek, 2016, p.74.
33 Lifton, 1986, p. 418.
34 Lifton, 1986, pp. 423–4.
35 Lifton, 2003.
36 Lifton, 2003, pp. 28–9.
37 Lifton, 2003, p. 29.
38 Bollas, 1992, pp. 193–217.
39 Orwell, 1946, p. 967.
40 Bollas, 1992, p. 203.
41 Burleigh, 2010, p. x.
42 Burleigh, 2006, p. xii.
43 Sebek, 1996, p. 290.
44 Arendt, 1951.
45 Arendt, 1951, pp. 311–12.
46 Arendt, 1951, p. 318.
47 Havel, 1986, p. 46.

3
HOME AND IDENTITY

The psychic home

In order to clarify some psychological elements basic to the current political and social unrest in Europe and beyond, I have suggested that it would be helpful to look at how the place of a psychic home can add a dimension to the understanding of conflict between people from different geographical areas. In order to clarify what I mean by a psychic home, I would suggest that having such a home, an internal sense of a secure home base, is a key feature of identity. The psychic home provides an organizing psychic structure for the sense of emerging identity. Such a home base must be built up from a number of different elements, as with the physical home, which forms its substrate. There are intra-psychic elements but also inter-subjective elements, involving the social world.

1. There is the basic structure of a home as a protected and hopefully welcoming space for shelter, providing the core of the internalized psychic home. The physical space of the home has an important function in helping to shape the interior life. One may say that the psychic home has a dual aspect—as both physical and psychical container.

In this notion of a psychic home, the physical structure of the home has an important part to play in providing an overall, containing structure or psychic container, which becomes internalized as an organizing configuration. The English word home derives from the old Norse, Heima, and perhaps encapsulates something of the Viking longing for home and hearth as a stable physical base to return to after their many voyages of exploration and conquest.

The physical structure of the home has an interior marked out by defining walls. The boundary between the interior and the exterior may be firm and stable or flimsy or permeable; the bricks and mortar of the family home may be loose or secure, with a clear focus or none. One may recall here the story of the three little pigs—only the house built of bricks could withstand the breath of the hungry wolf. Indeed, it was the third pig's fireplace that eventually killed off the wolf as he climbed down the chimney.

The boundaries of the house also have to be seen in context, within a community of other homes, and within a society. The home must be permeable to external influences, or else it will become the source of unreal relationships, including intolerance *of strangers*, who are perceived as threats to the precarious psychic home.

2. There is already a pre-established inter-subjective symbolic space predating the building or setting up of the home. The home-to-be already has a place in the family history and narrative, already situated as an element in a complicated network of relationships. There is a lineage, reaching back generations. The individual in a family is already situated before birth in a complicated, mostly unconscious, network of symbols, or kinship structure. Influenced by the work of Levi-Strauss on how unconscious social laws regulated marriage ties and kinship, structuring them like language, Lacan called this network the 'Symbolic Order'.[1] It is the Order into which the emerging subject has to structure himself, language, for Lacan being the key element through which this structuring takes place. I would want to add the vital contributions to the emergence of the human subject of the rich pre-verbal world, the world in which language is beginning to take shape.

3. The contents of the psychic home, its mental furniture, consist essentially of identifications with family members making up the home's interior. In the secure home, the parents provide continuity over time in their home making, providing a supportive base for the children to eventually leave, and ultimately to build up their own home. A stable psychic home involves individuals being recognized as being autonomous yet dependent, and receiving respect for their own individuality, with secure attachments. One can perhaps see most clearly here how the psychic home is integral to the notion of identity with the adolescent, for whom identity formation is a crucial task. They need the home base from which to explore but also they need it to be there for their return. This is perhaps why it can be so traumatic for the adolescent when their parents split up at this crucial point in their development, supposedly as they are now 'old enough' to be able to cope.

One can also see how a sense of individual identity depends upon the mutual relationships in the family being respectful of personal autonomy; that is, boundaries *within* the home need to be respectful, with individuality being respected and recognized. If such boundaries are not respected, then it is likely that strangers from *outside* the family and community will also not be respected.

For any individual, alternative psychic homes will develop in time, particularly if their family of origin is unstable or rejecting. For those with a core sense of a psychic home, it may be less conflictual to settle in alternative homes, to feel at home in a number of different places, cultures, overlapping and interpenetrating, to be '*cosmopolitan*'. For such people, the stranger can be a source of positive curiosity not a threat to their stability.

4. The ordinary home consists of activities; it is not a static or frozen entity. What could be called the 'work of the day'[2] takes place within the home. This refers to significant events, which require thought and/or action. The ordinary work of the day, structured around everyday activities, involves attention to all the significant, and at times deceptively indifferent, thoughts, feelings, and experiences that occupy us during the day and provide the raw material for thinking and for dreaming. Much of this psychic work carries on automatically without us being particularly aware of its regular occurrence or of its everydayness. It is usually taken for granted, unless the family has major problems, of the kind where the family home has broken down, and where ordinary family life cannot be held together safely.

Thus one can see how the notion of a *psychic home* consists of a number of different and interacting elements, including the physical interior of a home but internalized as a psychic interior. The notion of 'personal identity' refers to the development and then maintenance of a person's character, how they put together in some way their various multiple identifications, as well as including wider issues concerning a person's cultural and social influences. I am suggesting that the basic elements of the psychic home can be seen to provide a way of organizing the person's identity, or can be seen as intrinsic to any notion of identity.

Like their patients, psychoanalysts carry their psychic home with them though it will manifest itself differently. The analyst may not reveal details of their private life to their patients, but they carry their psychic home with them into the session. The choice of interior design of the consulting room, not to mention the books and any objects, may well reflect the nature of the analyst's psychic home; there is an interaction between the subjectivity of the analyst and the interior space where they work. An alive psychic home can provide a sustaining space for the analyst, allowing them to cope with the inevitable loneliness of the work.

While the analytic work carries on in separate localities, that of analyst and that of the patient, they do intertwine in various ways, in a dynamic fashion. Sometimes the analyst may find that their psychic home is invaded by the patient, with little space to think or feel; or else there may be a confusion of spaces, with little sense of a boundaried psychic home. These experiences may occur at once or take time to develop through the strange unfolding of the transference and counter-transference. A patient comes into our consulting room for the first meeting. We may have spoken to them briefly on the telephone, or communicated by email, perhaps have found out a little about them, either directly or from a referring colleague. But the fact is, both analyst and patient are strangers to one another in a number of ways, both with regard to knowing about their lives and cultures, but also with regard to their strange inner life. We provide a potential home for the expression of this inner life, for the engagement of the analyst's and patient's psychic homes.

One can see a particularly poignant dilemma concerning the psychic home with adoptions, particularly when the adoptee reaches adolescence, as Betty Lifton[3] has pointed out. When adoptees reach adolescence, especially with closed adoptions, and when the adoptee cannot find their birth parents, or when the adopted parents deny the reality of the past, particularly difficult issues around identity may arise.

> If your personal narrative doesn't grow and develop with you, with concrete facts and information, you run the danger of becoming emotionally frozen. You cannot make the necessary connections between the past and the future that everyone needs to grow into a cohesive self. You become stuck in the life cycle, beached like a whale on the shores of your own deficient narrative.

If the adopted parents do not *respect* the reality of the child's past, the adoptee can grow up with a divided self, walling off essential aspects of themselves, and emotionally frozen, not feeling sufficiently *recognized* for who and what they are. They may remain hungry for a psychic home, bereft of the links to such a home.

There may be some overlap in conceptualization here with John Steiner's notion of 'psychic retreats'.[4] These are pathological organizations in more disturbed patients, referring to when patients can withdraw or retreat into states of mind experienced as if they were places in which the patient could hide. Such states of mind may appear as literal spaces, such as a house or a cave. One could add here, that if the patient makes a retreat, then presumably they are retreating from something, from live contact with the other, or from some living psychic home.

Where home life has broken down, where it is, for example, chaotic or dangerous, one can clearly see how the basic conditions for secure attachments and identifications cannot take place; the internalized psychic home then becomes precarious or dangerous. From such pathology, one can perhaps see how the core of the psychic home is probably linked to early experiences where psyche and soma are beginning to be linked together, when the psyche begins to feel 'at home' in the soma, along the lines described by Winnicott.[5] The infant's psyche begins to dwell in the soma, with a sense of being self-centred inside his body, and this process depends upon the mother's handling, her ability to join up her emotional and physical involvement.

I have given examples of how the notion of a psychic home comes into psychoanalytic treatment elsewhere,[6] but to give a brief example to illustrate its relevance:

Mrs. X now has a good home, with a stable family, but she never feels secure in herself; she carries around inside some deep anxieties, linked to the experiences of her early life. Her parents split up when she was very young, and the patient was sent to boarding school soon after. Until the analysis, she had never questioned what had led to the break-up of the family, or why she was sent away from home. She carries around quite a fragile sense of a psychic home, afraid of expressing dependent feelings, and quite emotionally inhibited as a person.

She struggled for a long time with the analytic setting. She wanted to come to sessions, but as soon as she arrived, feelings of dread and despair would quickly arise, making, as she said, the couch uncomfortable. She managed her discomfort by a sort of freezing, with her body stiff and immobile on the couch. The analytic setting for a long time thus became a necessary but dreaded place. She would often wonder why she wanted to come, when on entering the consulting room she would feel so awful.

One of the main themes was an almost complete absence of early home memories, particularly after the break-up of her parent's marriage. She could recall losing a precious soft toy, and that her mother took her to an expensive store to replace it, but no substitute was found to be suitable, though she made do with some hard toys. However, bit-by-bit over the years, some early scenes came to her mind, after we had gone over some of the difficult feelings she experienced at boarding school. There, she often felt lonely, cut off and not one of the group. She began to make connections with some of her current fears about intimacy and those boarding school experiences. One session seemed to convey something of a turning point. It was the first time that she had made a stand about coming to her analysis.

She began in a fairly animated way. She was annoyed because at work there was a new computer system, and she had been told that she will have to set aside some full days to learn it. That would mean missing both personal commitments and her analytic sessions. She was angered by her (female) manager who expected this of her. However, she was not going to go along with this and would leave early to come to her sessions. My patient was also annoyed that she herself was made to feel neglectful by not going along with her work's expectations.

I was immediately struck by her making sure she would come to her analysis despite the pressure to miss out.

She was also worrying about a vulnerable client who was angry about having their invalidity benefit being removed. She was not sure what he would do to himself. There were also worries about a close family member who was ill and still in hospital.

I said that she was telling me about a number of outside pressures that had to be overcome. She did overcome them when she had decided she would come to her analysis.

She said that in fact her manager was normally reasonable, but what annoyed my patient was that the manager herself was being put under pressure from above but that she could not stand up to it. My patient did not want to be the one who made a fuss. She feared both standing out and any retaliation—the latter was a real fear, as someone in the team had in fact been effectively excluded for making a fuss previously.

I said 'You mean, do people make a fuss, or do they have to put up with whatever comes their way'.

This comment made her think of her relative's treatment and they put up with whatever was done to them, even if the staff were incompetent.

(I was thinking, 'Do I put up with her or make a fuss? What kind of manager/analyst am I for her?')

She continued—her relative would not find out what is happening to them. Typically for her family, they just give themselves to the doctors.

I said 'Well, there is a doctor here, and maybe you fear giving yourself up to me'.

She agreed. She talked about it being difficult here, with issues of control and power. She has to fit in with the holiday dates I had recently given her. Though she also sees they are reasonable, given the reality of the summer holidays and her own children's school dates. But there is an imbalance of power. She cannot make me say things. She does not know when I will say things. She wants me to say more. She has 'Zero control' over me. She added that she often had a sense of deprivation here; she felt deprived for much of the time.

After a pause, she said that she was having thoughts about mothers and babies, and all that babies get from their mothers in terms of physical contact and visual stimulation, as much as talking.

I linked what she told me about her own possible early depriving experiences as a baby or young child, with a mother who came and went, and how she could not make a fuss, she had to put up with what she was given, the hard toys for the soft ones.

She said that when I do speak she can feel in contact, and that does give her enough to keep going, but the feeling of deprivation is still often there. So she felt better about being here, even though it was also difficult.

I acknowledged what she had told me and then finished the session.

While of course there were many different elements to the session and to what was going on in the analysis at that time, I would point to the fact that it was a new experience for her to take a stand about her sessions. This did seem to be linked to a developing, if fragile, sense of being more 'at home' in the analysis, even though that meant having to experience difficult feelings. Given the fact that home for her was so full of conflict—with a mixture of loss, displacement, and rejection, I did feel this was a significant development.

Identity and home

I have suggested that the notion of a psychic home is integral to understanding personal identity. Identity is a term that is of great relevance to issues of race, ethnicity, nationality, gender, and sexuality. Feelings about identity, who one belongs with, can override even such basic wishes as a wish for freedom. Identity matters in very immediate ways, when it becomes a question of belonging, of inclusion, but also of exclusion. The phenomena of terrorism and fundamentalism mean also that we need to look at how identities are formed, sustained and can also be distorted. The existence of the Internet and the pace of globalization in addition mean that larger forces, capitalist or otherwise, are more and more eroding individual identities. It has become increasingly difficult for people to assert their own local identities; there is a constant risk of people becoming subservient to powerful interests.

Identity is a vitally important but complex and at times elusive or indeterminate concept. There are various fixed or constant elements in the development of our identity, which can become the source of integration and of a sense of permanence, of achievement and coherence, and there are still issues about the nature of identity that challenge our thinking, such as its link with the processes of identification, the question of whether or not unity is an illusion or a real possibility. De M'Uzan[7] has suggested that one can talk of a 'spectrum of identity', that the sense of I-ness is neither in the ego nor the other, but distributed along both, which matches my own picture of the human subject,[8] as being organized between the individual and the network of others. I describe the human subject as having a structure where multiple paths are possible, held together in some ways and not in others. Being able to tolerate the shifting and multiple elements of the psyche, bearing degrees of fragmentation, is crucial to the individual's subjectivity. I coined the notion of a 'subjective organization' as the psychic organization that structures the subject, involving individual and social elements, distributed along both, rather as in de M'Uzan's 'spectrum of identity'. Such an organization can become pathological in the sense of being defensive and held together by perverse forces, as with the pathological organization. But under normal conditions, the subjective organization remains the organizing structure involved in one's sense of 'I-ness', as well as that involved in the way that the subject is organized in the social field. One of the essential aspects of the subjective organization is that it involves subjects in interaction with other subjects. The subjective organization is a dual structure made up of individual and collective elements in a complex interrelationship. I think that becoming a subject must intimately involve having the stable sense of a psychic home as the basis for psychic shifts.

This situation could be understood by borrowing a musical metaphor, that of the modulation between tonic and dominant in, say sonata form, or with the resolution of dissonance when music returns to a home key from various musical excursions in related keys. Daniel Barenboim[9] describes the 'psychology of tonality', which parallels the inner life. This is

> creating a sense of home, going to an unknown territory, then returning. This is a process of courage and inevitability. There is the affirmation of the key—you want to call it the affirmation of self, the comfort of the known territory—in order to be able to go somewhere totally unknown and have the courage to get lost and, then, find again this famous dominant, in an unexpected way, that leads us back home.

I would suggest that one of the constant elements is that of the psychic home and that this provides a basis for a sense of identity, for crucial questions such as 'Who am I? Who do I look and act like? Which religion and nationality am I?' They indicate a search for a place in life, an identity which provides a relatively stable sense of home, and that provides the core of the elusive and precarious notion of identity, whatever its complex vicissitudes, however much the human subject is distributed between other subjects.

Identity has always mattered, at least in Western society, certainly since the ancient Greeks, even before passports and the Internet, as I have already described. Religion gave people a firm sense of identity for many centuries, even if that firmness meant that it was also a factor in creating conflict. In contrast to Homer's epic grandeur, if one were to capture the modern concern with identity artistically, one could do no better than consider the troubling pictures of Francis Bacon. He highlights in a disturbing way how our modern, or indeed post-modern, notion of identity is precarious. There is a permanent sense of unease in his pictures, marking the fragile sense of human identity. Faces and whole bodies intermingle and merge, sometimes are transformed into animal forms; mouths scream, bending figures cry out or are threatened, sexual encounters are anxiety ridden, identities are uncertain. Home is no comforting place here, rather the site of terror, cruelty, perversion, and crude sexuality. In David Sylvester's book *Looking Back at Francis Bacon*,[10] he describes Bacon's Study for self-portrait (1985–6), a brilliant triptych, depicting the artist from three viewpoints. Bacon here seems to alternate between masculine and feminine identities, in one panel with his legs tucked primly under the chair like a modest lady, and in another panel more macho, emphasizing his massive arms and broad shoulders. Sylvester quotes the critic Richard Dormant when he states that in our 'struggle to achieve a separate and secure identity' we have to learn 'to distinguish between our own bodies and those of others, to work out that our bodies not only have weight and mass, but also boundaries, limits, perimeters'. If the figures in this triptych 'are seen as embryonic shapes desperately trying – and failing – to form a single, secure identity, then they speak of a universal human condition, the aboriginal calamity with which we struggle all our lives—and this is the stuff of the greatest art.'[11]

While Bacon's triptych may reveal the struggle to form a single secure personal identity, contemporary politics reveals a real danger when people claim a single and overarching social and cultural identity rather than a looser sense of crossing a number of different identities. The fundamentalist dangerously owns a singular identity, excluding the rest of humanity, with potentially hateful and explosive results. They are no respecters of other people's homes. Identity can be homicidal, when it becomes singular and disrespectful of differences. Much safer is to recognize that we belong to a variety of groupings, with a plurality of affiliations, including language, gender, profession, religion, class, interest groups, political associations, and belief systems.[12] Identity can then be humanizing when it respects otherness. Thus a 'positive' notion of identity, respect, and recognition of difference go together, as do a 'negative' notion of identity, disrespect, and misrecognition of otherness.

Zygmunt Bauman describes how finding identity comes along with 'a bunch of problems rather than a single-issue campaign',[13] a feature he shares with most people these days, living in what he calls the 'liquid modern era'. By the latter, he means that 'in our liquid modern times the world around is sliced into poorly coordinated fragments while our individual lives are cut into a succession of ill-connected episodes'. The modern dilemma is to be wholly, or in part, out of place, or one might say, not quite at home. 'Identities float in the air, some of one's own choice, but others inflated and launched by those around.' One can 'even begin to feel everywhere *chez soi*, "at home"—but the price to be paid is to accept that nowhere will one be fully and truly at home.'

We in the liquid modern world,

> seek and construct and keep together the communal references of our identities while *on the move*—struggling to match the similarly mobile, fast moving groups we seek and construct and try to keep alive for a moment, but not much longer.[14]

One is reminded here of the suitably named mobile phone, to which we have become powerfully addicted, and without which communication can only be slow and uncertain. What did we do without it? Well we obviously had slower communication, longer waiting times before knowing what others thought or wanted. We had to wait hours or even days for messages to be answered. But there is a price to pay for being in a liquid world; our identity is also liquid, and, like liquid, difficult to tie down and shape, unless kept in a solid container.

On one hand, we long for a secure identity, yet becoming 'fixed' and identified gets an increasingly bad press. Yet having too much flexibility is not conducive to 'nest building'. But we live in a world where it is increasingly difficult to feel one belongs to a workplace or neighbourhood, or even family. There is instead an emphasis on being on the move, having a 'network' of connections, swapping identities. 'We talk these days of nothing with greater solemnity or more relish of "networks" of "connection" or "relationships". Not only because the "real stuff"—the closely knit networks, firm and secure connections, fully-fledged relationships—have all but fallen apart.'[15]

While flexibility may be a useful capacity,

> floating without support in a poorly defined space, in a stubbornly, vexingly 'betwixt and between' location, becomes in the long run an unnerving and anxiety-prone condition. On the other hand, a fixed position amidst the infinity of possibilities is not an attractive prospect either.[16]

While Bauman here does not offer solutions to the dilemmas he so clearly defines, there is an underlying sense that these dilemmas are directly related to the loss of 'fully-fledged' relationships, where there is a living attachment to home and to the workplace.

One cannot ignore the now massive literature on how *culture* affects one's sense of identity. Edward Said's work is pivotal to this field. In his classic *Culture and Imperialism*, he defines culture as meaning two things. First, it means 'all those practices, like the arts of description, communication, and representation, that have relative autonomy from the economic, social, and political realms, and that often exist in aesthetic forms, one of whose principal aims is pleasure.'[17]

Second, culture is a concept that includes a refining and elevating element, the best that is known and thought in each society. However, and this is one of the main threads of his study, culture can be used aggressively by a nation state in order to impose itself on others, differentiating 'us' from 'them'. Culture in this sense is a combative source of identity.

His own approach in the book, through a detailed examination of the work of various writers, such as Austen, Dickens, Conrad, Kipling, Camus, and Yeats, is to challenge a static view of identity which has been the core of cultural thought during the era of imperialism. Rather than see culture and identity as unitary, he proposes throughout his book that all cultures are involved in one another, 'none is single and pure, all are hybrid, heterogeneous, extraordinarily differentiated, and unmonolithic' (p. xxv). That is, he argues for a flexible, open-minded notion of identity, which can embrace different cultures and not impose on them from the outside. Such a view contrasts with that of imperialism, which was essentially about acquiring territory and imposing a particular way of life on other cultures, that is about acquiring *other homes*. Imperialism is the attitude of a dominating metropolitan centre ruling a distant territory. The attitude of those who ruled the colonies, creating an imperial culture in these other homes, reflected the various tensions and injustices in the home culture. There arose a complex relationship between the home culture, which needed to be stable and prosperous, while exploiting overseas territories. Thus Thomas Bertram's slave plantation in Jane Austen's *Mansfield Park* is shown to be mysteriously necessary to the poise and beauty of Mansfield Park.

Imperial possessions are usefully *there*, in some other space, with an unnamed population, whose identity is scratched out, erased; while such places become the site for adventurers, disgraced younger sons, travellers who sow wild oats or collect exotica. Said describes how in the great Victorian novels, 'home' and 'abroad' became crucial dimensions for analyzing the nature of English society. Abroad

> was felt vaguely and ineptly to be out there, or exotic and strange, or in some way or other 'ours' to control, trade in 'freely', or suppress when the natives were energized into overt military or political resistance. The novel contributed significantly to these feelings, attitudes, and references and became a main element in the consolidated vision, or departmental cultural view, of the globe.[18]

Said shows how there was in fact considerably more resistance to the imperialist impositions than was openly admitted. He also describes how in the course of time, decolonization was very much about *reclaiming homes* which had been usurped. In these acts of reclamation, all nationalist cultures become dependent on the concept of a national identity. As necessary as this process is in the act of liberation, there is of course a danger of mirroring the dominating culture from which they wish to be liberated.

Said argues for a new concept of identity, one which respects different cultures, *different homes*, where connections are made between cultures, other languages and geographies, where it is accepted that none today is *one* thing. Identity in this sense is about inclusion not exclusion.

However, it does seem that currently, far from there being an end to excluding nationalist sentiments, there is an increasing tendency globally to look towards the idea of the nation as a way of trying to assert control over what is seen as too much interference from 'outside'. The concept of a nation is, as Eric Hobsbawm[19] pointed out, a relatively new one. The equation nation=state=sovereign people only arose during the latter part of the eighteenth and the early nineteenth century, with the French revolution and the Declaration of Rights of 1795. Most states of any size were not at all homogenous and were (as even now) made up of a wide variety of ethnic and linguistic groups.

Indeed, Benedict Anderson has defined the nation as a cultural phenomenon, 'an imagined political community—and imagined as both inherently limited and sovereign.' A sense of a unified 'home nation' then owes as much to imagination as to any hard political realities. Such a sense of unity was helped over time by the often haphazard spread of crucial developments—such as that of printing, of increasing education, and the development of a sense of national languages and the owning of particular religious affiliations. Political dynasties, wars, and conquests had their part to play in this development. But the crucial step was the role of *imagination*. The nation had to be invented, 'imagined, modeled, adapted and transformed.'[20]

Over time the imagined community called a nation state has developed in various ways, positively and negatively, depending upon current realities, owing as much to crises of the imagination as to economic and political realities. Thus on the negative side, Hobsbawm[21] described how the rise of the Nazi state, with the resurgence of militant nationalism arose as a way of filling 'the void left by failure, impotence, and the apparent inability of other ideologies, political projects and programmes to realize men's hopes.'

I have already described how Michael Burleigh has shown how the Nazis and their partners in crime fundamentally altered the moral understanding of humanity, and in another study how totalitarian regimes used pseudo-religious imagery and notions such as 'awakening', 'confession', and the remorseless search for heretics to sustain their power.

On the positive side, various national uprisings against colonial rule, liberation movements of all kinds, owe much to the *imagined* communities they are liberating. As Anderson put it, having looked at how the nation came to be imagined through looking at social changes and different forms of consciousness, it is 'doubtful whether either social change or transformed consciousnesses, in themselves, do much to explain the *attachment* that peoples feel for the inventions of their imaginations.'[22] Why should, he asks, people *die* for their community, unless their nation inspired love? It is love in many guises that often motivates such acts—love of the motherland or homeland, or what I have called one's psychic home.

Loving attachments to homes can have complex origins, often having to deal with issues of *trauma* and fractured identity, which can be reconstructed if attention is paid to historical details. For example, Stuart Hall[23] faced similar issues to those of Said in his exploration of visual representations of Afro-Caribbean and Asian 'blacks' of the Diasporas of the West—the new post-colonial subjects. Such subjects have to face complex identity issues. Historically displaced from their homes, they are not in a position to reclaim their homes, as those living in the colonies could do; they are, to use a term often associated with the history of the Jews, subjects of a diaspora, dispersal. They have found other homes, and yet still have fundamental connections, through culture, history, myth, narrative, fantasy, and transmitted memories, to their origins. Dispersal and fragmentation are the history of all enforced diasporas, and clearly involve trauma and loss of identity. Such loss can only begin to be healed when forgotten connections between past and present are brought to light and once more set in place. That is not to say that there can be a return to what was; people's identities have moved on and have a life of their own. There are similarities but also differences between then and now which have to be recognized. Hall rethinks the positionings and repositionings of Caribbean cultural identities in relation to at least three 'presences'—the African presence, the site of the repressed; the European presence, which is the site of exclusion and expropriation; and the American presence, the beginning of diaspora, diversity, hybridity, and difference. There is no simple way that these presences can be harmonized or unified in a comfortable identity. Rather, these presences, which represent different discourses, meet at various junction-points; they can become the site of different subjective positions, or sites of temporary attachment to different subject positions.

Yet at some point, these attachments may become permanent. The Lebanese author Amin Maalouf, who was born in Lebanon and lives in France, in his book *On Identity* asks:

> So am I half French and half Lebanese? Of course not. Identity can't be compartmentalized. You can't divide it up into halves or thirds or any other separate segments. I haven't got several identities; I've got just one, made up of many components combined together in a mixture that is unique.[24]

He points out that identity is certainly made up of a number of allegiances, but that it is also necessary to emphasize that identity is also singular, something that we experience as a complete whole. 'A person's identity is not an assemblage of separate affiliations, nor a kind of loose patchwork; it is like a pattern drawn on a tightly stretched parchment.'[25]

Maalouf is also realistic about how identities are not always positive; they can be lethal, especially when 'tribal', based upon narrow and sectarian allegiances, which deny difference and diversity. Such a view matches the theme of Amartya Sen's book, *Identity and Violence*. Identities may become 'reactive', when for example a country, which has freed itself from foreign domination, creates its own identity, as a reaction to what they have left behind, rather than seek or create a different and more open form of identity. Reactive self-identities can lead to dangerous fundamentalism. Instead, Sen talks of the need to pay attention to 'our common humanity'.[26] Such an approach counters the tendency in economic and social analysis to neglect the influence of any sense of identity with others, and of what we value and how we behave—what he calls 'identity disregard'. And such an approach also counters what he calls 'singular affiliation'—the tendency to assume that any person pre-eminently belongs to only one collectivity, thereby obliterating people's natural multiple loyalties and affiliations. It was one of Sen's great achievements to show how an economic theory which obliterated such differences, such as merely focusing on a free market without any notion of people's capacities and welfare, cannot address modern economic realities in the developing countries.

The work of Jack Goody adds a further dimension to understanding our common 'global' humanity. He charts how world history has been hijacked by Western dominated approaches which have ignored the common social-cultural development between Europe and Asia going back millennia. In his book *The*

Theft of History, he points out that since the beginning of the nineteenth century, the construction of world history has been dominated by Western Europe, following their presence in the rest of the world as the result of colonial conquest and the Industrial Revolution. While other civilizations have their form of history, what has characterized European history is a tendency to impose their own story on the rest of the world, ignoring the many and complex developments and achievements of other civilizations, not to mention the constant interchange of ideas and inventions between Europe and the rest of the world. There has been, he maintains with considerable documentary evidence, a constant hijacking by the West of ideas and values originating elsewhere, with the West arrogantly assuming that it has the monopoly of rationality and virtuous ways of living. He shows for example that the West was not the inventor of, for example, the arts, such as the novel, painting and sculpture, nor of mercantile life nor even of *haute cuisine*.

He points out that the early growth of societies, from about 3000BCE, took place in a broad sweep of 'Eurasia', with the rise of urban cultures based upon an advanced agriculture employing the plough, the wheel, and sometimes irrigation. They developed urban living and various crafts such as writing.

> These highly stratified societies produced hierarchically differentiated cultural forms and a great variety of artisanal activities, in the Red River Valley in China, in the Harappan culture of northern India, in Mesopotamia and in Egypt, later in parts of the Fertile Crescent of the Near East as well as in Eastern Europe. There was parallel development throughout this vast region and there was some communication. Indeed the Urban Revolution affected developments not only in those major civilizations but also in those 'tribes' that lived on their periphery and which are taken to have in part 'fathered' Greek society.[27]

This hijacking of world history is not merely of academic interest, but it also helps to understand many of the current ignorant and intolerant attitudes to 'foreigners' openly displayed by some Europeans and fostered by populist leaders, happy to maintain the myth of Western cultural dominance based upon an inaccurate account of historical origins.

Notes

1 Benvenuto and Kennedy, 1986, p. 89.
2 Kennedy, 2007, pp. 246–60.
3 Lifton, 1994, p. 65.
4 Steiner, 1993.
5 Winnicott, 1949.
6 Kennedy, 2014.
7 De M'Uzan, 2005.
8 Kennedy, 1998, 2007.
9 Barenboim, 2003, pp. 46–7.
10 Sylvester, 2000.

11 Sylvester, 2000, pp. 223–4.
12 Sen, 2006.
13 Bauman, 2004, p. 12.
14 Bauman, 2004, p. 26.
15 Bauman, 2004, p. 93.
16 Bauman, 2004, p. 29.
17 Said, 1993, p. xii.
18 Said, 1993, pp.87–8.
19 Hobsbawm, 1990
20 Anderson, 2006, p. 141.
21 Hobsbawm, 1990, p. 144.
22 Anderson, 2006, p. 141.
23 Stuart Hall, 1990.
24 Maalouf, 1996, p. 3.
25 Maalouf, 1996, p. 22.
26 Sen, 2006, p. 119.
27 Goody, 2006, p. 29.

4

THE EARLY HISTORY OF TOLERANCE

Tolerance is a complex phenomenon, and there is a massive literature on what one could call the tolerance/intolerance dynamic, most of it focusing on social, political and legal issues, and few looking at psychological tolerance. In general, the usual approach is to maintain that tolerance entails putting up with a person, activity, idea or organization of which or whom one does not really approve, at least initially. Or it can be seen as an attitude or practice, which is only called for in certain social conflicts. As Rainer Forst puts it, toleration involves conflict:

> The distinctive feature is that tolerance does *not* resolve, but merely contains and defuses, the dispute in which it is invoked; the clash of convictions, interests or practices remains, though certain considerations mean that it loses its destructiveness … The promise of toleration is that coexistence in disagreement is possible.[1]

Of course this leads to a number of questions such as what kind of conflicts call for or permit tolerance, who are the subjects and what are the objects of tolerance, what kinds of reasons are there for objecting or accepting what is to be tolerated and what are the limits of toleration in different cases, including how far can the intolerant be tolerated? What does 'putting up with' a person or people mean? And how far can tolerance be stretched when powerful economic and political fears come into the picture, such as recent fears about being 'swamped' by 'hordes' of foreigners?

I would argue for an enlarged notion of tolerance, not one just resting on living with conflict, based on my reading both of historical accounts of toleration and of an interpretation of the arts as the source of tolerant attitudes. In order to trace out this enlarged picture, I start with an historical account of some of the key issues as a way of piecing together the different elements of an overall account of the nature of tolerance and its relevance to contemporary life. Given the complexity of the history of tolerance, and the fact that there are many detailed histories available, I can only point out what I consider of most relevance to current preoccupations, particularly where past ways of managing strangers, both those within and those outside a culture or country, resonate with our contemporary life. After looking at the early history of thought on tolerance up to the work of John Stuart Mill, I will tackle some key modern thinkers on the subject, all of whom owe a considerable debt to their predecessors; indeed without examining the latter, the former cannot fully be appreciated.

This history involves looking at how much intolerance was put forward as a stand against certain practices, such as heresy, as much as when tolerance was put forward as a counter perspective. In addition, one can see how the modern notion of tolerance crystallized out at a time of crisis in the European mind, the period between 1680 and 1715. As Paul Hazard has shown in his classic study of that time, new developments in the sciences, arts, and philosophy began to undermine the classical world of tradition and stability, causing a crisis in religious belief, political assumptions, and views about nature and reality. Extensive travel, particular to the East, opened the eyes of people to different ways of managing their lives and non-Christian values, so that the 'conscience of the old Europe was stirred and perplexed'.[2]

It was also a time when, as now, there was an *information explosion*. It was a time when information first became a commodity, not through books but through what became a thriving industry of manuscript newsletters, most of them concerned with the political issues of the time. People were hungry for information and so the distribution of such material became economically profitable. At the same time, governments increasingly realized that it was in their interest to put out their own information and control its flow.

> [T]he urgent request for versions of contemporary events, flattering to the ruler and edifying to the subjects, blurred the distinction between fact and fiction ... Hard-pressed by disastrous wars and lured by the prospect of enhanced reputation, governments offered money and favors to whoever could place their actions in the most favorable light.[3]

Truth and reality became blurred, a new age of doubt and skepticism was the result, all of which added to the crisis of the time. The dissemination of falsehood and fraud by the end of the seventeenth century 'produced skepticism about the very possibility of understanding the contemporary world or the recent past.'[4] The developing confidence in the new empirical science could not give enough of a counter to this increasing doubt. 'The political stuff of history seemed more and more impervious to investigation as governments appeared to spin ever more complex webs of deception.'[5]

It is striking how much current concerns about truth, post truth, fake news, and such like, mirror what was taking place in Europe around the late seventeenth century, which makes it particularly pertinent to examine the period for possible lessons.

While the modern notion of tolerance arose in the Enlightenment period there were of course many precursors, many ways in which strangers were welcomed, going back to Homer and the Bible, which are still relevant, not only as historical sources for contemporary attitudes to strangers, but as offering relevant ways of managing current encounters with those seeking refuge.

I have already mentioned how Odysseus as a stranger was given hospitality by his as yet unknowing wife Penelope. The Homeric concept of *Xenia* refers to a code of practice governing relations between strangers (*xenoi*) or different communities. The stranger is entitled to be treated within the host home with respect and given hospitality or *xenia*, with the offer of food and drink, a bed for the night, and a gift on leaving. Depending on the status of the stranger, he may be allowed to sit and eat with the host and be given more elaborate gifts. Host and guest both follow the appropriate etiquette. *Xenia* is also a way of managing through a particular etiquette potentially difficult potential encounters with a stranger. Such an attitude to a powerful stranger was a forerunner of political and military alliances.[6]

There are a number of scenes in the Odyssey where *xenia* takes place, cementing relationships and understanding between strangers, but also those where it is broken or not followed correctly, with usually destructive consequences. The latter is seen when the monstrous Cyclops eats Odysseus' companions. When Odysseus calls for a gift of hospitality, the Cyclops says to him that the only gift will be to eat him last of all. When Penelope's suitors invade her home rather than treat her and Odysseus' memory with respect, they are punished with death at Odysseus' own hands. Thus *xenia* towards strangers, as well as survival from the destructive results of its abuse by endurance and cunning, is a major theme of the Odyssey, no doubt reflecting its importance as a civilizing element of early Greek culture.

Both the Old and New Testaments and indeed the Koran make hospitality a positive virtue in similar ways to that described by Homer, with various rituals, including the washing of feet or care of the stranger's animals. In Judaism, hospitality, *hakhnasat orchim* (the bringing in of strangers), to guests is considered a blessing. When one knows of strangers who are hungry or need a place to relax, it becomes a legal obligation. The Bible contains many examples of the importance of being hospitable toward strangers and the rewards that one receives for the act of kindness.

There is also in the New Testament the parable of the Samaritan, the generous bystander, who comes to the aid of a man left for dead after having been beaten up by robbers. He tends to his wounds and cares for him at an inn. This is not a heroic act but an ordinary act of caring or beneficence, one which took place after others had passed by the wounded man, leaving him for dead. The parable no doubt has many potential meanings, but it is hard to ignore the basic message about the need for an ethics of caring for those who are evidently vulnerable, and against indifference to suffering.

But in addition there are more powerful commandments in the Bible to go beyond mere hospitality, or even beneficence, towards active engagement with those just that bit nearer than the stranger, towards neighbours, or when the stranger begins to live within a society where they were once strangers. Thus from the Old Testament:

> And if a stranger sojourn with thee in your land, ye shall not vex him.
> *But* the stranger that dwelleth with you shall be unto you as one born among you, and thou shalt love him as thyself; for ye were strangers in the land of Egypt.
>
> *(Leviticus, 33–34)*

Hence one should not 'vex' the stranger who lives in a neighbouring community, they should be left alone. Whereas if the stranger actually lives within your home area, they should be loved as you would love your own community; not left alone but taken into one's loving home vicinity. The memory of past trauma is a reminder of the need for an empathic response to the stranger, also like the Jews an exile in a foreign land.

And from the New Testament, where Jesus links up with his Jewish heritage:

> When asked what is the great commandment of the law, Jesus replied:
> 'Thou shalt love the Lord thy God with all thy heart, and with all thy soul, and with all thy mind.
> This is the first and great commandment.
> And the second is like unto it. Thou shalt love thy neighbor as thyself.'
>
> *(Matthew, 22: 36–9)*

Thus within the biblical tradition, welcoming and then loving the new arrival who then stays becomes a central moral position, involving the moral law, something which was evidently lost sight of in later religious wars and intolerant attitudes to different faiths. Even today we can learn from this tolerant attitude to the guest; we need to relearn the art of hospitality. But of course they first of all need to be seen as potential guests rather than as merely threatening presences, and for that another attitude is required, more like formalized tolerance. Accepting someone as a guest already implies one has a home.

The term *Tolerantia*, a precursor to the modern notion of toleration, was first used extensively in Stoic writings, for example by Cicero and Seneca, as a term for the virtue of an individual enduring pain and suffering. The capacity to bear emotional pain remains embedded in the modern notion of tolerance, from the obvious sense of having to put up with something irritating in an ordinary social context, to more complex mental states when emotional growth may have to involve tolerating emotionally challenging feelings, such as in a psychoanalytic session.

The notion of enduring suffering was probably incorporated into the subsequent Christian attitude to accepting pain and suffering during the years of persecution. Of course Jesus set the example of such a patient suffering in the face of persecution.

Subsequent early Church Fathers wrote of overcoming despair as a test of faith for the believer in the Kingdom of God. With regard to those of different faiths, there is early on a general attitude of charity and love to others, provided they are not wicked—the typical model for the latter is that of Jesus expelling the money changers from the Temple, as they had turned it into a 'den of robbers'. The latter action of course unfortunately was at times subsequently interpreted as an excuse for persecution of Jews because of their being allowed to lend money, rather than seeing it as Jesus wanting the Temple to be kept purely as a place of worship.

The different and rather conflicting attitudes shown by Augustine towards the justification of toleration became central to later attitudes to religious differences. Early in his thought, he maintained the principle of *credere non potest nisi volens*, that is a man cannot believe unless he is willing. Thus faith was based upon an inner conviction, freely embraced—a view to be taken up in the early thinking of Martin Luther. The virtue of love, nourished by love of God and inner grace comes in as well, in which the good Christian is urged to show compassion and patience even to the bitterest of enemies; such a view is also commended as facilitating unity of the church rather than division. Being tolerant towards other faiths then provides a model for one's own faith.

However, later Augustine, when confronted with the possibility of dangerous church splits, changed his view. The Catholicism of Augustine began to reflect the political reality of the church in that it was by then a group increasingly in a dominant position rather than a persecuted minority, and 'hungry for souls'.[7] Augustine proposed the notion of 'good coercion', in order to show the apostate the error of their ways. He cited the passage from Luke (14: 23), where a man was giving a banquet and no one was turning up, so he was urged to get his servants to 'Go out into the highways and hedges and compel them to come in, that my House may be full.' Jesus was in fact urging the man to invite the poor and disadvantaged from the hedges and highways, but the point is that one cannot just expect people to turn up and enter the Kingdom of Heaven; they needed some persuasion or 'good' *compulsion*. Augustine summed this up in one word as '*disciplina*', an 'active process of corrective punishment', a 'softening-up process', a 'teaching by inconveniences'.[8] And Augustine cited the case of the wayward Israelites who needed just such a discipline to curb their evil tendencies; they had needed the imposition of the Mosaic law virtually by force and 'compelled, by fear, to remain in a compact unity under the Law, even though the Law's significance had been understood and loved by only the very few "spiritual" men among them.'[9] He considered that this blatantly coercive regime had thus deterred the Jews from the woes of polytheism and had kept their unity.

Furthermore, 'Augustine's view of the Fall of mankind determined his attitude to society. Fallen men had come to need restraint. Even man's greatest achievements had been made possible only by a "straight-jacket" of unremitting harshness.'[10]

Unfortunately this interpretation of the Luke passage and the slogan *compelle intrare* (compel them to enter) led to the justification of increasingly militant and intolerant attitudes to dissenters and different faiths. It became to be seen as a legitimation of compulsion of heretics and schismatics back into the true faith. It was even used much later, for example by the writer and preacher J.-B. Bossuet in support of the revocation of the Edict of Nantes in 1685, when French Huguenots lost civil and religious freedoms, previously granted by Henry IV in 1598 after divisive religious wars and massacres of Huguenots. It was also this particular passage and its re-interpretation that became the focus of Pierre Bayle's radical views about tolerance in his *Philosophical Commentary* (1686), to which I will return below.

Augustine proposed that heretics could be forced to reenter the faith by 'moderate' forms of punishment. However by the time of the Crusades, and the establishment of various inquisitions in parts of Europe, more extreme measures, including execution were also used.

Much of the anti-heretical and anti-schismatic literature from Augustine and into the Middle Ages and to some extent beyond, saw heresy not only as a terrible crime, polluting and poisoning the human soul, but also as 'a contagious, polluting, and insidiously spreading disease requiring amputation or segregation, and held to be sexually based and associated with "lustfulness", "sodomy", and "libertinism"'.[11] These kinds of links between heresy and sexuality were repeated many times in early Modern Europe in arguments for the justification of intolerance, revealing how intolerance and fantasy often interweave.

The question of the peaceful co-existence of different monotheistic faiths was a focus of attention in the Middle Ages. The Islamic world of the Middle Ages, such as during the period when the Iberian peninsula was under Muslim rule, was a period of considerable tolerance towards other faiths, albeit with some restrictions. Both the major philosophers of Judaism and Islam of that time (who also both grew up in Muslim Cordoba)—Maimonides and Ibn Rushd (Averroes)—produce arguments for a certain amount of tolerance towards other faiths. They both defend the search for philosophical truth against religious dogma.

Ibn Rushd has the more compelling argument for toleration, asserting that Christianity, Judaism, and Islam have a number of equivalent ethical positions; that there is much in common at a high level of thinking, with the common search for a form of faith, of reasoned arguments and morality. Forst points out that 'modern justifications of toleration will in different ways take this as their starting point.'[12]

However, subsequent history of relations between the faiths consisted more frequently of ongoing clashes between doctrines. One may focus on relations between Jews and Christians from the Middle Ages as an illustration.

Jacob Katz in his book *Exclusiveness and Tolerance* [13] charts these relations in exemplary fashion, from the viewpoint of the Jews towards their non-Jewish environment from the Middle Ages to the Enlightenment era. What is both significant and helpful in this study is how he looks at the way that *both* faiths frequently maintained stereotyped attitudes to one another, preventing *mutual* understanding when such attitudes predominated. Indeed there were clearly reciprocal relationships between

Jews and Christians, each conditioned in their behaviour by the other, though with different emphases on each side.

On the one hand, Jew and Christian share a common bible tradition with considerable overlap in values and even moral commandments. However, they have different attitudes to religious truth. On the one hand the Jews believed that they had a special covenant with God, while for the Christians that covenant no longer stood with the appearance of Jesus. On both sides there was an ideology of separateness, with the Jews feeling the chosen people, with a special and at times mystic union with God, while the Christians believed in a 'new covenant' with the appearance of Jesus, with Jews now seen as covenant breakers. In turn the Jews considered Christians to be idol worshipers, seeing themselves as the upholders of the pure faith.

Meanwhile for much of the time, the existence of the Jews as a community depended upon economic relations with their Christian rulers as well as varying amounts of political protection. While economic relations were important, the underlying religious differences based upon attitudes to the covenant with God remained as the driving force for relations between the faiths with varying intensity, depending upon particular societal circumstances. While there were periods of discrimination against Jews, there were also relatively peaceful periods, such as between the ninth and eleventh centuries, where for example in France and Germany Jews were allowed to transact business almost without any restrictions. Nonetheless Christian and Jewish communities remained virtually two distinct societies, and being in the same economic and political framework this eventually caused many problems.

While it was possible in earlier times for Jewish populations to remain relatively separate from other communities, this was increasingly untenable as a position for those settling in Europe, and Jewish scholars and rabbis found various ways of trying to manage the need for more contact by reinterpreting aspects of Jewish everyday law, for example acknowledging the Christian deity as having much in common with their own, being the maker of heaven and earth.

The point to make here is that if there is to be toleration, then two sides need to restrain themselves as well as opening up to the other; there is a mutual process of acceptance; that is, there is an *inter-subjective* dimension.

I mention this sort of detail as a reminder that in looking to improve inter-faith relationships in our days, a matter of increasing urgency, there is clearly from these examples, a need to look at *both* sides. The history of how Jews and Christians struggled with these issues may well be instructive and relevant today.

It was only in 1215, with the 4th Lateran Council that a new attitude to Jewish contact with Christians came into existence, with the branding of Jews as an inferior social grouping, the compulsory wearing of the Jewish yellow badge and warnings not to mix freely with Jews. This was also the period when religious inquisitions against heretics and schismatics came to the fore. By then, there was widespread limitation of Jews in social life and active discrimination against them, probably fuelled by the religious crusades, whose aim was to liberate the holy land from Islamic rule. One can see here then how religious belief can become intolerant when mixed with military ambitions—a phenomenon visible in, for example, Syria and Iraq in our times.

As I have mentioned, Jews had some tranquillity in the Iberian Peninsula, until they were expelled in 1492 from Spain, in 1497 from Portugal, having already been expelled from England in 1290 and also from various European centres in the fourteenth century. The Spanish Inquisition then began as a way of trying to distinguish any heretics in those many Jews and Muslims who had converted to Christianity, though it then widened its scope towards any heretics. The Jews who left had to survive where they could, a haven being the Turkish Ottoman Empire, which had a particularly tolerant attitude to non-Muslims, through the use of the 'millet' system, a way of managing *group rights*. The millet was an autonomous self-governing religious community, each organized under its own courts of law and headed by a religious leader, who was responsible to the central government for the fulfilment of various responsibilities and duties, particularly those of paying taxes and maintaining internal security. In addition, each millet assumed responsibility for social and administrative functions not provided by the state. Jews in centres such as Salonica, Smyrna and Constantinople found havens of peace and prosperity, thanks to the millet system, for centuries, in fact until 1856 when a series of imperial reform edicts introduced secular law codes for all citizens, and much of the millets' administrative autonomy was lost.

While Islam remained the dominant religion in the Ottoman Empire, there was a relatively easy accommodation with other faiths, mainly Jews and Christians, through what one might call *'bureaucratic'* tolerance,[14] with the use of various rules to maintain the relations between communities. This was effectively a pragmatic way of managing an immense and multi-cultural empire. The barriers between Muslims and non-Muslims were pretty fluid, and allowed such a useful cultural and commercial interchange between faiths that the Empire grew in wealth, as evidenced for example in Constantinople where mosques, churches, and synagogues were both abundant and often in close proximity to one another.

Such tolerance was in striking contrast to the Habsburg Empire at the time of the thirty years war (1618–1648), where cohabitation between those holding different religious beliefs was impossible. Indeed, looking over the broad sweep of history, one could even say that in the last thousand years or so, Islam has been the most tolerant of the monotheistic religions, often giving hospitality to other faiths, something which can be easily lost sight of in the contemporary context. Indeed, the tolerationist writers of the seventeenth century often pointed to Islamic toleration as an example to be imitated.

It is also worth mentioning the subsequent formation of the Italian Ghetto, following the diaspora of Jews after the expulsions from Spain and Portugal, most famously in Venice from 1516, as this represented a new period in Jewish–Christian relations, and one which in a number of ways was quite creative for both sides, in contrast with the derogatory sense that the term ghetto has today.

On the one hand the Venetian ghetto was created in 1516 as a compulsory segregated quarter in which all Jews were required to live. Jews had already been reasonably well tolerated, as there was need for their economic help after a period of war with Genova. The Venetian senate then decided to provide a protected space for the Jewish population. The term ghetto probably arose as there was a foundry (*getto* in Venetian) on this site. While the ghetto separated the Jewish and Venetian populations, there was considerable contact between them, and indeed during the day Jews were permitted to circulate freely throughout Venice. It was really an 'open ghetto'. While there were restrictions at night, there were a number of allowable exceptions, such as the passing through the ghetto gates of Jewish doctors attending on Christian patients. The ghetto was also later enlarged to take account of the increasing number of Jewish residents, who had grown considerably due to their increasing prosperity, and it then also included a wave of migrants who had been forcibly converted to Christianity but had retained their faith in secret.

While the ghetto limited the freedom of the Jewish population, it also offered them a number of benefits. It offered an urban experience in the heart of Venice and in immediate proximity to the Christian population. The boundaries between the ghetto and the rest of the city were porous, and thus created a new sense of intimacy between both sides. From the Jewish side, the ghetto then enhanced Jewish cultural interaction with the outside world, and Jewish culture, the printing industry, music, and architecture flourished. It also gave them a basic sense of security, even with the restrictions; they were not being expelled and their own experience was given some legitimacy. They felt they had a home. Interestingly, while doctrinal differences between Judaism and Christianity in medieval times constituted the 'primary demonstration of the existence of a mutual awareness of diversity',[15] the situation in the ghetto became one in which Jews did not define their faith in terms of comparison with Christianity, and polemics against Christianity virtually ceased in the sixteenth century.

From the Christian side, there were benefits from contact with Jewish merchants and professionals, and even the Kabbalah, the Jewish mystical writings, became of great interest and influenced Christian intellectuals. Such writings had already influenced one of the most important of Renaissance philosophers—Pico Della Mirandola.

The administration of the ghetto became more formalized as it enlarged, with its own Councils, which had in time to take account of different ethnic Jewish populations—the Ashkenazi, Sephardic, and Levantine communities. In short, the ghetto came to function like a small republic at the heart of the larger Venetian republic.[16]

While of course ghetto formation has become associated with the Nazi past, the Venetian ghetto was unlike the Warsaw ghetto for example, and there may be lessons to be learned even now from the Venetian experience (and that of the tolerant Ottomans) about how to manage the close proximity of different cultures and religions within an urban context. For example, they show how the acceptance of differences can have a reasonable side, if managed well, that if communities are to remain in ghettos or ghetto-like areas, they need to be porous to the world outside the ghetto, and also close to administrative centres, as well as open to close cultural exchanges.

The further history of relations between Jewish and Christian populations has to be seen in the new context of the Enlightenment, which represented a fundamental break in how the human subject was conceived and when modern notions of tolerance were developed in the context of widespread intolerance.

Jonathan Israel's magisterial histories of the Enlightenment[17] delineate two forms cutting across nations and communities—*Radical* and *Moderate Enlightenment*, each type involving either wider or lesser amounts of tolerance to other faiths. Enlightenment thinkers of both streams all wanted to improve the human condition by means of reason, through a 'fundamental, revolutionary transformation, discarding the ideas, habits, and traditions of the past either wholly or partially.'[18] The more moderate enlighteners wanted a step-by-step change, while the more radical argued for a complete transformation of society. Israel's overall approach to his historical study of the Enlightenment is more of a focus on intellectual history, or the 'republic of letters', as the prime channelling and guiding force of social and intellectual change. For Israel radical enlightenment thinking is still relevant for today. Indeed, controversially, he goes very far in asserting that:

> For anyone who believes human societies are best ruled by reason as defined by the radical Enlightenment, ordering modern societies on the basis of individual liberty, democracy, equality, equity, sexual freedom, and freedom of expression and publication clearly constitutes a package of rationally validated values which not only were, but remain today, inherently superior morally, politically, and intellectually not only to Postmodernist claims but to *all* actual or possible alternatives.[19]

Nor does he confine such radical thinking to the Western tradition, being open to for example relevant Chinese and Islamic thought.

This view of the Radical Enlightenment contrasts with that of the Frankfurt School thinkers such as Adorno and Horkheimer[20] who, from an Hegelian and Marxist perspective, considered, in brief, that Enlightenment values themselves are not automatically radical and progressive and that potentially liberating processes revealed by the Enlightenment are undermined by our enslavement within the totality of capitalist social relations, bringing about *alienation* between people. Such a view, which has clearly influenced Zizek, is not referred to in Israel's histories, but it is possible that their analysis is more relevant to the limits of Moderate Enlightenment thinking.

Various governments and influential factions in the churches supported moderate Enlightenment thinking, which represented the mainstream. Newton and Locke were its main spokespeople in England. This form of Enlightenment aspired to conquer ignorance and superstition, establish toleration, and revolutionize ideas, education, and attitudes by means of philosophy but in such a way as to preserve and safeguard what were judged essential elements of the older structures, effecting a viable synthesis of old and new, reason and faith.[21]

In contrast, the radical Enlightenment thinkers aimed to sweep away existing structures. Radical Enlightenment thinking, which for Israel is above all epitomized by Spinoza's thought, involved a fundamental 'revolution of the mind'[22] including toleration, equality, democracy, republicanism, individual freedom, and liberty of expression and the press, which caused revolutions and near and actual overthrow of authority, tradition, monarchy, faith, and privilege.

Key and emblematic thinkers, in the radical tradition approach to tolerance are Pierre Bayle and Benedict Spinoza, and for the moderate tradition John Locke, though I will argue that Locke is still radical enough, with his new views about the individual's liberty of conscience and the need for the individual to be free from external interference, to be an aid for contemporary tolerant practices. Locke and to some extent Bayle argue for universal toleration, but not for the 'intolerant'. Locke for example excluded Catholics, as they were beholden to the Pope for their authority, which then prevented them from having liberty of conscience, and atheists as he saw them as disruptive to society. Bayle was accommodating towards atheists, while Spinoza alone argued for a fully encompassing universal toleration and against religious authority, and for that reason was seen as a dangerous thinker in his time, even in the relatively tolerant Holland where he lived.

Notes

1 Forst, 2003, p. 1.
2 Hazard, 1935, p. 28.
3 Dooley, 1999, p. 5.
4 Dooley, 1999, p. 6.
5 Dooley, 1999, p. 6.
6 Finley, 1954, p. 102.
7 Brown, 2000, p. 209.
8 Brown, 2000, p. 233.
9 Brown, 2000, p. 233.
10 Brown, 2000, p. 234.
11 Marshall, 2006, p. 222.
12 Forst, 2003, p. 89.
13 Katz, 1961.
14 Lacorne, 2016, p. 81.
15 Katz, 1961, p. 134.
16 Lacorne, 2016, p. 91.
17 Israel, 2001, 2006, 2010, 2011.
18 Israel, 2011, p. 7.
19 Israel, 2006, p. 869.
20 Adorno and Horkheimer, 1947.
21 Israel, 2001, p. 11.
22 Israel, 2006.

5

SPINOZA, LOCKE, AND BAYLE

Spinoza

The Preface to his *Theological-Political Treatise* summarizes Spinoza's approach to countering human prejudice and superstition in ways that are remarkably relevant today. He points out how much the human mind is swayed by hope and fear in times of doubt, each struggling for mastery. Led on by unscrupulous leaders, men's minds can become enthralled by prejudices, for example under the specious garb of religion or quasi-religious sentiments. He wonders how people,

> who make a boast of professing the Christian religion, namely love, joy, peace, temperance and charity to all men, should quarrel with such rancorous animosity, and display daily towards one another such bitter hatred, that this, rather than the virtues they claim, is the readiest criterion of their faith.[1]

He argues that men's habits of mind differ, so that some more readily embrace one form of faith, some another, for what moves one to pray may move another only to scoff. Therefore he concludes that,

> everyone should be free to choose for himself the foundations of his creed, and that faith should be judged only by its fruits; each would then obey God freely with his whole heart, while nothing would be publicly honoured save justice and charity.[2]

From the argument for liberty of faith and tolerance of different faiths, or what one would now call an argument for religious *plurality*, he moves onto more general issues about liberty, starting with what he calls the natural rights of the individual, putting forward the notion that no one is bound to live as another pleases, but is the guardian of his own liberty.

The treatise is then occupied with reinterpreting the Bible as an historical text that had a basic and simple moral message about loving one's neighbour and knowing and loving God. The texts of the Bible, thrown together by various authors over time and not dictated by God were not to be taken literally and certainly not to be worshipped. They did not provide actual evidence for so-called miracles and other supernatural phenomena. The status of any ceremonial practices was questionable; they were put there to help that particular community at that particular time to stick together, but had no relevance or universal application beyond that. Instead, they were described as part of the moral message aimed at ordinary people; they contained no philosophical truths or convincing doctrines about the nature of God; instead they were often merely allegorical stories aimed at illiterate followers. Philosophy and religion covered separate realms, and by reducing the Bible's message to a basic moral one free from superstition, speculation, and irrelevant ceremonies, everyone was free to interpret religion as they wished— hence one should be *tolerant* towards those with different religious beliefs.

Having undermined the divinity of the Bible, there is no justification for the Jewish people to see themselves as chosen and no reason to observe ceremonial laws or accept the authority of the rabbis.

While Spinoza was specifically addressing the Jewish Old Testament, his arguments were obviously aimed beyond this to any religious text. His was a universal vision of religion, which was to be shared by all humans, without any one religion having a privileged access to the truth. Hence it was hardly surprising that his views were both widely abhorred yet also widely influential as part of the radical enlightenment movement.

The *Treatise* then argues that people, through the right use of their reason, must necessarily come to an agreement to live together as securely and well as possible, if they are to enjoy the rights that naturally belong to them as individuals. In order to live securely they will need to do to all as they would be done by, defending their neighbour's rights as their own, restraining irrational desires to control others. He acknowledges that it is not the case that reason alone leads men on, and that they may be led by fear and prejudice, and that there are dangers in the way that sovereign power may be used against others. However in a democratic society, there is the best chance of restraining sovereign power, so long as men are given freedom of expression and thought, each person maintaining the liberty to preserve their own existence. The individual may give up some freedom for the sake of the peace of the community, but they will not lose their individual freedom to reason, judge, express, and write and publish their opinions.

By the time he had written the political treatise, Spinoza had in effect become an internal exile in Holland, excluded by his Jewish community in 1656 at the age of 23. His exclusion, the *Cherem*, the ban or excommunication pronounced by the Sephardic community of Amsterdam and which has never been reversed, probably came about over confrontations around his attitude to Jewish observance, his philosophical thinking, and finally the financial ruin of his merchant father's business. He ended up living frugally in various parts of Holland, writing his radical works while making a living grinding lenses.

At the heart of his views about individual liberty and tolerance was his philosophical system, most of which was published posthumously. His *Ethics* contains the core of his thinking and the logical key to his radical views about tolerance. In it, he argues through a number of logical propositions, that by God, he means an infinite being, a substance consisting of infinite attributes, each one of which expresses the eternal and infinite essence. God is the infinite necessarily existing, uncaused, and unique substance of the universe. There is only *one substance* in the universe and that is God, and everything else that is dwells in God. Nothing can be conceived without God. God and nature are the same. Nature is an indivisible, uncaused, and substantial unity. This has been described as a form of 'pantheism' where God is equated with the material universe.

To summarize:

> I have explained the nature and properties of God. I have shown that he necessarily exists, that he is one: that he is, and acts solely by the necessity of his own nature; that he is the free cause of all things, and how he is so; that all things are in God, and so depend on him, that without him they could neither exist nor be conceived; lastly, that all things are predetermined by God, not through his free will or absolute fiat, but from the very nature of God or infinite power.[3]

This picture of God was radically different from the traditional one of a being who looked over mankind and who could judge our actions or who caused the world to exist out of nothing. Spinoza's God is the cause of all things because all things follow causally and necessarily from God's nature. God cannot perform miracles because that goes against nature. The belief in miracles is only due to ignorance of the true causes of phenomena. We need to *understand* nature with clear and distinct intellectual knowledge.

This logical or mathematical or 'pantheistic' picture of God was, not surprisingly, seen as heretical. If God existed only in a philosophical sense, it once again took away the necessity for ritual and organized worship, and appeared to many at the time as arguing for a form of atheism. But it also removed controversial differences in belief systems and alternative interpretations of scripture that were the motors of religious intolerance.

Spinoza's monism extended also to understanding the nature of human beings. The human mind is part of the infinite intellect of God. Nothing stands outside nature, not even the human mind. A person is a unity of mind and body; indeed it is more accurate to talk again of *one substance*, which can be viewed in two ways, or from two different perspectives, as extension or thought. This does away with the mind/body duality as mind and body are two different attributes of the same substance, and this has made it popular with neuroscientific followers of materialism, who claim that the mind and the brain are co-extensive, one material substance.

Spinoza's model of freedom is complex and involves his elaborate theory of the emotions. A main point is that freedom involves knowledge of causes. We are slaves to our passions if we do not understand them and what has caused them. The ordinary notion of freedom is an illusion due to ignorance of true causes. Thus:

> Further conceive a stone, while continuing in motion, should be capable of thinking and knowing, that it is endeavouring, as far as it can, to continue to move. Such a stone, being conscious merely of its own endeavour and not at all indifferent, would believe itself to be completely free, and would think that it continued in motion solely because of its own wish. This is that human freedom, which all boast that they possess, and which consists solely in the fact that men are conscious of their own desires, but are ignorant of the causes whereby that desire had been determined.[4]

For Spinoza, genuine freedom is knowledge of causes; and the life of the free man is the life free from external causes because of this knowledge. Freedom for a person consists of the possibility of acquiring rational understanding of nature and of himself or herself, and this included the true causes of emotions.

I mentioned at the beginning of this chapter how Spinoza began his *Treatise* by examining how humans are easily swayed by prejudice and superstition, and oscillate between hope and fear in times of doubt. To counteract such attitudes, one needs to understand these emotions, look for clear and distinct knowledge of their causes, so that we are no longer slaves to our emotions; this is the way leading to freedom.

Locke

Spinoza's appeal to natural rights of liberty and self-expression, moving from arguments for plurality of religious faith to general arguments in favour of universal liberty, contrasts with Locke's position in his highly influential *Letter on Toleration* [5] where he remained mainly within the bounds of the issue of 'freedom of worship, theological debate, and religious practice, in so far as these are an extension of freedom of conscience, rather than with freedom of thought, debate, and of the press more broadly,'[6] though he also made important proposals about the limitations of government interference on the individual, and argued for the separation of church and state, that reached its fulfillment in the American Constitution. He begins the *Letter* with the theme that sets the main tone of the text: 'You ask me for my opinion of *mutual* [my italics] toleration among Christians. I reply in a word that it seems to me to be the principal mark of the true church.'[7]

Locke proposed a system of religious toleration accommodating Christian plurality and freedom of choice in matters of faith, while not accommodating irreligion, unbelief, and a libertine lifestyle. But given the reality of the times, this limitation very likely meant that his views would be both easier to accept and more directly influential. It was also in his directly political writings that he opposed political tyranny and favoured resistance to political intolerance. Thus in his *Second Treatise on Civil Government*, he, like Spinoza, has a notion of natural man—Spinoza talks of natural rights, Locke of man being free, equal and independent by nature.[8] Once men come together freely and by consent to form a community for their self-preservation, then new conditions apply, whereby the public good limits the individual's liberty. However, and this is something that Locke retains in his *Letter on Toleration*, every man has 'the right of freedom over his own person, which no other person has a power over, but the free disposal of it lies *in* [my italics] himself.'[9] Such a view reflects how much the role of government had shifted from the medieval period, where the sovereign was often seen as someone who must help their subjects gain their salvation in the next world,[10] to Locke's times when the government of a state began no longer to concern itself with its subjects' salvation. His writings were among those pivotal in justifying this transition to a more modern world.

I would suggest then that his ideas in the *Letter*, put together with his other writing on knowledge and politics represent a synthesis of a new view of the human subject, or in his terms the self, with a particular emphasis on *inwardness* as guarantor of truth, and placing liberty of conscience and personal autonomy at the forefront of his thinking. While focused on the nature of religious identity in the *Letter*, he was also concerned with the general nature of the self, identity, and the nature and limits of human understanding, topics he would cover with breadth and vision in his *Essay on Human Understanding*. He would also argue there for a more general liberty of opinion and tolerance of different beliefs. Thus:

> Since therefore it is unavoidable to the greatest part of Men, if not all, to have several *Opinions*, without certain and indubitable Proofs of their Truths; and it carries too great an imputation of ignorance, lightness or folly, for Men to quit and renounce their former Tenets, presently upon the offer of an Argument, which they cannot immediately answer ... It would, methinks, become all Men to maintain *Peace*, and the Common Offices of Humanity, *and friendship, in the diversity of Opinions*.[11]

It was also Locke that had the most and immediate influence on his successors such as Voltaire, thanks to his new approach to human understanding as based upon *experience*. Locke laid the foundation for a radically 'open' view of human nature by arguing in the *Essay* that there were no innate ideas and that babies were born with a clean slate, a *tabula rasa*. The fact that Locke denies that there are any innate moral or any other innate principles in the mind has far-reaching consequences. He does not deny that a child or even an infant has inclinations or appetites or the capacity to perceive; but he asserted that they are unable to use their reason in a way that can lead to theoretical or abstract principles. All such principles can only be acquired by *experience*. If there are no innate principles, one must look to experience, not to inherited dogma, to discover the truth. And one might even apply this assumption to the attitude towards any inherited body of knowledge, which must be radically questioned in the light of experience, and only by a man, once he has the capacity to reason, reflecting wholly within himself.

Furthermore, if the mind were so radically contingent on experience, then, as George Makari in his history of the soul concept put it, 'If every impression and experience could twist a man toward insanity or evil, then every moment, every day, was filled with uncertainty and dread, for events and environments molded humans like clay.'[12] Makari points out that Locke's model of insanity based on the precariousness of the mind and the unclear line between madness and sanity, rather than the traditional Galenic theory of humours, profoundly changed the way that mental disorders were understood and treated.

Nonetheless it would be accurate to maintain that Locke was against radical democracy. His experiences of living through the crisis periods of the English Civil War and its radical social and political change, and the religious dissensions and economic instability both of that time and the succession of James II, made him no doubt suspicious of radicalism. In his philosophy he saw his task as a modest one, an 'under-laborer in clearing the ground a little, and removing some of the rubbish that lies in the way of knowledge,'[13] rather than creating an eternal system along the lines of Spinoza. This approach would become one of the pillars of Liberalism, with its skepticism towards overarching systems of thought and fear of governmental coercion. It paved the ground for subsequent liberal economic thinking, with the emphasis on inducement though the 'impersonal' free market rather than coercion though government interference. And his empiricism, in tune with the explosion of scientific experimentation and the success of Newtonian physics in explaining the workings of nature, has come ever since to dominate the British approach to understanding the world.

Locke wrote his seminal *Letter on Toleration* in 1685 while living in the Dutch Republic. He was living there as a precaution against being arrested in England after opposition to Charles II. Locke was part of an oppositional group associated with his patron Lord Shaftesbury. The work was published in 1689, after Locke's return to England and after the 'Glorious Revolution' of 1688 that had driven out the intolerant and Catholic James II and then replaced him with the Dutch Protestant William and his English wife Mary. Before commenting on the *Letter*'s content, it is worth summarizing some of its historical and political background, particularly as there are certain parallels with the current tolerance/intolerance dynamic, with a similar background of international crises, justification for intolerance as necessary for protection against insurrection, and the difficulties in maintaining a tolerant position.

Holland itself was certainly a place that offered asylum of sorts for many victims of religious persecution, and it was the place where Locke and indeed Spinoza and Bayle were able to write in relative peace, though it was far from being a place free from intolerance. On the one hand, the 1680s were one of the most religiously repressive decades in European history.[14] The Catholic persecution of the Huguenots in France, the Protestant persecution of Protestant dissenters such as Baptists and Quakers in addition to Catholic recusants in England, Catholic intolerance in Piedmont and against the Waldensian sect, contrasted with the shelter offered by Holland for many political and religious refugees. There were however limits to the Dutch tolerance; some of their tolerant attitudes were as a result of a failure to enact intolerant laws and there was also opposition to the open attitude to strangers (then as now one might say). One should also note that, as I outlined before, many supporters of religious tolerance in the seventeenth century pointed to Islamic societies as a model of the kind of tolerance worthy of imitation.

Nonetheless, by the 1680s extensive religious toleration in Holland was almost a century old, and it provides a model of the issues involved in managing multiple communities then and now. It can still provide an example of the possibility of how to have a respectful and human world in intolerant times. Freedom of religion or conscience were:

> ...declared to be at the centre of Dutch identity from the period of the Dutch Revolt against Spanish rule. The 1579 Union of Utrecht officially provided for 'freedom of conscience'. Such freedom was placed at the legal and constitutional centre of the 'republic' created by the Dutch Revolt ... In the century following the ... Revolt, the Netherlands accommodated large communities of every one of the most significant denominations of Protestant 'heresy' and heterodoxy who were burned, banned, and banished from other European countries.[15]

The fact that Holland became the European banking centre was probably not unrelated to its tolerant position, as this helped to create a comfortable bourgeois and democratic society, one with a social conscience and leisure to foster the arts. As Hazard pointed out, it was banking that really made the Dutch state wealthy as well as enabling a generous attitude to strangers.

> A man who tries his best to convert a Jew is doubtless a good Christian; but he is a poor man of business. Holland stood for freedom of conscience, because long and bitter experience had taught her what it was to be persecuted for one's religious belief ... That was one consideration. Another was that you cannot carry on a banking, or any other business, if you have to start by asking your customer to produce his certificate of baptism.[16]

In these days when bankers have had such a bad reputation, it is as well to recall that they also at one time had a civilizing influence.

Jews, mainly Sephardic in origin from the Iberian peninsula, were also admitted and tolerated in significant numbers, though they were also limited in how and where they could practise, and were initially at least excluded from long-established craft guilds. The toleration of Jewish worship grew as Jewish economic power grew significantly.

The Netherlands also became the most important centre for publishing in Europe and more open than other societies in welcoming political as well as religious refugees, partly as a society aware of the economic benefits of immigration, partly as understanding itself as a refuge from persecution elsewhere, and partly because of strong support for republican 'freedom'.

It was also in seventeenth century Netherlands that the family *home* emerged uniquely, reflecting the growing importance of the family in Dutch society. Special rooms for sleeping were for the first time differentiated, children were given special attention and a 'snug' [a Dutch word] home atmosphere began to be created, In Dutch society,

> 'home' brought together the meanings of house and of household, of dwelling and refuge, of ownership and of affection. 'Home' meant the house but also everything that was in it and around it, as well as the people, and the sense of satisfaction and contentment that all these conveyed.[17]

One can see this transition in seventeenth century Dutch paintings of domestic scenes, which became popular items to hang on household walls. One can see in them the beginnings of a sense of a separate and special interior space. Simultaneously, the Dutch home acquired a special feminine atmosphere, thanks to the significant and increasingly dominant role played by women in the home. It must be said that this view of Dutch paintings has been challenged as reflecting later family values projected backwards onto them. Instead, others have emphasized the way that the paintings mark out a new visual space rather than reflecting a new domesticity.[18] My own view is that looking at these paintings provides a new way of seeing the human subject, one in which the subject is beginning to look inwards in a complex way, culminating in the work of Rembrandt. In that sense, I would agree that comfortable domesticity is not merely being represented but something more complex and challenging.

I think that there may well be a link between the seventeenth century Dutch sense of a secure home and a new sense of internal space and their tolerance to strangers, their ability to have a *tolerant internal space*, to open up both their external and internal borders.

But Dutch tolerance, like tolerance anywhere one might say, was also fragile, and suffered reverses and interruptions, with a number of Dutch writers arguing against full religious tolerance and with a failure to receive full legislative support. There was light but also plenty of darkness. But at its best, Dutch society at this time was able to represent both the light and the dark in some balanced way, as evident in Rembrandt's work.

Nonetheless, it should also be noted that Dutch society was 'not less, but more prone than other European societies to repress bawdiness, eroticism, undisguised homosexuality and street prostitution.'[19] In addition, the influx of certain relatively intolerant communities also had an effect on the general attitude to religious differences. For example the Protestant Huguenot community (in Holland and

England) 'attempted to maintain in exile their orthodox faith for which they had gone into exile and attempted to police the beliefs of their fellow ministers.'[20] This was noted by Bayle, who commented on the recent increase in support for intolerance in the Netherlands due to the influx of Huguenot ministers wanting to impose their own orthodoxy on others. Locke had many affiliations with the unorthodox and tolerationist Huguenots. There was thus a multiple and international context of intolerance for both Bayle and Locke.

Arguments for and against tolerance became a feature of much Dutch writing, providing the grounding and framework for Bayle and Locke's subsequent syntheses. There were a number of major Dutch contributors to theories of tolerance, stressing freedom of conscience, opposition to dogmatic imposition of beliefs (against that is the Augustinian compulsion to believe), the economic benefits of tolerance, and emphasis on human fallibility and error. There was support for a public but non-compulsory church and a desire to reduce controversy by not contradicting others unnecessarily. There was a kind of compromise between allowing other faiths to worship in private but not to be too demonstrative in public, perhaps as a way of managing the notable arguments still present against tolerance by, for example and notably the Dutch Reformed Church, who shared orthodox Calvinist views with their brethren in England and France.

> Toleration as practiced in the Netherlands had largely evolved as the allowance alongside one public church of various private practices of worship, occurring in buildings which did not appear to be churches from the outside, and with processions disallowed or discouraged for Catholics and Jews. Sources of public enmity and disputation were thereby strongly discouraged or removed, and religion was increasingly rendered for the tolerated in the Netherlands what tolerationist writing often declared it to be, an essentially private matter between worshippers and their God.[21]

The obvious point to note is that intolerance is an inevitable part of any complex society, but that Holland at that time had a way of managing intolerant beliefs and practices that on balance made it welcoming to strangers.

In order to maintain such a tolerant attitude, arguments for intolerance and counter arguments for tolerance had to be actively faced—this was possible because of the relatively open publishing of books in Holland. The argument for toleration also required the active participation of tolerationist organizations.

The tolerationists had to face considerable arguments in favour of intolerance from a number of sources, from Catholics and Protestants. Tolerance was often associated with sedition, heresy, treason, and an attack against their religious faith, while intolerance of the 'other faith' was seen as supporting their own 'true' faith. The Augustinian use of force or compulsion to enter the true faith became the driving force of much of this intolerant thinking—it has even been described as the 'life-blood' of intolerance in Restoration England.[22] It was often believed that intolerance was justified because religious uniformity would be more likely to guarantee civic peace. There were grounds for such a belief, for example in England, where Protestant Dissenters were very much involved with rebellion and resistance to authority during the Civil War and prior to the Restoration. Intolerance thus became justified as a response to genuine fears about peace and security, a common reaction even today.

With the support of various tolerationist associations of like-minded thinkers gathered in Holland, the tolerationists developed various political, economic, historical, and epistemological arguments for tolerance. Locke's *Letter* and Bayle's *Philosophical Commentary* have become the most famous of all the various tolerationist writings and indeed are still influential for liberal thinking on tolerance.

Locke's *Letter* produces a number of arguments for toleration, not all of them consistent, though the overall emphasis is on establishing the appropriate boundaries for religion and politics. He has been criticized for paying so much attention to religious toleration and for being inconsistent in his philosophical arguments. But whatever the *Letter*'s shortcomings, it has had tremendous influence since it appeared, particularly in conjunction with Locke's other writings on politics and on the nature of human understanding. It also easy to forget that when Locke wrote the *Letter* it was in the context of terrible wars of religion, which led to many atrocities. Though the *Letter* could not solve all the difficulties of that time, it was a breath of fresh air in the face of so much armed conflict and religious hatred.

The *Letter* came out at a crucial time, when, as I have outlined, tolerationist thinking was active in Holland where Locke was living; it covered some of the crucial issues concerning the nature of tolerance which are still relevant, it had enormous persuasive power as a piece of writing, it captured both an important 'spirit' of his time, and even now when religious conflicts have risen to the surface once more at a global level producing a new religious intolerance, it raises some of the most crucial issues that need thinking about in that area, and indeed it is one of those seminal texts that promotes thinking.

Locke's *Letter* begins, as I have quoted, with an appeal to mutual understanding, or what one could call 'horizontal' tolerance, tolerance between subjects of equal if different standing, as opposed to 'vertical' or top-down tolerance from a paternalistic sovereign power. Such horizontal tolerance has its roots here in the Bible's appeal to neighbourly and brotherly love. The shift in attitude required of mutual tolerance does not imply having to lose one's own belief; indeed a secure sense of one's own beliefs may make it less threatening to accept another's belief as valid. However, there is inevitably a tension between one's own and other beliefs and values. It may be easier to see polarized positions rather than common ground. Locke very quickly appeals to the basic and pre-Augustinian values of Christianity as a counter to this latter tendency, pointing out that Christian values involve charity, gentleness, and goodwill towards all human beings, though he does add, toward those who profess the Christian faith in particular. He will argue for tolerance towards other faiths, but only within certain boundaries, as I have already indicated.

One of Locke's overall concerns is the saving of souls, but not in the way that robs humans of their dignity and not through forceful means from the outside, that is, not from the Augustinian threat of compulsion, whether that be from the church or by the state. As the basis for his argument, he makes a fundamental distinction between the area of the person's immortal soul for whose salvation before God they alone are responsible and which requires 'actions and beliefs that are necessary to win the Deity's favour and which God has prescribed',[23] and the area of man's life in the world, a fragile life of uncertain duration which requires earthly goods to sustain it by labour and industry. So there is a kind of duality in how he sees the human subject, with a private and public self, and this can create difficult tensions for an individual and a society. Indeed, in this way of thinking there is a danger that the essential relatedness between individuals in a society can get lost. On the other hand it does point to the way that there may well be tensions between the tolerance of individual conscience and the ability of the group to tolerate individual differences.

Good morals, according to Locke, which are a major part of religion and go together with piety, also play a role in civil life. Locke describes how moral actions are subject to both civil jurisdiction externally from the government and *internally* from the 'individual governor' or one's conscience, the soul's guardian. One may have to follow society's rules and laws for the sake of civil peace, but there may occasionally be times when a ruler has decreed something that seems to the private conscience to be wrong. This may only happen rarely if the commonwealth is governed wisely, but if it does then Locke insists that 'a private person must not do any action that his conscience tells him is wrong.'[24] That proposition was later seen as giving sanction for rebellion against unreasonable authority.

Locke further argues that care of one's soul is for the individual and the individual's exclusive preserve and not the business of the government. Hence it would follow that there is a clear limit to 'vertical' interference from the government down to the individual, and matters of the soul override civil matters when it comes to moral questions. It follows from this 'separate spheres' assumption that there should be a strict separation between the administration of matters pertaining to the church and government, between political and religious matters, though defining the boundary between these areas may not always be so easy. The principle of the separation of church and state of course became of fundamental importance to the founders of the American constitution.

One could see then that from this perspective there may be two separate issues concerning tolerance, one pertaining to matters of the soul and the other to the civil world of the day-to-day running of society and government. However there must be some kind of relationship between the private area of the individual's soul and the public area of civil government and society. Thus if there is profound conflict in the public sphere, with war or revolution, that can hardly make for an environment where the individual can peacefully look after their private salvation. For the latter to be possible, there must be some attention to issues of *safety* and stability in the public world. Of course there may also be times when moments of extreme crisis in the public world test the individual's conscience, so that it is not really possible to maintain a constant separation between matters affecting the soul and the state, even if the administration of church and state is separated. But there are also times, as Locke points out at the beginning of the *Letter*, when fights over who holds the true religious faith, who is the most orthodox, are more to do with matters of power and domination than true religiosity. There is a difference between declaring war on one's own vices and actual warfare between competing religions; the former activity concerns the state of the individual's soul, the latter involves fanatics (or one could now add fundamentalists) who can perversely use cruelty and torture in the name of religion. Whereas toleration of those who have different views on religious questions is consistent both with the Gospel and with reason.

To define the boundary between church and state, Locke considers the nature of both in turn. The state, or commonwealth, is an association of people constituted for the purpose of preserving and promoting civil goods, that is, life, liberty, physical integrity, freedom from pain, as well as external possessions. The civil ruler is tasked with the preservation of these civil goods by means of fair laws. But the ruler cannot also be responsible for the salvation of the individual's soul. He has no more mandate than anyone else from God for this purpose. Nor can the individual be compelled by the power of the ruler to hold a religious belief; true religious belief only concerns the *inward* conviction in a person's soul. 'It is light that is needed to change a belief in the mind; punishment of the body does not lend light.'[25]

Locke has been criticized both at the time and more recently[26] for underestimating the power of some form of indirect coercion in affecting men's minds and their conscience, and not always in a negative sense. Locke argued that external influence could only change the person's will, not their beliefs. However, this does underestimate how much persuasion may not always be coercive. And even some more obvious direct coercion may be able to affect people's beliefs through a range of techniques, some of which could be seen as repressive and intolerant and others less so.

But I suppose the point is that, however true it may be that the powers-that-be can use coercion of whatever form to influence men's beliefs, this is not sanctioned by God and the gospel. Locke's argument rests on its religious basis, even if that means some philosophical contradiction. The only role for the state here is to help *safeguard* the individual's beliefs.

With regard to the nature of a church, Locke defines this as 'a free association of people coming together of their own accord to offer public worship to God in a manner which they believe will be acceptable to the Deity for the salvation of their souls.'[27] This is a 'free and voluntary' association, though with various laws for those who freely take part, and which concern the worship of God and the attainment of eternal life, not the possession of civil or earthly goods. Any sanctions used bring no benefit unless they 'sink deep into the soul and there receive the full assent of conscience.'[28] To that end exhortation, warning, and advice or even expulsion from the association may be used but not coercive force, which he will maintain is restricted to rulers, except in fact in self-defence.

He then discusses the various duties of mutual toleration, turning to human, civil, and religious rights as the basis for tolerating difference beliefs. Both individuals and individual churches should tolerate those who disagree with each other about their religious beliefs. Neither the individual (nor the church) has a right

> to attack or diminish another person's civil goods in any way because he professes a religion or ritual different from his own; all of that person's human rights as well as his civil rights are to be scrupulously observed ... the standard of justice is to be supplemented by the duties of benevolence and charity. This is commanded by the Gospel, and recommended by reason and the common society of human beings with each other formed by nature.[29]

Rulers have a duty towards mutual toleration at various levels, with regard to public worship and to belief and doctrine. The ruler's only concern is to ensure that no harm comes to the commonwealth and that no one loses their life or property. But the ruler also has to be very careful not to use this as a pretext for stifling any church's liberty; *justice* has to be maintained.

Different religions are to be tolerated, though he argues for certain limits to toleration, on civil and not religious grounds. He states that, '... neither pagans, Muslims, nor Jews should be refused civil rights because of their religion,'[30] and that the commonwealth accepts and welcomes everyone *provided* they are honest, peaceful, and hard working. He does however draw the line for who can and cannot be tolerated in the commonwealth as a result of what Forst describes as 'Locke's fear'[31] that of anything which basically threatens the stability of the commonwealth.

Locke has a basic assumption that tolerance can only extend to those who have a shared foundation in God. Without a belief in God one cannot trust a person to keep to the bonds of society. Nor logically can an atheist claim the privilege of toleration in the name of religion (the basis of Locke's arguments) since atheism does away with all religion. Locke is also suspicious of excessive religious enthusiasm as being irrational, and any religion that sets up a civil authority over religious matters—such is the case with Catholicism with its dependence on the Pope for legitimating religious practice, as well as Muslims who turn to the Ottoman emperor in a similar fashion.

Though Locke has been criticized, for example by Jonathan Israel, for basing his arguments on religious foundations, the *Letter* greatly extends the realm of tolerance in a number of ways—through the separation of church and state, through the recognition that any religious followers who accept the new mercantile world of honest and industrious labour earn the right to be tolerated, and through asserting that the refusal of diversity of opinion not its tolerance is the source of civil disorder. 'It is not diversity of belief (which cannot be avoided) that has caused most of the quarrels and wars that have occurred in the Christian world, but refusal of toleration to those who have different beliefs.'[32]

Finally, Locke also makes points about the nature of civil sedition which resonate today. Thus he points out that,

> if people contemplate sedition, it is not because they meet for religious purposes, but because they are overwhelmed by misery. Just and moderate governments are everywhere quiet, always secure; unjust and tyrannical governments will face a backlash from those they oppress.[33]

While seditions are common, they are 'often started in the name of religion. But it is also because of religion that subjects are badly treated and suffer discrimination.'[34] Even forgetting religion, he points out the bad consequences if discrimination were based upon a physical feature such as black hair (or we could add black skin), which then meant that such people were prevented from having citizens' rights and all the activities that bring people together.

> A common interest in buying and selling brings people together to do business, leisure brings others together to enjoy themselves, a common city and a shared neighbourhood unites people in living together, and religion brings yet others together for the purpose of worship. But there is only one thing that unites people on sedition, and that is oppression.[35]

Take away unjust legal discrimination and people will be safe and secure. He exhorts mutually dissenting churches to act as guardians of peace by keeping a sharp eye on each other's behaviour in order to check any tendency towards subversion.

All these points of course could be directly applied to current threats from terrorist subversion, radicalization and fundamentalism from whatever source. More emphasis on commonality, on uniting neighbourhoods rather than dividing them, and on mutual and alert safeguarding can only bring communities together and thereby reduce the threat of subversion.

Locke also extends these sorts of arguments to international relations. As Lacorne[36] points out, the *Letter* reveals a new principle of reciprocity in international relations. If a ruler discriminates against a minority religion in his country, there is a great danger of reciprocal discrimination in other countries with different predominant religions. Instead Locke founds a new and universal concept of peaceful and tolerant international relations based upon a virtuous circle of reciprocal tolerance of different beliefs, rather than a vicious cycle of intolerance and conflict.

Bayle

Unlike Locke, Bayle's arguments for toleration of different religions and for the toleration of atheism, provided it does not imperil social order, are not reliant on theology, though issues of religious tolerance and intolerance also provide the personal background for his thought. While the wars of religion certainly provided the backdrop to Locke's *Letter*, he retained his belief in the primacy of religious arguments for mutual toleration. Bayle cites the wars of religion as evidence that religious intolerance is morally wrong and that God could never have advocated those wars.

Underlying his views is a form of skepticism and an appeal to the ubiquity of uncertainty, increasingly typical of the age, in that time and again he points out the unreliability of reason to account for religious beliefs. Religious views are held on the grounds of trust and faith not from proof. As it is reasonable to both accept and reject religious beliefs, it cannot be reasonable proof, which grounds religious belief but faith, so-called 'Fideism'. This entails a move towards secular arguments for tolerance and acceptance of the rights of atheists to hold their beliefs. Unlike Locke, he does not see atheism as subversive of societal order, though in fact like Locke he condemns Catholics, but citing their intolerance as his reason not their allegiance to a potentially subversive authority.

Bayle had to flee to Holland from France to escape persecution. Following years of conflict, the Edict of Nantes proclaimed by Henry IV in 1598 had granted the French Protestant Huguenots freedom of conscience and limited freedom of worship. The aim was to promote internal peace, support the power of the King and yet also protect the dominant Catholic majority. The protection of the Huguenot minority however still depended on the goodwill of the political authority. Forst[37] describes how this situation represents what he calls the '*permission*' concept of toleration. The political authority gives top-down permission for the minority to have certain rights and freedoms, but there is also a certain amount of constraint on their freedom of action, which is no doubt better than no toleration, but comes at a price. Such toleration 'not only remains unstable and susceptible to revocation, but also represents a particular form of the rational exercise of power, a particular practice of imposing discipline through restriction of freedom,'[38] even though it could be argued that it is at least an advance over violent intolerance, and did represent a genuine political willingness to extend the field of tolerance.

Louis XIV revoked the Edict of Nantes in 1685, with the supposed excuse that there were no longer any Protestants in France who needed protection. This may have been a reflection of his own wish to extend his authority over his realm, to create the perfectly organized monolithic state, but it probably also reflected both an anxiety about the disappearance of faith following the reformation, a main theme of the counter-reformation, and a nostalgia for the church's lost unity. However, it was also essentially the use of state terrorism both to suppress Protestantism but also to enforce conversion to Catholicism. This move was supported by the arguments citing the Augustinian compulsion as a support for imposing Catholic beliefs by coercion. The revocation led to renewed and cruel persecution of the Huguenots, and Bayle, being the son of a Huguenot pastor, was brought up in that intolerant atmosphere, where, for example, men were imprisoned, women sent to convents, children taken from parents and baptized as Catholics and sent for adoption. But ultimately the revocation and its accompanying extreme repression, as is often the case, only led to increased revolt, and was a crucial turning point in history, representing both the high-water mark of the counter-reformation and the moment the tide turned.

France was of course not unique in using state power to impose religious belief. Catholics were persecuted in England, and the principalities of Germany, from the time of the Peace of Augsburg in 1555, were divided into Catholics and Lutherans, according to the religion of the ruler. But the revocation went beyond what these other states imposed, as there was not only civil intolerance but also an attack on the individual's liberty of conscience, akin to modern totalitarianism. Protestants were even officially forbidden to leave the country, so that they could be subjected to enforced conversion if necessary, while many Protestant places of worship were destroyed. Such impositions were strongly opposed by Bayle, arguing effectively that the state should not be forcing assimilation, and that each faith, including Jews and Muslims, should be allowed its own place of worship.

Whether or not the state should impose assimilation of those with different beliefs obviously has resonances with modern problems of how to facilitate racial and cultural integration. Though the use of state power, through, for example, laws banning the wearing of the hijab, may not appear to be as ruthless as that involved at the time of the revocation, there are nonetheless uncomfortable parallels, particularly of course in France.

The complexity of Bayle's position is revealed by his conversion at the age of 22 to Catholicism after visiting a Jesuit seminary, but then recanting a year later, which was seen as an even worse position than being a Huguenot and risked major punishment. Meanwhile his brother was imprisoned, where he died six months later. Fleeing to Holland, Bayle, cut off from his family and home and permanently in exile, then carved out his career as journalist, editor of the radical *Nouvelles de la Republique des Lettres*, and writer of books arguing for the new idea of tolerance from a fully philosophical position.

His earliest book, *Letter on the Comet* (Bayle, 1682), argued that a society of atheists could endure, that atheism would not lead to social instability, that belief in God was not essential to social cohesion, and that atheists could be virtuous. There are many examples of atheists living exemplary lives and orthodox believers being immoral. For him, superstition and religious fanaticism were worse evils than atheism, but in addition, it was not fear of God that drove people to moral acts but other motivations, and, 'hence that atheists are also capable of moral action, and that even a state composed of atheists could exist. Just as Heathens and Christians are capable of committing serious crimes ... so too are atheists capable of doing good.'[39] Hence Bayle was putting forward a realm of morality *separate* from religion—in striking contrast to Locke. This new kind of morality was to be judged by reason not by God. He would also later argue that the

> right to suppress others ... is inconsistent with the Christian religion, that it cannot be upheld on the basis of common human reason and the universal morality of reciprocity and that this is the source of all evil in existing societies.[40]

The *Philosophical Commentary*, his main text on tolerance, is pretty unreadable *in toto* these days, with its very detailed commentaries on biblical passages, though his arguments there are still relevant. In it, Bayle argues against two principles that justified religious intolerance—the Augustinian constraint and the nature of orthodoxy. Bayle argues that the use of force to compel religious belief is by nature bad and against Jesus' teachings. The intolerant use of force and the imposition of religious dogma merely makes people adhere to a faith but not believe it; it produces mere compliance. It has resulted in effect in conflict and religious wars. Force has only created more force. If neither side wants to listen to the other freely then it is a waste of time trying to debate issues.

Instead, Bayle wishes to push the level of thinking into another and moral region separate from religion, as he had in the *Letter on the Comet*. The light of reason, *la lumiere naturelle*, becomes the judge of actions, not religious beliefs. The basis of the moral rightness of actions, how for example to manage irreconcilable or very different belief systems is not about whether or not such actions conform to the 'true' church, but whether or not they can be judged by the natural light of reason.

He argues that there are no absolute beliefs. Referring to his tolerant precursor, Montaigne, *where* we live is just as likely to determine what we think and believe, given the enormous variety of beliefs in the world. The sincerity of individual conscience becomes the standard of morality, not what we are compelled to believe. External compulsion will not produce genuine religiosity; it may well produce orthodoxy but this is compliant belief not belief that comes from the inside and from the subjects themselves. Hence Bayle proposes a revolution in how we judge moral actions. There is no absolute truth in matters of religion, for,

> Now it is impossible, in our present state, to know certainly that the Truth which to us appears such (I speak here of the Truths of Religion in particular, and not of the Propertys of Numbers, or the first principles of Metaphysics, or Geometrical Demonstrations) is absolutely and really the Truth.[41]

He concludes that, 'the first and most indispensable of all our Obligations is that of never acting against the Instincts [*inspiration*] of Conscience; and that every Action done against the Lights [*les lumieres*] of conscience is essentially evil.'[42]

Forst points out that Bayle's key insight is, 'is that only a generally valid justification of toleration which rests on higher-level conceptions of reason and morality could lead to a generally intelligible, binding and fair form of toleration.'[43]

At that time, it was probably the case that tolerance of different faiths was seen as a license for blasphemy, heresy, and sexual perversion. The notion of a different and enlarged tolerance of difference founded on the lights of reason and the subject's conscience, rather than an appeal to religious belief and dogma, was thus revolutionary.

If atheists and religious believers of different faiths are all capable of sincere moral beliefs and have the capacity to reason, then this 'opens the way for a conception of toleration based on mutual respect and the justification of one's own claims on a common rational basis which is no longer tied to particular religious assumptions.[44] From this would follow that the state should not be intervening in matters of personal conscience, which in some ways parallels Locke's position, but from a different, secular basis.

Bayle subsequently became famous for his *Historical and Critical Dictionary* (Bayle, 1697), which became the epitome of his multi-determined thinking. It is a fascinating text, as the notes take up much more space than the actual entries, and there are also notes to the notes, so that one finds oneself as a reader being led through all kinds of side tracks and almost at times free associations. Reading the text requires a certain amount of patience and tolerance and a willingness to be led down multiple pathways.

> [H]is most daring ideas, his most provocative utterances are to be found *passim*, or tucked away in the notes. The result is that the things he was really anxious to convey are, except in a few instances, to be met with anywhere, rather than the places one would naturally expect to find them.[45]

The work would not be out of place in a modern bookstore under a section devoted to 'Post-modernism'.

Bayle's style is also a complex mixture of the erudite, the playful, and the ironic. One never quite knows how to interpret his essential position. Perhaps such a tone was necessary in an age where opinions and beliefs were literally a matter of life and death. Nonetheless the *Dictionary* had a profound influence. For example, his long article on Spinoza, even though critical of the latter's one-substance doctrine, was highly influential in spreading interest in Spinoza's thought, which itself resembles that of Bayle's in relation to the separation of moral thinking from religious dogma.

There are different ways of approaching Bayle's attitude to the role of reason in matters of religious belief. The traditional interpretation of his thought is that reason and faith are incompatible due to the limitations of reason, its inability to resolve complex moral problems such as the nature of evil or the mysteries of the Trinity. Reason is too weak to understand ultimate things, while faith and the best lights of one's own conscience resolve the paradoxes and complexities that reason cannot fathom.

Yet there is another more radical approach to interpreting his thought, which argues that his Fideism was more of a mask than a genuine position. Perhaps Bayle's own rapid oscillations between Protestantism and Catholicism and back again in his youth show this to be a possibility. One could say that he held a paradoxical view about the role of reason—on the one hand he held to an ethic of the natural light of reason, and on the other he often pointed out reason's limits to grasp the ultimate mysteries

There are a number of parallels in the lives and work of Spinoza, Locke, and Bayle. Their pioneering works concerning freedom and tolerance were all written in Holland where they were exiles, with Spinoza an 'internal' exile, having been cut off from his Jewish community, and the other two forced to flee their countries for fear of incarceration or death. Their thinking about different aspects of tolerance took place in the context of a century of unprecedented religious conflict and cruelty towards those holding different beliefs.

Locke and Bayle were certainly influenced by Spinoza, and by one another. All three thinkers to a greater or lesser extent criticized arbitrary political authority, with Spinoza being probably the most radical in his arguing for a variety of freedoms. Locke, being a diplomat and an adviser to government when he returned to England, was unlikely to be as radical as Spinoza. Yet his thought as a whole, with his new approach to human understanding and the nature of the self, would have considerable and international influence. All three thinkers displayed the increasing emphasis on the role of *reason* in making judgments about human affairs, which in due course was to become the watchword of enlightened European thought in the eighteenth century. It was on their shoulders that thinkers such as Voltaire would chart new territory in the fight against intolerance and injustice, and being still relevant today, they have provided key elements of the modern liberal approach to tolerance, with the assumption that people pursue different goals and maintain different beliefs and that these differences should be respected. We no longer claim that disagreements about religious and political issues are evidence of error, sin or treason. Yet the tendency to condemn those with differing beliefs and ways of life remains a constant possibility, as is the use of powerful external authority to impose beliefs on individual citizens, and thus new reasons for maintaining intolerant attitudes constantly arise. As I discussed before, the fear of the stranger in our midst has become a modern reality, from the McCarthy witch hunts of the last century to current anxieties about 'waves' of immigrants invading our homes. These classic texts on tolerance have for that reason become ever more relevant as a starting point for opposing such intolerant attitudes both from government and from citizens.

Notes

1 Spinoza, 1670, p. 6.
2 Spinoza, 1670, p. 10.
3 Spinoza, 1677, p. 74.
4 Spinoza, 1678, Letter LXII, pp. 390–1.
5 Locke, 1689.
6 Israel, 2006, p. 139.
7 Locke, 1689, p. 3.
8 Locke, 1690, p. 164.
9 Locke, 1690, p. 214.
10 Foucault, 2004, p. 4.
11 Locke, 1690, p. 559.
12 Makari, 2015, p. 148.
13 Locke, 1690, pp. 9–10.
14 Marshall, 2006, p. 17.
15 Marshall, 2006, pp. 138–9.
16 Hazard, 1935, p. 74.
17 Rybczynski, 1986, p. 62.

18 Hollander, 2002.
19 Israel, 1995, p. 683.
20 Marshall, 2006, p. 189.
21 Marshall, 2006, p. 358.
22 Goldie, 1984.
23 Locke, 1689, p. 32.
24 Locke, 1689, p. 33.
25 Locke, 1689, p. 8.
26 Waldron, 1988.
27 Locke, 1689, p. 9.
28 Locke, 1689, pp.11–12.
29 Locke, 1689, pp. 12–13.
30 Locke, 1689, p. 41.
31 Forst, 2003, p. 223.
32 Locke, 1689, p. 42.
33 Locke, 1689, p. 38.
34 Locke, 1689, p. 38.
35 Locke, 1689, p. 39.
36 Lacorne, 2016, p. 28.
37 Forst, 2003, pp. 145–6.
38 Forst, 2003, p. 146.
39 Forst, 2003, p. 239.
40 Forst, 2003, p. 239.
41 Bayle, 1686, p. 261.
42 Bayle, 1686, p.227
43 Forst, 2003, p. 241.
44 Forst, 2003, p. 246.
45 Hazard, 1935, p. 105.

6
LATER ENLIGHTENMENT
From Voltaire to the American Revolution

As the seventeenth century came to an end, the century of war, conflict, and crisis would lead into a new and more human and reasonable world, at least potentially. What had changed was a world where philosophy abandoned metaphysics and aimed to restrict itself to what could be directly perceived by the human mind, with an idea of nature as powerful, regulated, and consonant with reason, from which was derived natural law, freedom, and equality. The right to happiness on earth was seen as a main aim of morality, and in order to achieve such an aim, there was an attack on absolutism, superstition, and war, with science as the new way that could ensure man's progress and happiness. 'All is now ready. The stage is set for – Voltaire!'[1] By the end of the century, after the American and French Revolutions, there were in place many of the basic elements of modern tolerance.

Voltaire

Voltaire's *Treatise on Tolerance*, written in the latter stages of his life, was published in 1763 and was a passionate defence of freedom of conscience and an attack on injustice and religious intolerance, a position that became very influential to the founding fathers of the American constitution. One could say his was a 'skeptical' tolerance, opposed to all forms of dogmatism, and driven by a belief that we cannot be certain about absolute truths, a stance similar in our times to that of Karl Popper[2] who, in his own essay on tolerance, even quotes Voltaire about our being fallible and prone to error. The *Treatise* was written soon after a 68-year-old Protestant Toulouse merchant Jean Calas had been falsely accused of murdering his son (who had actually hanged himself) and then tortured and executed. As it became clear that there had been a miscarriage of justice incited by mob rule and prejudice, Voltaire began an ultimately successful three-year campaign to clear Calas' name and that of his family. The *Treatise* used philosophical arguments as well as a good deal of effective rhetoric to make its points, but was not a closely argued work such as that of Bayle; it was in some parts more like campaigning journalism, a model for Zola's subsequent defence of Dreyfus, and in that sense Voltaire speaks to us now as immediately as he did then as a crusader for the truth.

Voltaire was a man of letters, a highly influential thinker, journalist, playwright, poet, and all-round *philosophe*, who came to wield considerable international influence, being seen as the foremost champion of tolerance, liberty of thought and philosophy. After an earlier period as the object of persecution, censorship, and intermittent exile, he ended his life returning to Paris as esteemed patriarch and sage, with his bust crowned on the stage of the *Comédie-Française*.

Voltaire had retreated to his property on the Swiss French border at Ferney around 1758, well placed if he needed to make a quick escape from French persecution. Ferney became something of an international crossroads for European intellectuals, with a stream of visitors passing through and exchanging ideas. At one time he complained about the absence of peace there and that he had become the 'innkeeper of Europe', but as a result of his position he was able to keep in touch with the latest ideas and significant events.

Voltaire's formative experience was his brief exile in England from 1726 to 1729, after which he published the *Philosophical Letters* (1734), a somewhat idealised celebration of English society. I have already quoted from the letters his famous proposition about England living in peace due to its multiplicity of religions. He praises English liberty, enterprise, and freedom of thinking. Unlike the French, the English had no need to fear a tyrannical and monopolizing church or a despotic king, while even their aristocrats were not above becoming involved in trade. All had to pay taxes regardless of birth and in proportion to their wealth, and hence there was equality of justice at all levels.

Voltaire contrasts Descartes' talk of innate ideas, for example intuitions about the perfection of God or that the angles of a triangle add up to 180 degrees, with Locke's view that our knowledge comes from experience. English science, epitomized by the great Newton, was founded on experience not on some elaborate hypotheses. He contrasts Newton's theory of gravitation, based upon the phenomena of experience and mathematical principles, with Descartes' fanciful theory of vortices. The contrast between British empiricism and continental rationalism persists to this day, if only as a myth, perhaps still over-influenced by Voltaire's views. This can make conversation between the UK and its neighbours at even a political level challenging, with the two sides probably unconsciously at odds over contrasting views of the world.

Voltaire's voice as a thinker came to fruition at this time. One wonders how much his skeptical stance owes to the English literature he also encountered at this time, such as that of Jonathan Swift.

The *Treatise* begins with the events of the Calas case. Jean Calas, a Protestant, had been a Toulouse merchant for 40 years and was known as a good father and family man, even tolerant of one of his sons converting to Catholicism, and allowing his children to be cared for by a Catholic servant. But another son was troubled; unable to enter business because he could not obtain the necessary certificate of Catholicity, he hanged himself in his father's storeroom, after losing money gambling.

Voltaire described Toulouse as a generally intolerant society, known for its hostile attitude to non-Catholics. Hearing of the hanging, a crowd gathered around the house and whipped up in a frenzy, Jean Calas was accused of murdering his son, as the boy was supposedly due to recant the next day, and so had been strangled out of hatred for Catholicism. The local magistrate subsequently had the Calas family, the family servant, and a visiting friend put in irons. The whole affair coincided with the bicentenary of the annual celebration of the massacre of 4000 Huguenots, whipping up the crowd and producing increasing rumours about the father's murderous intent. Thirteen judges were then assembled to hear the case for the prosecution. Only one of the judges, convinced both that the accused was innocent and the crime impossible based on the evidence, argued in the family's favour—'against the passion of intolerance he opposed the zeal of humanity.'[3]

Despite the obvious lack of evidence, the father was found guilty and condemned the next day to be executed by means of pretty hideous torture, finally dying without complaint on the wheel, though the rest of the family were released, with the daughters being locked in a convent. The mother did eventually escape to Paris, where she was greeted with help and sympathy, and eventually she was reunited with her daughters.

Given the facts of the case, Voltaire's aim in the *Treatise* is to 'examine whether the true religious spirit is more consistent with charity or with cruelty',[4] and in order to do so, he ranges his arguments widely, examining the nature of intolerance, its history in different countries, including India, Persia, China, and the American colonies. He asks if tolerance is dangerous, and cites various national and international examples to show that the opposite is the case, and that the dogmatic spirit and the misuse of religion is the cause of disaster and mayhem. 'In the end, tolerance has been responsible for not a single civil war, whereas intolerance has covered the earth with corpses.'[5] It is thus foolish and against the new spirit of the times, the Age of Reason, to promulgate religious intolerance or to base policy on it.

Voltaire promotes the use of Reason as an antidote to fanaticism, religious 'enthusiasm', and other forms of 'madness', as it is the 'one slow but infallible route towards enlightenment. Reason is gentle, humane, tolerant; she smothers discord, strengthens goodness, and renders obedience to the law so attractive that coercion is no longer necessary to uphold it.'[6] Furthermore, he argues that there is no natural right to persecute; that would be the law of the jungle and would have ended up in the extermination of mankind.

Citing Locke's 'excellent letter on tolerance', Voltaire maintains that each individual citizen should be permitted to believe only in what reason tells him, to think only what his reason, be it enlightened or misguided, may dictate, provided that he does not threaten any disturbance to public order. 'For a man is under no obligation to believe or not to believe. His duties are to respect the laws and customs of his country.'[7]

He argues that intolerance produces either hypocrites or rebels. In contrast he uses the example of how the evangelists gave at times very different details and descriptions in the Bible about different facts concerning Jesus and his ancestry. If this had taken place in his own times, no doubt this would have produced masses of squabbling. However, these apparent contradictions were reconciled by the early Church Fathers.

> There exists no greater example than this, to teach that we should be tolerant with one another in our disagreements and humble when faced with something we do not understand ... If to persecute those with whom we disagree were a pious thing to do it would follow that the man who managed to kill the greatest number of heretics would be the most holy saint in Paradise.[8]

He gives various examples of tolerance, including what he calls the extraordinary tolerance of the Jews, who have harsh laws yet in reality show the most extraordinary spirit of tolerance in their application.

Voltaire also tackles the passage from Luke concerning the host who tells his servant to compel guests to come to the banquet, a passage which, as I have already described, became the basis after Augustine of considerable persecution. Voltaire considers that too much has been made of the words 'make them come in'. For it stands to reason that this means no more that to ask, implore, entreat or desire them to come in. He asks what on earth this request and this dinner have to do with the subject of persecution.

Voltaire describes how the spirit of intolerance distorts everything, and also depends upon *poor evidence* for its justification, as it is always on the lookout for the most trivial pretexts, in contrast to every other word and act of Christ which exhorts patience, gentleness, and forgiveness. He gives the familiar examples of the latter, such as the Good Samaritan, the parable of the prodigal son, the forgiveness of sinners and tolerance towards a woman taken in adultery and the guests at the wedding feast at Cana who asked for more wine and for whom Christ turned water into wine. Nor did Christ turn Judas away, despite knowing he would betray him, and told Peter to put away his sword, and the children of Zebedee not to destroy a city by fire because they had not received lodging there.

The only cases in which intolerance is justified is when society is threatened to be undermined by criminal acts or by fanaticism. Therefore, to be entitled to society's tolerance, men should start by renouncing fanaticism.

Finally, Voltaire argues for 'universal tolerance', that not only should Christians tolerate one another, but also every man as our brother, including Jews, Turks, the Siamese, and Chinese, for 'are we not all children of the same Father and creatures of the same God?'[9]

In his postscript, Voltaire pleads for cooperation among mankind, and hopes that he has sowed a seed from which one day there might be gathered a harvest, with the hope that the spirit of reason will spread enlightenment everywhere.

One may consider this plea overoptimistic in today's intolerant and violent world, and yet one cannot accuse him of ignoring injustice and violence. On the contrary, he faces it head on, arguing why intolerance goes against religious principles and is also the cause of conflict rather than just an end product. He points out how *intolerance distorts reality* and is on the look-out for every easy pretext for promoting conflict because it is usually based on flimsy evidence. And he offers a humane view of mankind, as vulnerable, error prone, and fallible. Our fallibility is not to be used as an excuse for persecution but as an example of human commonality.

The eventual rehabilitation of the Calas family became for Voltaire an example of the progress of reason and enlightenment, both for the narrow world on which he was focusing but also at a universal level.

Soon after the *Treatise*, Voltaire wrote an article on tolerance in his *Philosophical Dictionary*, where he repeats that tolerance is the 'prerogative of humanity. We're all steeped in error and weakness; let's forgive each other our follies; that's the first law of nature.'[10] He also repeated there his example of how a multiplicity of religions is conducive to a tolerant society. In addition he argues, with international examples, including referring to the Quakers, Hindus, Jews, and Muslims, how conducting business in the various trading exchanges is in itself conducive to tolerance; business is a leveller. Even Ancient Rome was tolerant towards any religion that focused on making money rather than proselytizing. Furthermore, he supports again the separation of temporal and spiritual powers. Any state religion is bound to become intolerant, as it will use state power to enforce religious beliefs and practices.

As in his *Philosophical Letters*, he extols the Quakers as a good example of tolerance, being a religion without priests, dogma, rituals, or sacraments, and regarding as brothers all who believe in God. They were also not allowed by their members to enter Parliament, to hold a state office nor even to serve on a jury, so as to keep their beliefs free from state interference, only permitting themselves to do business. Voltaire was also skeptical enough to think that this was a position which could lead to considerable financial benefits for their children, who would be bound then to become less ascetic. Even such tolerance had its limits and risks.

There are also other limits to Voltaire's notion of tolerance, for not only does he exclude fanatics, but also, like Locke, atheists and all supporters of any 'superstitious' religion that may incite political instability. Voltaire ultimately is seeking a rational religion, one which is consistent with the age of reason; his justification of tolerance is a secondary aim, his hope that reason will be able to oppose dogmatism and fanaticism. Of course one could say that not only does this underestimate the power of the irrational to undermine any reasonable undertaking, but this attitude in a sense makes a religion out of reason, something which Rousseau will take up in his notion of a 'civic religion'.

Rousseau

The intellectual preoccupations of the early to mid-eighteenth century could be seen as a debate about different models of the self. There were many debates about the nature of the human soul and how the mind can think. There were differences in view about whether or not the mind is incorporeal, whether or not the mind consists of a unified substance, and how these different models are related to religious belief. I have already sketched out how the thought of Locke and Spinoza represented two different approaches to the nature of reality, and these thinkers were often used as baselines for these debates. In parallel, there was a sea change in the attitude to authority, with centralised authority, most clearly represented in the rule of Louis XIV, being challenged. One can even see this change in the move from the massive classical architecture of Versailles to the flowing and complex Rococo style seen in, for example Germany, where there was no centralised authority but a multiplicity of principalities.

In addition, and particularly under the influence of Jean-Jacques Rousseau, there developed a new model of the self, one where sentiment and not reason came to play a central role, while the relationship between the individual and society was also given a new dimension. In some ways Rousseau has been seen as anti-Enlightenment, and he certainly quarrelled with a number of key Enlightenment thinkers, including Voltaire and Diderot. But maybe that is too simplistic a notion. I think one could see him struggling with the Enlightenment vision as based on the central role of reason, but I would suggest that he was still very much a child of the Enlightenment, extending the vision by paying focused attention to sentiment and feelings, rather than overturning Enlightenment thinking.

Rousseau's discussion of civic religion towards the end of *The Social Contract* is his main explicit discussion of tolerance. He argues that 'tolerance should be given to all religions that tolerate others, so long as their dogmas contain nothing contrary to the duties of citizenship.'[11] In his notion of a civic religion, there are only a few dogmas, such as the existence of a 'mighty, intelligent and beneficent Divinity, possessed of foresight and providence, the life to come, the happiness of the just, the punishment of the wicked, the sanctity of the social contract and the laws.'[12] While the only negative dogma is that of intolerance.

Rousseau sees religion of some sort as necessary in order to preserve the social 'bond of union' between people. Not surprisingly, given the central importance of religion in those times, he did not envisage a purely secular state being possible or desirable; indeed, like Locke, he considered atheism as dangerous to the unity of society. The problem as Rousseau saw it was how to reconcile the claims of religion with allegiance to the sovereign. Initially people believed their leaders were gods, so that there was a kind of social unity. However, he maintained that Christianity introduced a radical but divisive kind of religion. (And hence he was considered a dangerous heretic.) Although seemingly based on the brotherhood of man, he maintained that Christianity also separated the political and spiritual realms, subverting the political order and creating social disorder. It did this by preaching that salvation comes in the next world not in this world, by teaching indifference to political events in encouraging inwardness, and it taught people to be slavishly dependent by fostering martyrdom. Jesus, thus, 'came to set up on earth a spiritual kingdom, which, by separating the theological from the political system, made the State no longer one, and brought about the internal divisions which have never ceased to trouble Christian peoples.'[13]

One could see then that once this form of religion was established it would be inevitable that those internal divisions would be the cause of further conflicts both within Christianity and between Christian states, let alone between Christian and non-Christian states. Rousseau's aim was to conceive of a form of religion that would provide a new kind of unity between the spiritual and political realms. He noted that of all Christian writers it was only Hobbes who proposed to remedy this situation by welding the state and religion together into an absolute sovereign. But he must have seen that the masterful spirit of Christianity was incompatible with his system, and that the priestly interest would always be stronger than the state.

Instead of this divisive form of religion, Rousseau then proposed a purely civil profession of faith, 'of which the Sovereign should fix the articles, not exactly as religious dogmas, but as social sentiments without which a man cannot be a good citizen or a faithful subject'.[14] Rousseau, as so often carried away as it were by the power of his 'sentiments', proposed that one should banish anyone from his ideal state, or even execute them, if they did not believe the articles of faith—not for impiety, but as an anti-social being, incapable of truly loving law and justice, an argument of course soon to be taken up by the revolutionary Jacobins under Robespierre and his followers.

Thus, overall, Rousseau proposed a form of tolerance within certain limits; those limits are those beliefs or assumptions that are consistent with the unifying bonds of society, similar to what Durkheim,[15] influenced by Rousseau, was to call 'social solidarity'. Though Rousseau's views would appear to justify a totalitarian society, in fact he was also clear that the Sovereign's power over the individual citizen was to be limited to only what was in the public interest. 'They owed the Sovereign an account of their opinions only to such an extent as they matter to the community.' Rousseau, prefiguring Mill's harm principle, noted that each man in a republic was free in what did not harm others.[16] In this sense, some have argued that Rousseau is 'consistent in his commitment to tolerance as an essential mark of a properly ordered society'.[17] However, one can also worry about this notion of 'public interest', which of course can be used to justify all sorts of state repression, as indeed became the case during the Reign of Terror of the French Revolution.

Rousseau would seem, perhaps reflecting his contradictory character, to be oscillating between on one hand a new and radical form of social relationship, where social unity and social bonds are primary, where common sympathy between human beings is to replace the old hierarchical power structures, and on the other hand a form of potentially totalitarian society where public interest, or the so-called 'general will' may trump the individual's personal interest. One can see both these trends in Rousseau's writings. Indeed, as Sheldon Wolin has described, 'Few men have been more deeply at odds with society than Rousseau; fewer still have spoken as powerfully for the need for community.'[18] Wolin does not see that as paradoxical but as reflecting Rousseau's deep alienation. He cites a number of examples of this in the writings, where Rousseau describes mankind as no longer at home with himself, or as at war with himself and with his essential nature. Society, with all the inducements to rivalry and ambition has trapped man into adopting a social self, which has stifled the authentic, natural or what one might call the 'true self'.

For Rousseau then, society has distorted man's fundamental nature, creating a form of social dependence, which has only created inequality and discontent. Freud saw such discontents as an inevitable part of civilisation, which had to be accepted as the price for sublimating our primal drives. Rousseau would not accept such a thesis, instead proposing a vision where society should fulfil man's emotional needs through a close social interdependence, a corporate community, a *moi commun*, 'where each simultaneously discovered himself in the closest solidarity with others'.[19] This would entail a close identification of each person with the communal whole, the general will.

The issue of community values and how they may or may not conflict with individual values, whether or not a society can function when it loses homogeneity and how much heterogeneity it can accommodate, will become important issues for any theory of liberal tolerance in our own times. It was Rousseau who really first brought to the fore the issues that need to be faced, even if in so doing his solutions were contradictory.

One view of Rousseau's vision is to see it as potentially dangerous, and leading to a totalitarian society terrorising those wishing to express their individuality in contradiction to the 'general will'. As Hannah Arendt described in her book *On Revolution*,

> Rousseau took his metaphor of a general will seriously and literally enough to conceive of the nation as a body driven by one will, like an individual, which also can change direction at any time without losing its identity. It was precisely in this sense that Robespierre demanded: 'il faut une volonté UNE'.[20]

It was a short step from this demand to Robespierre, like subsequent dictators, taking on himself the role of embodying the 'One will'.

However, on another track, Nicholas Dent has argued persuasively that one can construct a humane form of tolerance in Rousseau's writings, one which prioritizes *respect* for others, and this seems linked to his model of the self and the nature of human sentiments.

Dent begins his paper by making the point, to which I shall return when considering tolerance in current circumstances, that tolerance can be seen as one important aspect or component of affording due respect to others.[21] Though respect has wider connotations than tolerance, having a tolerant regard towards others involves granting them the respect they are due, provided of course that the other is not acting harmfully, such as being about to murder someone, or expressing extremely intolerant attitudes.

Dent maintains that Rousseau was above all concerned with the harmfulness of a system of social and personal relations where what was dominant was the contempt for the person and life of others and intolerance was pervasive. Instead, he was concerned to offer an alternative of a society where social and personal relations were such that respect for others was the fundamental ordering principle. These considerations developed in Rousseau's early *Discourse on the Origin of Inequality* (1755) as well as in his book on education—*Émile* (1762).

Rousseau's ideas here turn around his moral psychology, where he makes a distinction between *amour de soi* (self love) and *amour propre* (self concern, pride or vanity, or perhaps, more accurately, narcissism) and adds the role of *pitié* (compassion). There are various ways of interpreting these three essential elements of his psychology. In the *Discourse on Inequality, amour de soi* seems to be a natural feeling which leads every animal to look to its own preservation, 'and which, guided in man by reason and modified by compassion, creates humanity and virtue',[22] whereas *amour propre* is a 'purely relative and fictitious feeling, which arises in the state of society, leads each individual to make more of himself than of any other, causes all the mutual damage men inflict on one another'.[23]

These distinctions arise from Rousseau's picture of the evolution of man, from his natural state, where incidentally he has not acquired a home, where he lived on instinct and without competitive and destructive relations with others, to that of organized settlements, where rivalry and competitiveness began to create inequalities and conflicts. Civilization and the creation of settled *homes* have thus, according to Rousseau, alienated man from his natural or true self, creating instead a kind of false self in order to manage conflictual relationships. Yet as the quote above shows, guided by reason and compassion, the natural *amour de soi*, or perhaps true self, can be cultivated. Compassion is engendered in relation to the sufferings of others, which becomes the basis for giving others the respect which is due to them. Intolerant relations would reflect the dominance of narcissistic *amour propre*. In Dent's view,

> the presence of tolerance is not merely the absence of intolerance in Rousseau's ideal community. Rather, tolerance will be a matter of the positive welcoming and prizing of human individuality where that is expression of that integrity of mind and spirit of life which is affording to everyone a fundamental confidence in their value and worth as persons.[24]

Thus tolerance towards others would be a major mark of a community constituted by respect for others.

This model is not without problems and contradictions. Rousseau's natural man is of course a myth, however much he considered it to be based on historical considerations. My own view is that the development of a sense of home was a civilizing moment, allowing people to become social beings. Yet of course it is true that once people start living near one another on a regular basis and in stable communities, conflicts inevitably occur, though at the same time so do cooperation and sociability. I suppose the point is that Rousseau is emphasizing that man has natural good sentiments from which he can become alienated. The task for any society is to find ways of tapping into these positive sentiments—whether guidance by reason and compassion is sufficient for this task is debatable. There would also need to be focused attention on the way that *amour propre* or narcissism of the more destructive kind can hinder our best efforts to afford respect to others.

Besides Rousseau, there were a number of his contemporaries, particularly those in Scotland, who elaborated a theory of moral sentiments, challenging what appeared to be the overly rigid division between reason and emotion, or mind and body as put forward, at least in most of his thought, by Descartes. They also challenged the model of human nature as essentially selfish, based on the solitary human subject exemplified in Hobbes and Descartes. Against this, David Hume, Adam Smith, and Francis Hutcheson defended 'sympathy' as a natural moral sentiment involving others, a social passion, which is very close to compassion or Rousseau's *pitié*, and the glue for society to remain together. As Smith put it, 'The word sympathy, in its most proper and primitive signification, denotes our *fellow-feeling* with the sufferings, not that with the enjoyments, of others.'[25] He makes the important point that being sympathetic does not mean being in perfect harmony with the other person, which he calls 'approbation'. 'We do not weep, and exclaim, and lament, with the sufferer. We are sensible, on the contrary, of his weakness and of the extravagance of his passion, and yet feel a very sensible concern upon his account.'[26] This provides the basis for human social relations, and I think, a basic element in thought on tolerance.

Smith describes the role of this fellow feeling, when considering how two people engage with one another over objects that may affect either of them.

> Though your judgments in matters of speculation, though your sentiments in matters of taste, are quite opposite to mine, I can easily overlook this opposition; and if I have any degree of temper, I may still find some entertainment in your conversation, even upon those very subjects. But if you have no fellow-feeling for the misfortunes I have met with, or none that bears any proportion to the grief which distracts me, or if you have no indignation at the injuries I have suffered, or none that bears any proportion to the resentment which transports me, we can no longer converse upon these subjects. We become *intolerable* [my italics] to one another. I can neither support your company, nor you mine. You are confounded at my violence and passion, and I am enraged at your cold insensibility and want of feeling.[27]

Thus the basis for tolerant relations between people is compassionate, sympathetic fellow feeling, without which we remain distant from one another. It is a short step from 'cold insensibility' to rage and violence towards others, and intolerant social relations. Compassion is thus 'the cornerstone passion of our sense of justice'.[28] But in order to counter intolerant social relations, we need an understanding of how people can become 'coldly insensible' to the plight of other humans, a reality unfortunately only too familiar in the modern world.

The American experience

Whatever one feels about current American political life, the early history of the American colonies and the foundation of the American constitution obviously turn on the central role of tolerance and the general influence of Enlightenment thinkers such as Locke, Diderot, Montesquieu, Voltaire, and others. In order to fully grasp current political realities in the US, including the way that the religious right has become so influential today, it is helpful to look at some aspects, relevant to my theme, of the complex origins of American society, its revolution and the way that the issue of how to accommodate a multiplicity of religious beliefs came to play such an important role in early American history.

The American Revolution 'from the outset acted as a seismic shock, inspiration, and agent of change not only in North America and continental Europe but also within Britain itself as well as Ireland, the Caribbean, Ibero-America, Canada and South Africa.'[29] But it is difficult to see it as a consequence of 'radical' Enlightenment, given the fact that several of the major figures (with the exception of John Adams) such as Washington, Jefferson, and Madison remained aristocratic landowners with slaves or came from slave owning families. However, it must also be said that their views about slavery did change, with Washington freeing his slaves with his death, and Jefferson and Madison becoming increasingly abolitionist. In the event they shared radical enough views about the equality of all men (albeit white men), the importance of human dignity and religious tolerance. Furthermore, they escaped the extreme consequences of radical Enlightenment soon evident in the chaos of the French Revolution. Overall, as Israel describes, albeit with his usual sharp and critical tone towards the followers of 'moderate' Enlightenment,

> The Enlightenment maturing in mid- and late eighteenth century North America ... was predominantly a Lockean-Newtonian construct formed within a religious culture, characterized by an unparalleled plurality of churches espousing a certain conception of toleration and insisting on 'balance' and 'moderation' as basic principles.[30]

The context for the American Revolution was also much more 'moderate' than the subsequent French Revolution. In the American colonies there were already a considerable amount of relatively stable political organization, with the 13 states having their own organized political bodies. Hannah Arendt pointed out that this was unlike anything available in France.[31] The general social situation in the colonies and in France was also very different. In the latter extreme poverty was common, while this was not the case with the former. Furthermore, the most 'obvious and the most decisive distinction between the American and the French Revolution was that the historical inheritance of the American Revolution was "limited monarchy" and that of the French Revolution was absolutism, which apparently reached far back into the first centuries of our era and the last centuries of the Roman Empire.'[32] Thus, the more absolute the ruler, the more absolute the revolution will be which replaces him—as indeed was the case with the Russian Revolution. It was thus the good fortune of the American Revolution that it occurred in a country that knew nothing of the predicament of mass poverty (unlike now of course) and among a people who had a widespread experience of a form of self-government which had grown out of a limited monarchy.

With this social and political environment as the context, although there were many radical ideas swimming around the founding fathers, in the end, and after much reasoned debate led by James Madison, they came up with a workable constitution in 1787, followed soon by the remarkable and more radical Bill of Rights, with ten amendments, such as the seminal First Amendment guaranteeing religious plurality, and others guaranteeing personal freedoms. This constitution balanced the needs of the diverse individual states while keeping some sense of central governing control; it followed the thought of Montesquieu in keeping separate the powers of the different branches of government in order to limit the power of one element of government; and overall, with the Bill of Rights, it retained core beliefs around equality and freedom of conscience. Thus the original constitution maintained the separation of powers, while the first amendment consolidated the separation of church and state.

Of course these two forms of separation were never going to be fixed. With the first kind of separation there would always be conflicts between the different elements, times when for example there would be attempts on the part of the executive to prevent the legislature from fulfilling their function and vice versa. And with the second kind of separation, there were bound to be attempts by religious groups to have undue influence over government, given the great influence in the US of religion in daily life; or when elements of government might become attached to one form of religious belief, or, as recently, attack a religion (Islam) in the name of government security. The point is to provide a structure where such inevitable conflicts could be both made visible and then manageable; for that to happen there would inevitably be much debate or legal argumentation about the meaning of the constitution.

The founding fathers were preceded in the mid-seventeenth century by an influential Puritan thinker, Roger Williams, who espoused radical views about tolerance, freedom of conscience, and the governance of a society and was the originator of the need for a 'wall of separation' between church and state, a notion which became highly influential in later interpretations of the First Amendment, both by Thomas Jefferson and by the US Supreme Court in the mid-twentieth century. Williams very probably influenced Locke's writing on tolerance, and thereby directly and indirectly helped create the conditions that would lead to the First Amendment. As Nussbaum[33] has argued, Williams also provided a template for a uniquely American form of thinking about tolerance and liberty.

Born into a wealthy middle-class family in London, he became a Puritan during his student years in Cambridge, and facing persecution migrated to Massachusetts Bay in 1631, where he became a teacher in the church at Salem. However, he was soon excommunicated and expelled for his 'dangerous' opinions, in which he denounced 'the intolerance of the Puritans and especially the proposal to create a Christian commonwealth'.[34] He argued, like Locke years later, that it was no business of the civil magistrate to concern himself with the beliefs of his subjects, nor impose any kind of religious uniformity. The true aim of the authorities was to create the conditions for civil peace and prosperity. Freedom of conscience applied to everyone, including Jews and other non-Christians, even atheists.

Incidentally, Williams' experience of persecution exposes the powerful myth, still active today in certain quarters and shaping the American identity, that the first New England colonists were fleeing religious persecution in England in order to establish a regime of religious liberty in America. As Lacorne points out, this myth does not stand up to empirical investigation, since 'the Puritans had a single overriding interest: to establish a genuine and durable religious orthodoxy ... Punitive laws, arrests and convictions, along with a few executions, served to terrorize dissenters, primarily Quakers and Baptists.'[35]

However, despite the absence of religious liberty, political liberty did develop, beginning with the original Mayflower Compact, which emphasized that they were loyal subjects of King James, and undertook before God to create a colony in north Virginia where they would form a civil political body with 'just and equal laws'. Notwithstanding this noble aim, the reality of the compact was that its signatories were a small group of 18 pilgrims and 23 'strangers' out of a total of 102 passengers, with women, children, and servants being excluded. The just and equal laws were likely to be only applied to the core group of male pilgrims.

Williams managed to escape his persecutors partly with the help of some native Americans (he was an early supporter of their culture), and found refuge in the New England wilderness, eventually founding the colony of Rhode Island and Providence Plantation as a shelter for all victims of religious persecution. In order to acquire the charters for the colony he made frequent trips to London, where his writings appeared and caused considerable outrage both in England and back in the colonies.

His book *The Bloudy Tenent of Persecution for Cause of Conscience*,[36] based on a controversy with the leading Puritan theologian of Massachusetts, John Cotton, and written mainly in the form of a dialogue between Truth and Peace, contains his essential thoughts and was highly influential, though the House of Commons condemned it to be burnt. Much of it is rather indigestible these days with many biblical references from both Old and New Testaments on every page and highly emotional language, but its basic 12 tenets are powerfully stated.

To summarize in modern language, he begins with a statement that Jesus, the Prince of Peace, did not require or accept the blood of so many Christians in the many religious wars, that scripture on the contrary argues consistently against the doctrine of persecution for cause of conscience, and that the latter doctrine is guilty of all the blood of the souls crying out for justice. He argues against the civil magistrates having any authority over spiritual matters and the individual conscience, the latter being God's realm—this was the origin of his argument for the wall of separation between church and state. Also, that it is the will and command of God, since the coming of Christ, to allow all non-Christians (including Native Americans) freedom of conscience and worship, that it is no business of the state to enforce a common religion, nor to force Jews for example to convert to Christ.

And finally that allowing freedom of conscience and worship provides a firm and lasting peace for a state, allowing people of different faiths to flourish, which is the manifestation of true Christian civility.

Forst[37] points out that all of the arguments about tolerance, which would later be found in Locke, are found in Williams' writing. Yet paradoxically, though Williams is much more attached to religious argumentation, he also makes a much clearer separation between spiritual and civil matters, with the state's role being confined to the defence of people and the punishment of uncivil actions. God alone is the ultimate judge concerning matters of faith, and human beings are not permitted to make any judgment about this that would justify force. Coercion of conscience is both futile and illegitimate, which is basically an argument from 'natural law', given to us by God. Intolerance is the greatest sin of all as it usurps God's judgment and curtails the freedom of the faithful, including the possibility that those who are 'soul-killers' may become 'soul-savers' by God's grace.

Martha Nussbaum in her book *Liberty of Conscience* has an extensive commentary on Williams as a pioneer of the American approach to liberty and tolerance. As she writes, 'The free conscience, and the civil peace it requires, became the foundation of America's distinctive approach to religious liberty and equality. The equal status of religious minorities was its most persistent concern.'[38]

She writes that Williams inaugurated a distinctive emphasis on the importance of a 'mutually respectful civil peace among people who differ in conscientious commitment';[39] that, influenced by the experience of both solitude and space and precariousness of daily living in the New World, he began a distinctive feature of American tradition as a 'personal, highly emotional sense of the preciousness and vulnerability of each individual person's conscience ... To impose an orthodoxy upon the conscience is nothing less than what Williams, in a memorable and oft-repeated image, called "Soule rape"'.[40]

Against the urging of the Puritan John Cotton to seek the comforts of orthodoxy in a time of stress 'Williams shows us a different way of living with uncertainty, a way involving civil peace and equal respect for each person's conscience.'[41]

Although there were many in the colonies who fought against Williams' openness of spirit, the general tone of his writings became in time the dominant ethos of the colonies, as ideas of religious liberty and fairness gradually took hold, even where Williams' own name was abhorred.

Rhode Island became an oasis of tolerance, without any of the witch trials prevalent at the time (encapsulated dramatically in Arthur Miller's play *The Crucible*); in 1652 it passed the first law in North America to make slavery illegal, Jews acquired full rights there, and Native Americans were given respect and protection. All this was based upon Williams' idea of the preciousness and dignity of the individual human conscience, that everyone has inside something infinitely precious, something that demands respect from us all, and something in regard to which we are all equal, and thus different cultures and religions need to be accommodated within a society, not excluded.

The major figures of the American revolution may or may not have had firsthand knowledge of Williams' writings, but these works had become embedded in the American cultural and political landscape and together with the more familiar works of Enlightenment thinkers, drove them to fight for liberty of conscience as well as freedom from their colonial masters.

Although it is not my intention to go over the complex history of the American Revolution, it is worth examining the tipping point where the future leaders of the revolution were galvanized into open rebellion as relevant to the issue of tolerance. This was when acceptance of British rule broke down, with the passing by the British Parliament of what they called the 'Coercive Acts', but were suitably named the 'Intolerable Acts' by the American patriots. These were passed in 1774 after the Boston Tea Party and meant to punish the Massachusetts colonists for their defiance of throwing a large tea shipment into Boston Harbor in reaction to changes in taxation by the British to the detriment of Colonial goods. In the belated attempt to reassert Royal authority, the acts took away Massachusetts' self-government and historic rights, triggering outrage and resistance in the Thirteen Colonies. This led to the convening of the First Continental Congress at Philadelphia where a boycott of British goods was agreed, which was thus a key development in the outbreak of the American Revolution in 1775. The acts produced rage amongst the colonists, increasing the influence and numbers of the radicals. Thomas Jefferson from Virginia described it as a deliberate and systematic plan of reducing the colonists to slavery, and the attempt at imposition on the colonists turned him into an active radical.

Jefferson wrote *A Summary View of the Rights of British America* for the First Congress, a tract addressed to King George, which was seen as too radical to accept, but led to his being made a delegate to the Second Congress, which ultimately took the step of declaring independence. In the pamphlet he argued for the autonomy of colonial legislative power. Jefferson appeals to 'nature' as justifying his arguments for freedom from British legislation,[42] a later constant theme of his writings, including the Declaration of Independence. His writings are full of references to nature, natural right, natural law, and the laws of nature. In the Declaration he invoked 'the laws of nature and of nature's God' which entitle a people separate and equal station in life. If there were a universal and uniform human nature, then it would follow that there should be no hierarchical relations in society. Of course it must be said that his notion of human nature, unlike that of Roger Williams, did not extend to women, African-Americans or Native Americans; there is always the danger when appealing to human nature of having a fixed view of its meaning.

Jefferson's Virginia *Bill for Establishing Religious Freedom* [43] contains arguments for religious freedom extending what was contained in the Declaration of Independence. The use of force by either civil or ecclesiastical powers, which consist of fallible men, to assume dominion over others is seen to go against the natural right to profess and by argument maintain their opinions in matters of religion. And later in a letter to Connecticut Baptists[44] he agrees with them that religion is a matter which lies solely between man and his God, and that the rights of conscience are fundamental and natural, and that an individual 'owes account to none other for his faith and worship'. He reminds them that the Declaration of Independence affirmed that the legislature of the American people should 'make no law respecting an establishment of religion, or prohibiting the free exercise thereof, thus building a wall of separation between church and State.'

This wall of separation was necessary to make sure that freedom of conscience was maintained against pressures to conform with whatever body was in power. He argues strongly against uniformity of opinion, and, anticipating John Stuart Mill, that difference of opinion is advantageous in religion, that a plurality of opinions is inevitable given man's fallibility and is also beneficial to society as it enriches it and requires religious groups to limit one another. That implies there must be no official state or national religion. The wall of separation must be maintained if plurality of views and religious freedom and tolerance of difference were to be protected. This became enshrined in the First Amendment, enacted in 1791.

There has been much criticism in the US since then of the metaphor of the wall of separation, with some religious groups arguing that it poses the danger of an 'iron curtain', where there should instead be much freer circulation between the political and religious spheres, given the reality of the importance of religion to so many Americans. Of course one could argue that for that very reason there is a need for such a wall, one with few 'doors', because of the risks of undue religious influence on political leaders.

The situation in the UK however is that there is no wall of separation as the Anglican Church is the official religion of the country, with the monarch pledging at the coronation to 'defend the faith'. The difference however with the American context is that in reality the Christian religion, or any religion in the UK, does not wield such powerful influence on political life. Compared to the US, religion in the UK is weak, and therefore there is really no need for a wall; one exists without it being even legislated for, a wall of indifference.

In contrast, Americans have experienced several so-called 'Great Awakenings', going back to the first one initiated by Jonathan Edwards in 1734, preaching in Northampton, Massachusetts, and the British Evangelical George Whitfield on his tours of various states at a similar time. These preachers appealed to the common man with intense emotionality, often appealing to the heart and offering an intense religious conversion; the born again Christians were indeed born out of this national movement. According to Jonathan Israel's commentary on this phenomenon,[45] this New Light revivalism was powerfully anti-intellectual, basically conservative and represented a counter-Enlightenment movement, in the form of either emotional evangelism or conservative ultra-Protestantism, hostile to intellectual and social innovation.

It must be said, however that there is another side to this religious revivalism. It did provide a levelling of hierarchy, placing individual religious experience over established church doctrine and in that sense had a democratizing effect. It led to the flourishing of many sects, and offered a kind of unity throughout the nation.

In the US, according to Denis Lacorne, the wall of separation is sometimes unbreachable, sometimes full of doors, depending on the circumstances and the requirement of a complex multi-ethnic and multireligious culture.[46] There are, he points out, two different historical narratives of the formation of the American identity; American identity is dual in nature. One side remains convinced that the American identity has been shaped by the influence of Enlightenment thinkers, based on a rational philosophy that excludes or sidelines religion, and the other side, influenced by a romantic rediscovery of the Puritan ancestors, is convinced that the nation is at its core religious, and therefore government should support the free exercise of religion, even supporting faith-based schools and organizations with public funding. The Supreme Court at various times has wavered between these two narratives, finding it difficult to reconcile them. One cannot understand the American interpretation of tolerance, nor indeed American politics today, without understanding this duality at the heart of the American identity.

Notes

1 Hazard, 1935, p. 332.
2 Popper, 1987.
3 Voltaire, 1763, p. 7.
4 Voltaire, 1763, p. 11.
5 Voltaire, 1763, p. 22.
6 Voltaire, 1763, p. 25.
7 Voltaire, 1763, p. 49.
8 Voltaire, 1763, p. 52.
9 Voltaire, 1763, p. 89.
10 Voltaire, 1764, p. 242.
11 Rousseau, 1762, p. 277.
12 Rousseau, 1762, p. 276.
13 Rousseau, 1762, p. 270.
14 Rousseau, 1762, p. 276.
15 Durkheim, 1893, pp. 22–3.
16 Rousseau, 1762, p. 275, note 1.
17 Dent, 1988, p. 134.
18 Wolin, 2004, p. 330.
19 Wolin, 2004, p. 332.
20 Arendt, 1963, p. 71.
21 Dent, 1988, p. 115.
22 Rousseau, 1755, p. 66, note 2.
23 Rousseau, 1755, p. 66, note 2.
24 Dent, 1988, p. 131.
25 Smith, 1759, p. 55.
26 Smith, 1759, p. 55.
27 Smith, 1759, p. 27.
28 Solomon, 2007, p. 66.
29 Israel, 2011, p. 443.
30 Israel, 2011, p. 464.
31 Arendt, 1963, p. 180 ff.
32 Arendt, 1963, p. 154.
33 Nussbaum, 2008, p. 34 ff.

34 Lacorne, 2007, p. 147.
35 Lacorne, 2007, p. 27.
36 Williams, 1664.
37 Forst, 2003 pp. 183–4.
38 Nussbaum, 2008, p. 37.
39 Nussbaum, 2008, p. 36.
40 Nussbaum, 2008, p. 37.
41 Nussbaum, 2008, p. 40.
42 Jefferson, 1774, p. 64 ff.
43 Jefferson, 1777, p. 390 ff.
44 Jefferson, 1802, p. 396.
45 Israel, 2011, p. 463.
46 Lacorne, 2007, p. 160.

7

JOHN STUART MILL, LIBERTY, AND THE HARM PRINCIPLE

Towards modern liberal tolerance

In tackling the thought of John Stuart Mill, we reach the threshold of the modern treatment of tolerance, and with his book *On Liberty*,[1] written under the influence of his partner then wife, Harriet Taylor, we come to the last of the classic texts on tolerance and freedom and still the basis for much modern liberal thought.

Mills starts the book with a quotation from Wilhelm von Humboldt's book on *The Sphere and Duties of Government*—'The grand, leading principle, towards which every argument in these pages directly converges, is the absolute and essential importance of human development in its richest diversity.'[2] Von Humboldt anticipated a number of Mill's arguments and those of libertarians today, in that he considered that the state had only a limited role in the life of the individual citizen, being confined to general *security* but little else, as the individual's free development, their ability to choose a '*plan of life*' was more important than anything else. For example, with regard to the state's role with regard to children:

> The State must see that the parents strictly fulfill their duty towards their children, that is, to befit them, as far as their situation allows, to choose a plan of life of their own; and that the children, on their part, discharge the duty they owe to their parents, that is, to do all to enable the latter to fulfill their duty with regard to them; while neither parents nor children be allowed to overstep the rights which the discharge of their mutual duty puts into their hands. To secure this object alone must be the State's endeavour; and every attempt to bring out positive ends through the pretence of this solicitude—as, for example, to encourage a particular development of the children's powers—must be regarded as foreign to its appropriate sphere.[3]

While Mill follows Von Humboldt in prioritizing the value and development of human individuality, he provides a much more complex picture of the relation between the individual and their society, and where the state may have a legitimate role in intervening in the life of an individual, for example, if the latter is in danger of harming others. Mill retains Humboldt's role of 'security' in establishing where the state can intervene in the individual's life, but Mill's picture of the human subject is not one where they are cut off from others in isolation from society. Indeed, Mill had already given considerable attention to the nature of society and the theory of sociology, for example in his book on the *Logic of the Moral Sciences*, the sixth book of his *System of Logic*.

In the latter, Mill considers that consideration of the laws of the formation of character is the principal object of scientific inquiry into human nature. By a law he is referring to the discovery by observation and experiment of uniformities of experience, such as successive states of mind, or what his father James Mill called the law of association of ideas. Mill looks at the working of the individual mind, or the science of the individual, but then moves onto the science of man in society, 'of the actions of collective masses of mankind, and the various phenomena which constitute social life'.[4] Such a study is necessarily even more complex than studying the individual mind, but it is still a human task; when humans come together, he states, they are not converted into a different substance—perhaps a debatable point from our perspective, when we have seen how group phenomena can indeed turn individuals into inhuman creatures incapable of seeing the humanity of the individual.

Mill offers detailed considerations of how to study social phenomena, how observation and experiment can be applied to complex social situations, and what method is most suitable for so doing. He eliminates the use of methods such as chemistry and geometrical abstractions as unsuitable ways of comprehending human social affairs, for example conducting experiments on people, as if they were part of a chemical experiment, is completely unrealizable and inappropriate. This leaves first of all the physical method, with deductions based upon the laws of human nature applied to a given state of society. This can provide certain predictions and observed tendencies, for example with the use of statistics to look at the behaviour of human populations, or the way that a study of the political economies in different countries provides solutions to how industries and businesses work. However, the phenomena are so complex that our current theories invariably fail to take account of the observed phenomena.

This leaves the less precise but more applicable historical method, which starts from what he calls 'inverse deduction', where one starts with generalizations suggested by general examples and circumstances from history, and then looks for underlying causes; what are the causes which 'produce, and the phenomena which characterize, States of Society generally'?[5] It is with Mill's notion of a 'state of society' that we come to how one can understand and study the essential relatedness of individuals with one another.

A state of society is the 'simultaneous state of all the greater social facts or phenomena,'[6] which includes society's material elements such as economic development, the state of industry, and wealth and its distribution; political elements such as the forms of government, class divisions, and relations between classes; and elements of belief, matters of aesthetic taste, and cultural interests.

It is implied that there exists a natural correlation between all these different elements; 'that not every variety of combination among these general social facts is possible, but only certain combinations; that is in short, there exist Uniformities of Co-existence between the states of the various social phenomena.'[7] And he makes the point that information we have with regards to the history of societies is valid for understanding current societies, as that information when duly analysed will discover uniformities. The fundamental problem of the social sciences is to find the laws according to which any state of society produces the state that succeeds it and takes its place. What keeps society together in a condition of stability is a mixture of a number of essential elements—education, which involves training the individual to subordinate his personal impulses towards the ends of society; feelings of allegiance and loyalty towards some common and durable good or aim; and lastly a strong and active principle of cohesion among the members of a community.

With the regard to the latter, he further makes the powerful and still relevant point that

> We need scarcely say that we do not mean nationality, in the vulgar sense of the term; a senseless antipathy to foreigners; indifference to the general welfare of the human race, or an unjust preference of the supposed interest of our own country; a cherishing of bad peculiarities because they are national, or a refusal to adopt what has been found good by other countries. We mean a principle of sympathy, not of hostility, of union not of separation. We mean a feeling of common interest among those who live under the same government … We mean, that one part of the community do not consider themselves as foreigners with regard to another part; that they set a value on their connection—feel that they are one people, that their lot is cast together.[8]

One might consider these wise words a manifesto for contemporary tolerance, an open-minded ethics of acceptance of otherness.

Overall, Mill proposes that there is something called a state of society defined by a number of different and interacting elements, in which one can detect various continuities between these elements, and that every state of society is caused by its preceding state, that is, it is shaped by its complex history. Different states of society will show different and distinctive characters, some progressive, others less so, though degrees of progressiveness are difficult to judge. The state of 'civilization' of a given society seems to be related to its political stability, including the three basic elements of education, allegiance, and cohesiveness.

When it comes to considering the ends to which society should aim in order to improve itself, one is no longer in the realm of the sciences but that of the arts, or what in this context, Mill, following von Humboldt, calls the 'Art of Life', in matters of morality, aesthetics, and human conduct. It is here that Mill finally brings in what he considers the ultimate principle of human development and conduct—that of happiness. The promotion of happiness is not the sole end of human actions but a reference point by which to judge human actions. But what is essential for Mill is the development of a particular kind of 'noble' character. However Mill, having come to the end of this book, does not enlarge on what he means by such a character. One can assume, based on the preceding pages, that this must involve an appreciation of society's cohesion and stability, not some model of the individual in isolation from their society, for it would otherwise be puzzling why he spent so much attention prior to these last pages of the book describing the state of society and how it can be understood. But it is with his book *On Liberty* that one can begin to have a more coherent picture of Mill's notion of an individual's link with their community.

The main subject of his book is civil or social liberty—'the nature and limits of the power which can be legitimately exercised by society over the individual',[9] and hence from the beginning of his text the nature of the relationship between the individual and their social environment is a central focus. While traditionally individual liberty meant protection from the tyranny of political rulers, the society of Mill's time faced a new situation, still relevant today, where the individual additionally needed protection against what he called, following de Tocqueville,[10] the 'tyranny of the majority'. This meant the

> tyranny of prevailing opinion and feeling; against the tendency of society to impose ... its own ideas and practices as rules of conduct on those who dissent from them; to fetter the development ... and prevent the formation of any individuality not in harmony with its ways.[11]

Mill will take up in detail what he means by the fostering of individuality in the third chapter of the book, but individual development and its protection against intrusions remains a major theme, and how this may or may not be compatible with the interests of society. Mill's own personal development was famously crucial in emphasizing this theme. As he wrote in his *Autobiography*[12] at the end of his life, his philosopher father James Mill, a disciple of Jeremy Bentham, brought him up in a very intellectually strict environment, learning the classics and other topics from a very early age. But he had a mental breakdown as a young man, or rather what one could call a 'breakthrough', because it revealed to him a new way of being, one where feeling was to be treasured as much as intellectual achievement. While he could agree with his father that happiness and the improvement of mankind was a main aim of life, when it came to the happiness of the individual, this was not something that could be imposed in a machine-like way, with a rigid imposition of discipline. During his breakdown Mill was oppressed by the thought that all feeling was dead within him. It was when he 'accidentally' read the *Memoires d'un Pére* by Jean-Francois Marmontel, the French historian and writer and one of the *Encyclopedistes*, that he found a way through his despair. Mill was overcome with feeling when he came to the passage that related the father's death when Marmontel was a boy, and how the young Marmontel then felt that he would be everything to his family, in order to supply what had been lost. From that moment, Mill's burden began to become lighter, and he realized that his was not a hopeless case, and that he was able to feel. There of course must have been an intimate connection with reading about a dead father and Mills' own dead feelings—the fact that it was his father's mechanical, 'deathly' approach to education and the devaluation of the role of feeling that had brought Mill to the point of breakdown. Perhaps the reading of this passage provided a route for the expression of unresolved Oedipal issues. But whatever the precise psychological explanation of Mill's turnaround, this led to a transformation in how he saw the world and adopting 'a theory of life' where personal happiness was more likely to be attained by indirect than direct means. He considered from that moment that just enjoying life for its own sake, rather than actively seeking happiness in some planned way, was more likely to achieve a happy state of mind. It was from then that Mill also 'for the first time, gave its proper place, among the prime necessities of human well-being, to the internal culture of the individual.'[13]

He did not abandon intellectual pursuits, nor fail to consider analytical thinking as essential to individual and social improvement, but 'The maintenance of a due balance among the faculties, now seemed to me of primary importance. The cultivation of feelings became one of the cardinal points in my ethical and philosophical creed.'[14] This emphasis on personal development as something inward rather than imposed from the outside very much pervades the book on liberty.

In the introduction to the book, Mill reveals his vision or theory of life as one where the individual should be free to cultivate their individual development from within, and without undue external interference. He does look at some of the social and historical reasons for how societies can create social divisions by tyrannizing individuals, such as through class interests, slave labour including that in slave plantations in the US, and differences between the rights of men and women. It must be emphasized how much Mill was opposed to the way that women remained bound by convention and prejudice, often subjected to a form of slavery in constricting marriages, and he subsequently argued in detail for their liberation in his book *The Subjection of Women*. [15]

Mill mentions the issue of religious belief as one where it seemed to be virtually the only case where the rights of the individual against society had been asserted on broad grounds of principle, and the claim of society to exercise authority over dissent openly opposed. He states (no doubt thinking here of Locke and other early Enlightenment thinkers) that:

> The great writers to whom the world owes what religious liberty it possesses have mostly asserted freedom of conscience as an indefeasible right, and denied absolutely that a human being is accountable to others for his religious belief. Yet so natural to mankind is intolerance in whatever they really care about, that religious freedom has hardly anywhere been practically realized ... In the minds of almost all religious persons, even in the most tolerant countries, the duty of toleration is admitted with tacit reserves ... Wherever the sentiment of

the majority is still genuine and intense, it is found to have abated little of its claim to be obeyed.[16]

Thus, even in societies where there is some degree of tolerance, the tyranny of opinion and belief still predominates, and any duty to be tolerant is pretty lukewarm, hardly an 'active' tolerance.

To counteract this state of affairs, Mill then expounds what has become one of the most influential principles governing the dealings of society with the individual, the so-called *Harm Principle*, or *Principle of Self-Protection*. This principle is essentially a development of those thinkers such as Locke, Bayle, and Spinoza who posited the primacy of individual conscience in matters of religious belief and practice. But Mill extends the arguments from religious belief into the social life in general, that is, to a form of 'social tolerance'.[17] Mill writes that the object of his text is to assert:

> one very simple principle, as entitled to govern absolutely the dealings of society with the individual in the way of compulsion and control, whether the means used be physical force in the form of legal penalties, or the moral coercion of public opinion. That principle is, that the sole end for which mankind are warranted, individually or collectively, in interfering with the liberty of action of any of their number, is self-protection. That the only purpose for which power can be rightly exercised over any member of a civilized community, against his will, is to prevent harm to others.[18]

This principle is quite a complex one involving both positive and negative elements. There is the protection of others from harmful individual action, which could be seen as a mixture of a negative action towards an individual but positive towards others. At the same time, the individual is him- or herself part of society and needs to be protected from the harmful action of others, and therefore any action taken to protect society should in principle take account of the effect on the individual of an excessive protective action. It is not always easy or indeed possible to find the right combination of actions which can both protect an individual and also keep society from experiencing harmful effects; there of course will be times, as with serious criminal acts, when the individual has to be harmed for the good of society. But there are many other less clear situations when the boundary between the individual and society needs to be constantly redrawn, revealing a constant interplay between the security of the individual and the security of society. One suspects that Mill himself would have had a high threshold by which the state could interfere with the individual's personal liberty for the sake of state security. And of course in our day, we have become used to how the language of security can be corrupted by authoritarian governments.

Mill essentially makes a rather artificial distinction between conduct that concerns the individual and that concerning others—between self-regarding and other-regarding actions. It is only behaviour that concerns others which can come under any kind of central control or influence, while 'over himself, over his own body and mind, the individual is sovereign'.[19]

Mill also clarifies that this principle concerns mature adults and not children or those who need to be looked after, including presumably those severely mentally ill or those with severe learning disabilities. The principle also only applies to relatively mature societies where free and equal discussion is possible, not for those who have yet to achieve this form of progress.

This principle does not imply that the individual is removed from society or from social responsibilities, but is aimed at defining the different 'spheres of action'—what belongs purely to the sphere of the individual and where society does or does not have a direct or an indirect interest in the individual's action. An individual's social or other-directed actions will include positive acts for the benefit of others, which may involve some element of compulsion, such as jury service, engaging in defence activities; or such actions may involve taking action to help someone in need or in danger—indeed a failure to act in these last circumstances would be unjustifiable. Hopefully, he adds, personal conscience would enable an individual to see when to take appropriate and responsible action with regard to others.

Mill then delineates the appropriate sphere of human liberty, of pure self-directed actions. There is first the inward domain of consciousness, a wide and crucial area on which he will focus for much of the text. This includes liberty of thought and feeling, including the freedom to express opinions on all subjects. I would add here the importance of *imagination* in enabling an individual to have a tolerant internal space that can allow for liberty of thought and feeling. Though the latter really concerns relations between the individual and others, Mill considers it to be almost as important as liberty of thought itself. Secondly, there is liberty of tastes and pursuits, framing our 'plan of life' to suit our own character, to undertake our pursuits without being impeded, provided we do not harm others—we can be seen to be foolish, perverse or wrong, but that is different from being harmful to others. Lastly, from this liberty of the individual, follows the liberty, within the same limits, of combination among individuals, that is the 'freedom to unite, for any purpose not involving harm to others: the persons combining being supposed to be of full age, and not forced or deceived.'[20]

Thus, once more, one can see how Mill's concern with individual liberty is not of a kind that neglects relations with others. Indeed, one could call his form of liberty a 'liberty to relate' as much as a freedom to pursue personal aims.

Mill ends the introduction with a warning, very relevant today, about modern pressures on individuals, due to the increasing size of political communities nationally and internationally. There is, he writes, an

> increasing inclination to stretch unduly the powers of society over the individual, both by the force of opinion and even by that of legislation; and as the tendency of all the changes taking place in the world is to strengthen society, and diminish the power of the individual, this encroachment is not one of the

evils which tend spontaneously to disappear, but, on the contrary, to grow more and more formidable.[21]

He will not give in this text much detail about how to curb this encroachment, except to mention the hope that a 'strong barrier of moral conviction' could be raised against it; his main purpose here is to give general guidance about where one should place the boundary between individual liberty and legitimate state interference, and under what overriding principle. That is, he is defining here the '*boundary of tolerance*', where the state should tolerate the individual's freedom to act, however much that action may be disapproved of, or be objectionable—up to the point, that is, of *significant harm* to others, harm which, for example, violates a moral norm, such as theft. That is, the law quite often provides a 'red line', the furthest limit to what can be tolerated. Of course where actions move over from being just concerning or offensive or eccentric or generally objectionable to being significantly and persistently harmful, is a matter of interpretation in a particular state of society.

The remainder of the book *On Liberty* expands on the basic issues in the introduction under the topics of liberty of thought and discussion, of individuality as one element of well-being where he creates a more detailed picture of the kind of character development that he would prioritize, the limits to the authority of society over the individual and finally a discussion of some practical applications of the general principles.

In the chapter on liberty of thought and opinion, Mill argues strongly for a positive model for how people should manage exchange of different opinions, what kind of social climate is conducive both to the discovery of the truth and at the same time is beneficial to what he calls the 'mental well-being' of mankind, perhaps something like enlarging our minds, opening them up, freeing them from ignorance, but also facilitating individual development.

Free and open debate, which will inevitably include a clash of ideas, opinions, and judgments, is a way of reaching a resolution of issues. All opinions, however in error, will contain some element of the truth; it is 'only by the collision of adverse opinions that the remainder of the truth has any chance of being supplied.'[22] Thus the toleration of different viewpoints has significant value, both for discovering the truth but also because this provides a model for how to relate in society by *valuing* others. How far one should go in tolerating others' views is a matter of debate. Mill seems to suggest that even evil opinions have to be allowed expression, for the greater good of society. That is he argues for a radical and unqualified tolerance.

I would suggest, however, that the boundary of what can be tolerated in this instance depends again on the wider harm principle. For example, tolerating an extreme opinion may have negative consequences; giving extremists a voice may unfortunately empower them to undertake harmful acts. There is, then, bound to be some curtailment of free speech, but any curtailment has to be open for examination as to the genuine risk of legitimate or significant harm, or the risk of suppressing individual freedom may be too great. There is no inevitable slide into censorship and tyranny as a result of imposing a boundary on what can be publicly tolerated, provided that due caution and attention to the risks is in the open. But that of course already implies the functioning of an 'open' society, where such issues can be monitored and open to examination without fear of reprisal.

The chapter on individuality fleshes out more of Mill's vision of the individual's life plan, a task he was first impelled to undertake after his breakdown in his twenties. Toleration of different opinions is linked to individual development, or what he calls 'different experiments in living'. Mankind is not infallible, their truths are often only half-truths, and

> unity of opinion, unless resulting from the fullest and freest comparison of opposite opinions, is not desirable, and diversity not an evil but a good, until mankind are much more capable than at present of recognising all sides of the truth ... As it is useful that while mankind are imperfect there should be different opinions, so it is that there should be different experiments of living; that free scope should be given to varieties of character, short of injury to others ... It is desirable, in short, that in things which do not primarily concern others, individuality should assert itself.[23]

Even if an opinion is wrong, he argues, it should be allowed to be expressed, as conflict of ideas in itself improves the level of debate and discussion, making the possibility of arriving at the truth more not less likely.

Thus tolerance of different of opinions for Mill is not 'merely a concern for the correctness of conclusions, but for the whole spiritual, moral, and intellectual health of the inner life.'[24] This makes tolerance a powerful and key element of Mill's thinking around liberty, consisting of both an epistemological and ethical justification for his views—the former concerning its role in working towards the truth, the latter due to its role in achieving a variety of human goods.

There is, moreover, no clear machine-like plan or model about how to 'become an individual'. There are indeed, he argues, multiple paths available in European societies for personal development. But making individual and spontaneous choices about how to live, exercising one's own individual spontaneity, owning one's desires and impulses, however modified by one's own culture, is essential to the formation of individual character. This may mean having to stand up against custom and despotic imposition as well as the tyranny of popular opinion. Society should be very cautious about imposing anything that could undermine the individual's free expression. And anyway, Mill states that a good argument against any such interference with an individual's personal conduct is that it is more likely than not to be done badly and in the wrong place, especially as public opinion tends to dislike anything that smacks of difference. This is particularly evident in the long history of religious intolerance and persecution.

Thus, overall, as Mill summarizes in his last chapter, individuals are not accountable to society for their actions, in so far as they concern the interests of no one but themselves. Society may give advice or instruction and use persuasion as measures to influence an individual, but no more, unless the individual's actions are prejudicial to the interests of others. In the latter case, the law may be used to provide suitable sanctions or punishment. There may also be cases where society will have to intervene actively to protect a vulnerable person, such as those who are mentally ill, or those who are slaves, including he argues many women enslaved by their controlling husbands. The most cogent reason for restricting the interference of government is 'the great evil of adding unnecessarily to its power'.[25]

Mill ends the book with a prescient vision of the terrible potential power of the state to stifle human individuality.

> A State which dwarfs its men, in order that they may be more docile instruments in its hands even for beneficial purposes—will find that with small men no great thing can really be accomplished; and that the perfection of machinery to which it has sacrificed everything will in the end avail it nothing, for want of the vital power which, in order that the machine might work more smoothly, it has preferred to banish.[26]

Mill's thought continues to be highly influential, both as an inspiration for liberal thinkers and a target of those opposed to liberalism. While one may quarrel with some of his arguments, he provides a detailed and reasoned justification for placing the individual's development of their capacities, their ability to form their own unique life plan, at the heart of his thinking, a view which grew out of his personal pain in confronting his father's master plan to create a child moulded by philosophy, with little place for human feeling.

As Isaiah Berlin wrote:

> Mill believes that man is spontaneous, that he has freedom of choice, that he moulds his own character, that as a result of the interplay of men with nature and with other men something novel continuously arises, and that this novelty is precisely what is most characteristic and most human in men. Because Mill's entire view of human nature turns out to rest not on the notion of a repetition of an identical pattern, but on the perception of human lives as subject to perpetual incompleteness, self-transformation and novelty, his words are today alive and relevant to our own problems.[27]

While Mill's notion of well-being was individualist, he nonetheless did not see the individual as isolated from their social environment, and saw the state as having a role in promoting individual development, albeit he was also extremely cautious about how much the state could become monolithic and mechanistic and hence interfere with personal spontaneity and growth. He also emphasized how public opinion can become tyrannical in its attitudes to individual differences. Though of course unaware of the degree to which irrational and unconscious forces were to be released with terrifying consequences for the course of history in the twentieth century, he nonetheless saw the dangers of mass thinking, the potential destructiveness of industrialization and the fragility of an open society, and hence the need to protect the individual's liberty against social coercion. However, one could argue that his attitude to mass public opinion was also somewhat elitist. If we have learned anything from the recent Brexit vote in the UK and from the election of Donald Trump in the US, it is that those who feel disenfranchised from the centres of power can make their views known if they are not heeded; the majority, however 'tyrannical', needs to be given a voice.

The principle of personal liberty, Mill's overriding principle, involved the ability to choose one's life plan, and had to be protected from state and public intrusion. However, he also argued that society had a role in facilitating individual development by promoting or supporting, or at least tolerating, open and free discourse, the free and open expression of different viewpoints. However, one had to be cautious about the state promoting particular opinions.

Mill showed that there are limits to how much an individual can cultivate their own plan of life, and in particular when the individual's actions may cause significant harm to the social fabric; society then has a right to protect itself from harmful acts by individuals or groups of individuals—from, for example, terrorists. As I have suggested, this is a complex principle, as issues of harm and self-protection go both ways, towards and from the individual. It can be difficult to distinguish any action that has no effect on others. And an action may benefit some while harming others, adding even more complexity and ambiguity in trying to assess the object of any harm. Presumably Mill would apply the principle of utility, what is best for society overall, at some point in order make a kind of calculus of harm, although he was always clear about protecting individual rights against majority pressure.

There are also issues about what counts for harm that Mill left ambiguous. The assumption is that the harm must be legitimate or significant, and is to be distinguished from upset, even offence, as the free expression of opinions creates the right environment to facilitate the well-being and flourishing of mankind. It can be difficult to know when speech becomes harmful, and how much regulation of what is publicly spoken is tolerable in a free society. Mill's view implies we need dissident and even hateful voices to be heard; regulating or censoring such voices would be anti-development and counter to truth finding.

Perhaps the best answer to the issue of what counts for significant harm is to have available a setting where this issue can be freely debated and a judgment then made on the individual case, as each situation can be difficult to decide in general terms. I would call this a setting for the establishment of a *Tolerance Process*, which would take place in a public space where a controversial act or belief or proposition is held up to ongoing scrutiny, in order to ascertain whether or not it causes harm to others. That is, any restrictions on individual freedom on the basis of harm to others need to be publicly justified. Sometimes the appropriate setting will be a court of law, but there will be many times when this would not be the correct place to settle a complex political or moral argument. Unfortunately, in the absence of the appropriate setting, what often happens is that matters of this kind are dealt with by poor public debate via the popular media and the Internet, and through prejudiced assertions rather than open-minded debate.

Of course this notion of a public setting for tolerant exchanges of opinions is somewhat of an ideal; yet there are already places where such an exchange is possible. For example, my experience of being on a jury was that it was possible for 12 people from widely different backgrounds to come together in a civilized and serious setting in order to establish the facts of a criminal case and without jumping to conclusions or betraying prejudices. Such an open approach, admittedly forced by circumstances of having no choice in being on a jury and who would be one's fellow jurors, can be contrasted with the recent attitude of a Labour member of parliament who maintained that she would 'never hang out with Conservative women, who could not be friends of hers, and that they were "the enemy"'. In an article in the *Sunday Times* (27 August, 2017), Katie Glass rightly in my view admonishes this MP for being bigoted and for using the 'politics of hate'. In contrast, Glass maintains that 'You have to build a rapport to wield influence in a parliamentary democracy. It takes cross-party collaboration and adult debate'.

Thus, an open and adult attitude to debate and tolerance towards those with, for example, different political views can start at the micro level, with individual citizens taking responsibility for their own behaviour towards others. This does require what James Mill had described in his last work, *The Principles of Toleration*, as not giving in to 'the habit of attaching oneself to one side of a question',[28] instead of being open to the evidence on different sides. This habit, he adds, is a tendency of those who are powerful in a community because of vested interests, thus providing a balance to his son's suspicions about the tyranny of the majority.

Notes

1 Mill, 1859.
2 Mill, 1859, p. x.
3 Von Humboldt, 1854, p. 181.
4 Mill, 1843, p. 61.
5 Mill, 1843, p. 100.
6 Mill, 1843, pp. 100–1.
7 Mill, 1843, p. 101.
8 Mill, 1843, pp. 110–12.
9 Mill, 1859, p. 126.
10 De Tocqueville, 1835, p. 199ff.
11 Mill, 1859, p. 130.
12 Mill, 1873.
13 Mill, 1873, p. 118.
14 Mill, 1873, p. 118.
15 Mill, 1869.
16 Mill, 1859, pp. 133–4.
17 Forst, 2003, p. 363.
18 Mill, 1859, p. 135.
19 Mill, 1859, p. 135.
20 Mill, 1859, p. 138.
21 Mill, 1859, pp. 139–40.

22 Mill, 1859, p. 180.
23 Mill, 1859, p. 185.
24 Edwards, 1988, p. 107.
25 Mill, 1859, p. 244.
26 Mill, 1859, p. 250.
27 Berlin, 1969, p. 189.
28 Mill, 1826, p. 21.

8

PLURALITY AND TOLERANCE

Some key modern views on tolerance

The thought of Hannah Arendt concerning the nature of political life has certain key similarities to that of J.S. Mill, particularly with regard to the 'need for free and open public debate of different views',[1] and in this sense Arendt has a significant notion of political tolerance, albeit not expressed in the customary language of liberal thought.

I have already described how Arendt conceived of the origin of totalitarianism as a form of social pathology arising under modern conditions, yet she also based her thinking very much on a somewhat idealized vision of the workings of the Greek city state, or *polis*, where the Greek citizen can openly debate in a public space. For her the ancient world was so much more experienced in all political matters than us. It was not so much that she thought that Athenian democracy was the best political system, given the reality of its systematic coercion of women and slaves, but, 'the first flowering of democracy was among the most vivid and intense. Athenian political life was a politics of talk and opinion, one which gave a central place to human plurality and the equality between citizens.'[2]

Arendt saw the Greek polis as one where there was a clear distinction between the public and private realms, between the household, the realm of coercion, and the public realm of freedom, where citizens (the adult male heads of households) met for deliberation and debate on matters of concern. This became the model of how she saw the human condition, where the public realm of acting together in concert is the ultimate expression of human freedom. Equality or, in Greek, *isonomy*, among citizens is a condition of politics; it is not natural to man, but in the polis people were brought together at the same level, not as private citizens but as equals in the public sphere; whatever their birth they remained equal in that public space, where they could engage in political action through public debate. She applies this *pluralistic* ideal to contemporary life, asserting that '[m]en in the plural, that is men in so far as they live and move and act in this world, can experience meaningfulness only because they can talk and make sense to each other and themselves.'[3]

The founding fathers of the American Revolution came nearest to this ideal when drafting and deliberating about their Constitution, though she acknowledged that their ultimate achievement was only partially successful in enabling equal participation of citizens.

Though there was a distinction between household and public space, the Greek polis also, in my view, revealed an additional connection between the individual and the city. For example, in Plato the individual soul (*psyche*) and the polis seem to be intertwined, or at least more closely attached than any modern theory of the relation between the individual and the state. His very notion, in *The Republic*, of the tri-partite division of the soul into the rational part (*logistikon*), the irrational and appetitive (*alogistikon*) and principle of high spirit (*thumos*) follows the division of functions within the polis; and the polis is not seen as some simple projection *en masse* of the structure of the individual soul. There is a subtle and dynamic 'connectedness' between the individual psyche and the polis. The polis is indeed a model of a community in touch with its various parts. Thus:

> That polis ... is best ordered in which the greatest number use the expression 'mine' and 'not mine' of the same things in the same way ... And the polis whose state is most like that of an individual man. For example, if the finger of one of us is wounded, the entire community of bodily connections stretching to the soul for 'integration' with the dominant part is made aware, and all of it feels the pain as a whole, though it is a part that suffers.[4]

Thus Plato has a model of a community where there is integration or connectedness (*suntaxis*), and the need for an awareness of the whole structure. Of course he adds an elitist slant by proposing in his model of the polis the presence of the small group of ruling Guardians or philosopher-rulers, who at least encapsulate these principles in their very function as they are supposed to put the interests of others not themselves to the forefront.

The Platonic model, which I think is an important element of Arendt's political thinking, is one where the individual is, anyway, close to the public world. In Plato, insights are revealed between speakers—in the *Republic* between Socrates and others. Reason is a property of *dialogue*, the interaction between speakers in a public place, revealing the truth. The form, through dialogues, of Plato's philosophical inquiry represents in itself the source of knowledge.

Arendt emphasized how the distortions of the social world are expressed in those developments such as totalitarianism, which threaten to destroy the possibility of public discussion of political affairs, giving the ideal of the openly communicative Greek polis as a model.[5]

Arendt collected together a group of essays written over 12 years titled *Men in Dark Times*, referring both to the contemporary scene which had witnessed the horrors of the mid-twentieth century, but also any period where the public realm is obscured and people no longer have a sense of sharing a common world. The opening and key text in this collection, 'On humanity in dark times, thoughts about Lessing', is an address given in Hamburg when received the Lessing prize in 1959. Gotthold Lessing, the German Enlightenment philosopher and dramatist (1729–81), was a firm believer in tolerance and religious pluralism. Thus in his drama *Nathan the Wise* (1779), he proposed that each of the monotheistic religions had an equal claim to truth, 'the precise extent of which can be determined only after an indefinite, and perhaps infinite, period of time.'[6] He held it to be valuable and indeed inevitable that there would be plurality not only of religions but also of views about truth in general.

Arendt's address consists of a number of themes, including the relation of truth to the kind of free thinking promoted by Lessing and the quality of relations between people that enables open and human communication. For her, 'We humanize what is going on in the world and in ourselves only by speaking of it, and in the course of speaking of it we learn to be human.'[7] But of course open and public discourse requires a tolerant public place and space in which to speak. Totalitarian regimes make this impossible. People may then withdraw into an interior realm, into what she called the 'invisibility of thinking and feeling', but this is not a fully human world. It must be said that Arendt was no lover of psychoanalysis, and she appears to prioritize the public world over the inner world, rather than see the realms as intimately connected. Freedom for her seems to be predominantly about public deliberation and communication rather than private or inner freedom.

Margaret Canovan, commenting on the Lessing address, proposes that Arendt's model of open public communication gives us new ways of approaching an understanding of tolerance. Canovan begins her commentary by pointing out yet another paradoxical element embedded in the notion of tolerance and its relation to truth. On the one hand, tolerance has a natural affinity with scepticism, with being doubtful that there is one truth, one way of doing things or seeing the world. Having a clear view of what truth is tends to be associated with those who have strong beliefs, such as religious faith; intolerance is more likely to appear in such situations. On the other hand, tolerance has often been defended as a way of attaining the truth, by for example allowing different views to be expressed, letting people have their say until the truth comes out, in a kind of jury of views, until there is unanimity. Mill considered this to be the way that mankind improves itself, through the free and open expression of viewpoints, gradually narrowing the bounds of multiple and diverse opinions, until one arrives at the truth.

There is a similar paradox when looking at the relations between tolerance of diverse cultural practices and love of humanity. There is a tendency for those advocating tolerance to suggest that once people are brought close enough together, differences will melt and people will be brought together in one common human world, implying that tolerance of diversity will ultimately lead to uniformity. Of course the art of community relations is to try to bring people together while respecting their differences; finding common ground does not necessarily imply losing all one's own beliefs and values. Nonetheless it would be well to keep in mind the dangers of uniformity and the risk that it may turn living truths into dead dogmas,[8] and spontaneous ways of living into mindless routines.

In order to avoid such impasses, Arendt proposes in the Lessing address that, like Lessing, one remains suspicious of the existence of a single compelling truth (though not evidenced facts), and that instead one rejoices in the unending discourse among people in search of the truth but never reaching a single source of truth; the notion of single truth only leads to inhumanity.

> Lessing's greatness does not merely consist in a theoretical insight that there cannot be one single truth within the human world but in his gladness that it does not exist and that, therefore, the unending discourse among men will never cease so long as there are men at all. A single absolute truth ... would have spelled the end of humanity.[9]

Arendt describes this as a special form of tolerance, involving the gift of friendship, openness to the world, and the genuine love of mankind. The ideal of absolute truth that she describes in its extreme form in totalitarian regimes threatens in all societies the political public space between people, which she prioritizes as the site of freedom. 'She wanted to defend the political space between people: a space in which there is room to consider different perspectives and reach sound political judgments and room to stand back from one's immediate feelings and loyalties and strive for impartiality.'[10]

If men united in single opinion,

> so that out of many opinions one would emerge, as though not men in their infinite plurality but man in the singular, one species and its exemplars, were to inhabit the earth ... the world, which can only form in the interspaces between men in all their variety, would vanish altogether.[11]

Canovan summarizes the implications for such a tolerant vision of the human world with the following points—that public debate has an intrinsic value, that this has implications for the tolerance of political differences, that diversity of views and opinions, provided one has access to the proper facts, is integral to politics, and that the political condition of *plurality* and freedom depends upon a commitment by all those concerned to maintain the common political world that guarantees rights as citizens to all of them. But, where groups endeavour to destroy that common political world, or refuse to share it with certain others, their right to tolerance must be forfeit.

Arendt thus proposes a powerful vision of a tolerant public space open to all, but needing to be guarded against the forces of intolerance, those who aim to limit open and public discourse, often in the name of some single and abiding 'truth'.

Apart from the importance of Greek thought in Arendt's thinking, another key influence was that of Immanuel Kant, much of which is revealed in her *Lectures on*

Kant's Political Philosophy.[12] Indeed, Kant's views of the role of tolerance in upholding reasonable and public debate between free human beings have played a significant part in the thought of several key modern thinkers in this field, perhaps the most influential being Onora O'Neill, John Rawls, and Jürgen Habermas.

For Kant, enlightenment was about the ability to use one's own understanding or reason; a revolution may put an end to despotism and oppression, but unless ways of thinking were changed, then there would not be true revolution, which requires new ways of thinking. Enlightenment of this kind requires freedom, and for Kant freedom, as described in his essay *What is Enlightenment?* is the 'public use of one's reason in all matters'.[13] Though Kant appeared in this context to refer to a scholar's freedom to write for a reading public, his construction of freedom can be interpreted in a wider sense, offering a substantial and pluralistic view of tolerance.

In this essay, Kant makes an unusual and particular distinction between the private and public use of reason, which was clearly a major influence on Arendt's own private/public distinction. Private for Kant did not refer to what was merely individual, personal or interior, but to the nature of the communication used. A private communication was one addressed to a restricted audience, such as when a clergyman addresses a religious gathering, and one defined by some external authority. A public communication was free and unrestricted, addressed to a plurality of other free human beings. A clergyman could make public use of his reason if as a scholar he addresses the world, enjoying then an unrestricted freedom to make use of reason and to speak in his own person. To enjoy such freedom would require tolerance within the public arena.

Arendt commented that the precedence accorded to public over private communication may appear as something of an inversion of traditional liberal priorities,

> but on this point Kant is unequivocal: the use of reason in addressing a domestic or private gathering is dispensable to freedom, whereas the right to publicity, the right to freely submit one's judgments for public testing before 'a society of world citizens' is not dispensable but is utterly necessary for freedom, progress and enlightenment.[14]

Kant recognized that his notion of enlightenment is more an ideal than a current reality, that we have a long way to go before men can be in a position of using their understanding confidently and well in what one could call a tolerant space. 'Enlightenment is a process.'[15]

Arendt builds on Kantian and Greek foundations as the basis for political life, emphasizing the importance of public freedom and the necessity of a public space where men face each other as equals and participate in the formation and testing of opinions through public debate.

Kant also offered Arendt important insights into the nature of public communication in his *Critique of Judgment*, particularly in the first part where he examined the phenomenon of aesthetic judgments, matters of taste about, for example, the beautiful and the sublime. Judgments in matters of taste seem at first sight to be far from relevant to political life, yet Kant points out that the faculty of judging is a special kind of reflective activity inevitably involving relations between people, and hence is of wide relevance and significance. The interest in the beautiful exists only in society, not in isolation, and

> if we admit that the impulse to society is natural to mankind, and that the suitability for and the propensity towards it, i.e. *sociability*, is a property essential to the requirements of human beings as creatures intended for society, and one, therefore, that belongs to *humanity*, it is inevitable that we should look upon taste in the light of the faculty for judging whatever enables us to communicate even our *feeling* to everyone else.[16]

This faculty of judging requires reflection, and a special kind of *enlarged mentality*, where one takes account of the views and judgment of others, putting oneself in the position of everyone else in the hope of coming to an agreement. This is a form of common human understanding, not to be confused with the ordinary meaning of common sense, but a special kind of *sensus communis*, or 'public sense'.

Kant proposes three maxims to elucidate different aspects of this common human understanding—the need (1) to think for oneself and avoid prejudiced thought, (2) to think from the standpoint of everyone else, and thus have a broadened way of thinking involving a plurality of people in one's horizon, and (3) always to think consistently, what he recognizes as the hardest maxim to achieve.

Arendt considered that the capacity to judge is a

> specifically political ability in exactly the sense denoted by Kant, namely the ability to see things not only from one's own point of view but in the perspective of all those who happen to be present; even that judgment may be one of the fundamental abilities of man as a political being insofar as it enables him to orient himself in the public realm, in the common world.[17]

There may be some connection here with what I have earlier called a 'higher order' kind of empathy, which also involves an appreciation of the other's point of view coupled with thought *and* imagination.

The early work of the Kant scholar Onora O'Neill provides a detailed account of tolerance based upon Kant's notion of the public use of reason. Tolerance is seen to have a fundamental role in providing convincing grounds for reason, for putting forward standards or norms for rational inquiry. This may seem of only abstract philosophical significance, and indeed Kant's writings can be difficult to penetrate because of their frequent preoccupation with universal issues, with possibilities and principles. Nonetheless his thought often has important practical consequences; indeed much of his focus in the area under consideration was on 'practical' reason, which he saw as more fundamental than theoretical reason.

As O'Neill points out, as Kant depicts it,

we reason only if we act, think or communicate in ways that (we judge) make it possible for others to understand, to accept or to reject our claims or proposals. If we merely assert, or assume, or appeal to 'authorities' that others do not (sometimes even cannot) follow, we fail to offer them reasons.[18]

For Kant, there are deep connections between reasoning and politics because both are activities in which a *plurality* of participants need to engage with one another's thought and action. But as there may well be disputes between participants, coordination and shared assumptions have to be *constructed* rather than just assumed.[19] Kant likened that kind of construction to that of a building project, one which has to be pretty modest given our capacities. Rather than build a Babel-like tower of reason reaching the heavens, we only have enough stock of materials to build a *house*, and rather than having workers each speaking their own language and hence unable to work in coordination, we need to find a common plan, which can provide a stable platform for a secure home—thus following Kant's three maxims of the *sensus communis*.

The central thought of Kant's account of public reason is that it cannot be derivative, cannot lean on external authority; instead of being like a cyclist trying to ride by leaning on passing objects, a reasoner has to let go of such supports if they are to find their balance.[20] Of course it remains most unlikely that in the reality of the messy public world of politics such unrestricted communication is possible; it is more an ideal to work towards, or a standard of possible enlightened thinking.

O'Neill points out that 'Kant's distinctiveness lies in the fact that his discursive grounding of reason presupposes plurality, and the possibility of community; it does not presuppose "atomistic" subjects, actual communities or ideal communities.'[21] Tantalizingly she does not develop any further how this may lead to an evaluation of Kant's account of subjectivity.

In her earlier essays, 'The public use of reason' (1986), which looks at the nature of tolerance (or toleration in her terms) within a Kantian framework, and 'Practices of toleration' (1990), which is concerned with communication in the media, she sees tolerance as intimately linked to the grounding of reason in the shared public world. This is not of merely abstract importance but has direct application to the political world, particularly how communication between people is preserved and sustained. She points to Kant's three maxims of judgment to guide us as to how communication between plural subjects is a possibility. Communication is not a solitary act; even a communication that fails and finds no audience must use socially established modes of communication.[22] She asks how communication is possible in a democratic society, how can people be enabled to speak together. For this to be possible there need to be '*practices of tolerance*'. Kant had maintained that it is wrong to conduct our communications on principles that cannot be universally shared, and it would thus be wrong to communicate in ways that destroy or threaten those who wish to communicate. Orwell's description in his novel *1984* of the language, Newspeak, used by the totalitarian state Oceania, where freedom of thought is limited, with a restricted grammar and limited ideologically based vocabulary,

> is an image of vile intolerance because it destroys the very possibility of communication. It damages not merely particular communicators and communications but whole practices of communication. In the end it destroys not just freedom of public speech but freedom of thought.[23]

For tolerance to be maintained she argues that it is not enough to demand non-interference with acts of expression. Instead there needs to be a more robust and active framework, one which is likely to be demanding, which will sustain practices of tolerance from which no one is excluded. That is, there needs to be an *obligation* to protect free and open communication, both by enabling practices of tolerance, but also by paying attention to how intolerance can undermine free public communication.

For John Rawls tolerance plays a central part in his notion of justice as fairness, in his ground-breaking book *A Theory of Justice* (1971), where liberty of conscience is fundamental; his first principle of justice is that each person has an equal right to the most extensive scheme of equal basic liberties compatible with a similar scheme of liberties for others. Tolerance (or toleration) and thereby moral and religious freedom is not derived from some practical necessity or for reasons of state but follows from the basic principle of equal liberty for all.[24]

While tolerance of other people's views is thus basic to the practice of justice, there are nonetheless times when tolerance of intolerance is not possible. This may happen when there are matters of security and where there is a threat to basic liberties, for example where a group of some kind such as an intolerant sect aims to impose their beliefs and practices on others. Here the first principle of justice comes into play as it describes how basic liberties need to be compatible *between* people. There thus follows from this that there needs to be some public setting where reasonable public debate about matters of what can or cannot be tolerated takes place. In Rawls' earlier thought he was using a model of a basically well-ordered society where such matters can be debated in reasonable ways by reasonable people, where people have the capacity for genuine tolerance and mutual respect.

In Rawls' later thought, in *Political Liberalism* (1993) and in his last book, *The Law of Peoples* (1999) he moved from his assumptions of a well-ordered society to trying to tackle the modern democratic society where diverse and often incompatible religious, philosophical, and moral world views live alongside one another in various comfortable and uncomfortable ways. Instead of a uniformity of assumptions and beliefs he proposes that such a modern society should work with 'overlapping consensus'.[25] In an overlapping consensus, citizens will have their own comprehensive doctrines. But when it comes to people joining together into a stable society, there needs to be a political conception that all these different citizens can share. Such a conception is bound to be a flexible one, or anyway not so comprehensive as to be incapable of allowing such sharing. He called such a political conception a *'module'*—'an essential constituent part that fits into and can be supported by various reasonable comprehensive doctrines that endure in a society regulated by it.'[26]

In order to achieve an overlapping consensus there needs to be a consensus of reasonable, as opposed to unreasonable or irrational, comprehensive doctrines. The crucial fact is not the fact of pluralism itself, which could just be chaotic, but 'reasonable pluralism,' where people can both come together but also disagree on reasonable grounds. An overlapping consensus is not just a mere *modus vivendi*, a way of putting up with people, what I earlier described as a state of 'mere tolerance'. It is a more active and positive political model, where tolerance is embedded in the way that people with different ways of life and ways of thinking can find common ground in order to come together in a just, stable pluralistic society.

Rawls provides a clear and fundamentally liberal view about what he considers would be a suitable 'module' for such a society. This would entail mutual *respect* for others, which would enable people with different doctrines to cooperate with one another and abide by terms of cooperation in the first place. The just principles he puts forward need to satisfy the criterion of *reciprocity*.

> This criterion requires that, when terms are proposed as the most reasonable terms of fair cooperation, those proposing them must think it at least reasonable for others to accept them, as free and equal citizens, and not as dominated or manipulated under pressure caused by an inferior or social position.[27]

As the requirement for the reasonable pluralistic society, there would need to be a commitment to certain core liberal values such as equal basic rights and liberties of citizenship, the right to vote and to participate in politics, liberty of conscience, freedom of thought and of association, the protection of the rule of law, and attention to managing economic inequalities.

Rawls was not unaware that his model was somewhat utopian, though he optimistically called it a 'realistic utopia'[28] one with practical postulates about how a 'decent' society should manage differences. In this vision of the possible, 'the necessary (political) virtues are those of political cooperation, such as a sense of fairness and tolerance, and a willingness to meet others half way',[29] Rawls also calls this approach one of a duty of 'civility', involving a 'willingness to listen to others and a fair-mindedness in deciding when accommodation to their views should reasonably be made'.[30]

While tolerance is integral to Rawls' whole thought, he only clarifies his concept of tolerance in his last book, and he does so rather surprisingly just in a footnote:

> The main points of this conception of toleration can be set out in summary fashion as follows: (1) Reasonable persons do not all affirm the same comprehensive doctrine. This is said to be a consequence of the 'burdens of judgement.' (2) Many reasonable doctrines are affirmed, not all of which can be true

or right as judged from within any one comprehensive doctrine. (3) It is not unreasonable to affirm any one of the reasonable comprehensive doctrines. (4) Others who affirm reasonable doctrines different from ours are reasonable also. (5) In affirming our belief in a doctrine we recognize as reasonable we are not being unreasonable. (6) Reasonable persons think it unreasonable to use political power, should they possess it, to repress other doctrines that are reasonable yet different from their own.[31]

He adds that, though every society contains many unreasonable doctrines, how far any such doctrine can be tolerated will depend not upon these various points but upon principles of justice and the kinds of actions such principles will allow. My own version of this standpoint is to pick out the harm and the respect principles as the most cogent and easily applicable to situations where a judgment is required about what kind of actions and/or beliefs can be reasonably tolerated in a diverse society.

Rawls' theory, particularly in its later developments, has the great advantage of being readily applicable to a modern essentially liberal democratic society. However, his thought does make assumptions about human beings being decent and reasonable, and able to have open public debate about different viewpoints. The model requires that such liberal traditions are already rooted in society; it does not clarify how to bring such a society about, or how such a society may rest on less liberal realities such as exploitation and inequality. It is assumed that the liberal society is the most reasonable one. That is, for his model to work, it requires a *setting* in which people are able to exercise their freedoms. For him, this setting is clearly a liberal society, and he does not really look at how the ideal fails to match up to reality. What if, for example, people are not decent and reasonable all the time, but are full of irrational desires and drives which make their acts and communications at the very least fallible?

Hobbes' solution to such realities was to argue for a powerful central sovereign to keep order. Modern China seems to follow this model closely. Classical Marxist theory would require a complete overhaul of the way that power is distributed. It would seem that liberal theory would distribute the sources of power over several institutions, in order to minimize the possibility of dictatorship, but it does rely rather heavily on people behaving well towards one another, thus going against the evidence that intolerance and prejudice are part of the human condition. The hope is that political institutions and the legal framework will be enough to maintain and safeguard a just and equitable society. I think that more is needed, and that involves a fundamental change in attitude of citizens towards their fellows, an act of imagination perhaps. One could characterize this shift as providing what I earlier described as a '*home for otherness*'.

Rawls does have a somewhat ill-defined psychological or moral theory, which tries to take account of human failings, by setting up the principles of respect and reciprocity, or civility, as guiding relationships, a kind of home for otherness. Hence a moral comprehensive doctrine underpins the whole political theory.

There is no neutral position from which the theory develops. While I suspect that no political theory can escape this dilemma, Rawls could have done more to clarify this moral base.

Jürgen Habermas tackles the public use of reason within the context of a theory of human communication, which in its earlier form at least was deeply influenced by psychoanalytic clinical practice. He argues that active tolerance, with human subjects able to communicate in an open public arena, not passive indifference, protects a pluralistic society from being torn apart as a political community by conflicts over comprehensive world views.[32] Tolerance enables subjects to have open, free, and non-coercive communication.

Habermas' aim was to delineate a critical social science, and in his first major work, *Knowledge and Human Interests* (1968), he considered that psychoanalysis is a human science not a natural science, and what is unique about it is its discovery of a particular kind of self-reflection, through which the human subject can free themselves from states in which they have become objectified. Psychoanalysis in his terms deals with 'distorted communication', which has inhibited the patient's life. Through psychoanalytic treatment the subject can move from a passive position with little sense of their own subjectivity and freedom to relate to others, to a more active and aware subjective position where open and relatively undistorted intersubjective communication is possible. This specific activity of self-reflection must be accomplished by the subject themselves with the analyst; there can be no substitute for it by, for example, the use of technology. Computers are no substitutes for genuine human communication. His concern for how communication can become distorted and objectified, and how modern technology can become the source of alienation and 'instrumental' rather than emancipatory reason, was undoubtedly influenced by his youthful experience of the perverse way that the Nazi ideology, with the help of the latest technological and bureaucratic developments, used violence and propaganda to promote their message.

Thus Habermas uses his reading of psychoanalysis to put forward a liberating or 'emancipatory' theory of communication in terms of what he calls '*Communicative Action*' between subjects in a community. Communicative action is a distinctive type of social interaction oriented to mutual understanding and is quite different from other kinds of social interaction which aim, for example, at achieving success, or which have some self-promoting 'strategy'. Such strategic thinking is essentially 'monologic' rather than 'dialogic'. The latter is integral to communicative action.

For Habermas, the human mind is essentially constituted through an intersubjective process in the social field; at the heart of our subjectivity is a social core. 'The infant becomes a person by entering the public space of a social world that receives him with open arms ... Intersubjectivity has the mysterious power to unite disparate elements without eliminating the differences between them.'[33] However, he also recognizes that free and open communication is fragile and needs some form of special protection from forms of coercion.

While one might criticize this model of communication as an ideal one because one could argue that it is rare for human communication to be free from some kind of distortion, Habermas is nevertheless pointing to a simple yet profound human reality – that from the beginning of life the human infant is driven towards communication. Working with children, one can see very clearly how development drives them on; it is a basic human fact that children want to communicate and are driven to do so, and that there is an inescapable reality of development moving them forwards. Difficulties in speech and language development can have serious consequences for the child's ability to relate. Habermas himself was well aware of this problem, as he was born with a cleft palate that needed surgical intervention and that affected his confidence in communicating yet also made him acutely aware of its importance.

With regard to adult relations and political life, the notion of an ideal communication community functions for Habermas as a guide that can be applied both to regulate and to critique concrete speech situations. Individuals would be able to raise, accept, or reject each other's claims to truth, rightness, and sincerity solely on the basis of the force of the 'better argument'—i.e. on the basis of reason and evidence—and all participants would be motivated solely by the desire to obtain mutual understanding. Although this is an ideal situation, it can serve as a model of free and open public discussion within liberal-democratic societies.

Habermas specifically discussed the notion of tolerance in the context of how religious tolerance was historically the 'pacemaker' for various kinds of cultural change leading to the improvement of human rights. Tolerance began with moving away from the 'authoritarian act of *unilaterally* declared religious tolerance towards a right to exercise one's religion freely based on the *mutual* recognition of everybody's religious freedom, which entails a right to protection against the imposition of alien religious practices.'[34] This, as Habermas added, became the basis for what Rainer Forst has called the 'Respect' concept of tolerance as opposed to the 'Permission' concept driven from above by a hierarchical authority, as I describe below. With the respect concept of religious tolerance there is intersubjective understanding and recognition across confessional divides, which involves an act of imagination where one looks into the other side's position, or imagines their point of view, in order to reach some sort of respectful appreciation of difference. This is in effect an example of Habermas' communicative action at work. He points out how the practice of such religious tolerance became an important driving force for the emergence of the modern democratic and pluralistic society, and in some ways remains so today as a motor of multiculturalism, protecting societies from fragmentation and disintegration.

Tolerance, Habermas maintains, is not indifference; it is a much more active process involving the burden for those who hold different world views to make the *effort to respect*, if not fully understand, other world views. Freedom of religion continues to test the neutrality of the modern state, where a majority culture can abuse its power 'to lay down what shall count as the generally binding political culture in a pluralistic society according to its own standards.'[35]

Examples of when such issues come to the fore include whether or not French Muslim girls can wear religious clothing in schools, whether or not a Jewish prisoner must be offered kosher food, whether Sikhs riding a motorcycle have to wear helmets, whether an employee can take time for religious festivals etc. Such disputes, which may well have to go to law for their resolution,

> show why the spread of religious tolerance ... identified as the pacemaker for the emergence of democracies, has also become a stimulus and model for the introduction of further cultural rights within constitutional states. The inclusion of religious minorities in the political community awakens and promotes the sensitivity to the claims of other groups that suffer discrimination. The recognition of religious pluralism can assume this model function because it throws an exemplary light on *the claims of minorities to civic inclusion*. [36]

For minorities in a pluralistic society to be fully integrated so that they feel comfortable with their own identity while feeling that they belong to the wider community, there needs to be a 'network of relationships of reciprocal recognition', and there may well also need to be some form of legal framework guaranteeing cultural rights.

Habermas argues that the 'advance in reflexivity exacted from religious consciousness in pluralistic societies in turn provides a model for the mind-set of secular groups in multicultural societies'.[37] At the same time, the equal coexistence of different ways of life must not lead to isolation and segmentation. He argues, perhaps rather optimistically, that, 'The citizens as members of a society may legitimately cultivate their distinctive cultures only under the condition that they all understand themselves, across subcultural divides, as citizens of one and the same political community.'[38] Of course this is easier said than done. One also needs to tackle issues such as competing identifications within communities, as well as the kind of fears about the loss of a psychic home that I described in earlier chapters, for there to be the possibility of the kind of integration of cultures which Habermas described.

Rainer Forst has written extensively on tolerance; his magisterial book *Toleration in Conflict* (*Toleranz im Konflikt*, 2003) provides a comprehensive account of the history of tolerance as the backdrop to his own theory. For the latter, he divides tolerance into four types, which can all be present in society at the same time, so that conflicts about the meaning of toleration may also be understood as conflicts between these conceptions.

There is first of all the *Permission* conception of tolerance. The Permission conception is about those in power allowing others, usually a minority, to live in accordance with their own convictions. This would be to accept a minority's minimal demands for freedom of belief and practice, but may be better than nothing, at least for a while. It is a kind of *'vertical'* tolerance, from top down. This is a hierarchical situation, where one party allows another party certain things on conditions specified by the first one. It has been a common form of tolerance found in many historical writings and at crucial historical moments such as the Edict of Nantes in 1598, proclaimed by Henry IV granting the French Protestant

Huguenots freedom of conscience and limited freedom of worship. The aim was to promote internal peace, support the power of the King and yet also protect the dominant Catholic majority. The protection of the Huguenot minority however still depended on the goodwill of the political authority, and that kind of paternalistic tolerance still informs our understanding of the term. The political authority gives top-down permission for the minority to have certain rights and freedoms, but there is also a certain amount of constraint on their freedom of action, which is no doubt better than no toleration, but comes at a price. Such toleration 'not only remains unstable and susceptible to revocation, but also represents a particular form of the rational exercise of power, a particular practice of imposing discipline through restriction of freedom'.[39] A minority may not be actively persecuted, but they are not given equal rights, and hence remain stigmatized in some way, for example tolerating gay relationships but not allowing gay marriage.

The second conception, the *coexistence conception*, is similar to the first one in regarding tolerance as the best means for managing conflict. What is different, however, is the relationship between the subjects with groups that are roughly equal in power, and who see that for the sake of social peace and the pursuit of their own interests mutual tolerance is the best of all possible alternatives. The Peace of Augsburg of 1555 is an historical example of this form of tolerance. This was a treaty between Charles V, the Holy Roman Emperor and the Schmalkaldic League, a military alliance of Lutheran princes within the Holy Roman Empire, signed at the imperial city of Augsburg. It officially ended the religious struggle between the two groups and made the legal division of Christendom permanent within the Holy Roman Empire, allowing rulers to choose either Lutheranism or Catholicism as the official confession of their state. The Peace established the principle *Cuius regio, eius religio* ('whose region, his religion'), which allowed the princes of states within the Holy Roman Empire to adopt either Lutheranism or Catholicism within the domains they controlled, ultimately reaffirming their sovereignty over those domains. Thus, the two sides preferred peaceful coexistence to conflict and agreed to a reciprocal compromise, to a certain *modus vivendi*. This is more of a *horizontal* form of tolerance between roughly equal groups. However, this may not lead to a stable social situation in which trust can develop, for once the power relationships change, the more powerful group may no longer see any reasons for being tolerant. It can provide stability if there is a legal basis to the agreement to the truce between the parties, some form of binding treaty. One could say this is by and large how modern states usually manage their mutual relationships.

The third form of tolerance is the *respect conception*, a more powerful and engaging and 'horizontal' form of tolerance, where the tolerating parties respect one another in a more reciprocal sense, as autonomous, or as equally entitled members of a community constituted under the rule of law. The various sides may differ fundamentally in their ethical beliefs about how they lead their lives and in their cultural practices, but they are guided by norms that all parties can equally accept and without favouring one specific ethical or cultural community.

Forst was very much influenced here by the thought of Pierre Bayle on tolerance. Forst points out that Bayle's key insight 'is that only a generally valid justification of toleration which rests on higher-level conceptions of reason and morality could lead to a generally intelligible, binding and fair form of toleration.'[40]

At that time, it was probably the case that tolerance of different faiths was seen as a licence for blasphemy, heresy, and sexual perversion. The notion of a different and enlarged tolerance of difference founded on the lights of reason and the subject's conscience, rather than an appeal to religious belief and dogma, was thus revolutionary.

If atheists and religious believers of different faiths are all capable of sincere moral beliefs and have the capacity to reason, then this 'opens the way for a conception of toleration based on mutual respect and the justification of one's own claims on a common rational basis which is no longer tied to particular religious assumptions.'[41]

There may be subtle and controversial distinctions in the practice of respect tolerance, where, for example private traditions are easily tolerated, so long as they do not create conflict in the public sphere. This 'weak' respect version of tolerance is clearly exhibited in the 'secular republicanism' of the French authorities who held that headscarves with a religious meaning have no place in public schools in which children are educated to be autonomous citizens. That is, all citizens are held to be equal when they are in public, and should stand outside or above their private convictions. However, this is a very narrow concept of what it means to be a good citizen. It could ultimately lead to totalitarian uniformity of views and values, with no room for the expression of cultural and political differences.

A more open and 'stronger' form of respect tolerance would accept fellow citizens as political equals with a certain distinct ethical-cultural identity to be accepted more thoroughly, accepting that expression of difference is compatible with being part of a political community. Social and political equality and integration are thus seen to be compatible with cultural difference, however, within certain limits. For example, female genital mutilation, though practised in certain ethnic communities, is unacceptable in a modern society that prioritizes the needs, rights, and safety of children. Apart from this extreme example, by and large this open form of respect tolerance does not demand that members of a community renounce their ethical and cultural beliefs and values.

The respect principle merges into Forst's fourth principle, the *esteem conception*. This implies an even fuller, more demanding notion of mutual recognition between citizens than what I have called his weaker respect conception, but I think that it is hard to distinguish it from the stronger version. The esteem conception implies that being tolerant does not just mean respecting others as moral and political equals, it also means having some kind of ethical esteem for their beliefs, even with some reservations. One may esteem a way of life, for example certain kinds of religious beliefs for their usefulness or efficacy, but still consider they are incompatible with one's own position. There is anyway a significant degree of reciprocal esteem and respect from both sides.

To answer the question which of these conceptions should be the guiding one for a given society, two aspects for Forst are most important. The first one requires an *assessment of the conflicts* that require and allow for toleration, given the history and character of the groups involved, and that requires judgment and I would add a tolerant material and imaginative space where such judgment can take place. The second aspect requires an adequate and convincing 'normative justification' of tolerance in a given social context. For Forst, the concept of tolerance itself does not provide such a justification; it does not stand alone but needs other and well-grounded normative resources to be a virtue. In practice, this seems to mean that:

> the art of tolerance is an art of finding proper reasons that can be presented to others when you think that they should conform to a norm that they don't agree with in their practices and beliefs ... It is focused on the proper justifications that can be given for subjecting people to political and legal norms.[42]

I would suggest that Forst's stronger respect and esteem conceptions could be merged into my notion of '*Subject Tolerance*'. As I described before, this form of tolerance requires a tolerant imaginative internal space, and it also implies that one *respects* the other and others as subjects *of* their experience, with agency and capacity for independent judgment. This contrasts with '*Object Tolerance*', when the other and others are seen as mere objects to be treated as subject *to* those in power. Those that are merely tolerated as objects may be confined in a ghetto or walled off from society in less visible ways, but their object status remains.

The degree to which others are treated as subjects will of course vary, providing a complex interplay between subject and object tolerance. In a clinical setting, one could imagine a patient moving from a position of object tolerance to subject tolerance as their capacity to 'become a subject' develops.[43] Seeing the other as a subject requires some self-reflection, where otherness in oneself is seen as part and parcel of being human. To recall Kristeva's words: 'How could one tolerate a foreigner if one did not know one was a stranger to oneself?'[44]

Subject tolerance thus requires some form of equal and respectful relationship between different parties holding different views. But for there to be such tolerance, there already needs to be an assumption of what Ingrid Crepell[45] calls a 'will to relationship'. Tolerance depends upon an initial will to interaction in the face of differences, which of course is far from being the case in many situations of conflict. This approach does require a shift in political attitude, and a considerable amount of good will, motivation, and imagination from those engaged in politics. In that sense this is rather an idealistic vision of the place of tolerance in our often diverse but also conflict-ridden societies.

The capacity for relationship is innate, though certain basic 'good enough' environmental provisions have to be available for a child to fully develop that capacity. Similarly, certain basic environmental or social and political conditions need to be in place for different groups to be able to access their innate sociability. Locke began his *Essay on Toleration* emphasizing that *mutual* tolerance was the essence of the true church. Crepell extends the importance of *mutuality* as a key feature of tolerance, enabling social relations in general to be managed for the mutual benefit of different groups and for society as a whole. This approach does not ignore conflict and disagreement; on the contrary these are inevitable accompaniments to any relationship. Tolerance does not come about by simply resolving disagreements and differences, but through a rebalancing of differences through 'seeing those their commitments and beliefs as broader than they did at the beginning of the encounter.'[46]

Tolerance as an ideal establishes

> the concept of an arena of accommodation between groups who had previously attempted forcible conversions or ejections of others. To be able to occupy this space of mutual existence, a majority of persons must be able to identify with the political sphere.[47]

Of course one of the most pressing of contemporary issues is the extreme alienation many people feel towards politicians, which then makes them suspicious about how change to their own lives can be brought about by public action. The public sphere has come to represent corruption, deception, and a failure to connect with ordinary people. In the UK it seems only the Royal Family, at least in their better moments, can provide a vision of communal good will.

In contrast to this pessimistic view of the common public sphere, Crepell offers an aspirational vision of tolerance with an ethical core at its centre, which

> explicitly supports the capacity of persons to adopt a complex moral attitude: stand for principles, respect for others who do not share the same principles, and sustain a common life ... This attitude does not say: accept all differences regardless of their consequences. Rather it says: make policy decisions to resolve conflicts so that the reasoning and results sustain the mutual benefit of our common but diverse lives.[48]

For tolerance to be a sustainable long-term feature of a just society, she argues that it must be supported by mutuality as an end, 'enabling continuous adjustment and negotiation without expecting a conflict-free consensus.'[49] This process of intersubjective, mutual judging and adjustment does not just exist on the level of ideas to be debated but also at the level of beliefs and practices, all within the bounds of a common life. There is a hope, perhaps at times utopian or anyway idealistic, that identification with the common life can balance strong group allegiances, that accommodation between groups can become a society's primary commitment.

The term *accommodation* has a number of resonances, which probably overlap at a subliminal level. In this context it primarily refers to a commitment to peaceful and non-coercive relationships with persons with whom we disagree. It also implies granting special exemption from majority expectations and requirements, such as allowing exemptions from activities such as serving on juries or military service due to religious beliefs, or allowances made in the workplace for those with physical disabilities.

In biblical interpretation, which may well have influenced its first use in a political context, the accommodation principle is the concept that God uses language that accommodates our human understanding. Accommodation was also used by Jean Piaget[50] to refer to part of the adaptation process in child development. The process of accommodation involves altering one's existing schemas or ideas, as a result of new information or new experiences. New schemas may also be developed during this process, where a small child needs to *alter* the pre-existing schema inside their mind to make sense of new things that he or she encounters in the outside world. It is different from assimilation, which is the process of adaptation where ideas and concepts are made to *fit in* alongside pre-existing ideas and concepts to make sense. Such processes of accommodation and assimilation are also clearly relevant to how adults cope with the world and new and strange information, experiences and different cultures.

Martha Nussbaum has written extensively on contemporary politics and its links to past thinkers and movements, laying particular emphasis on the place of political accommodation. I have already quoted her commentary on the American pioneer Roger Williams as a precursor of the American approach to liberty of conscience and wide accommodation of different faiths and cultures within a whole society. In her books *Liberty of Conscience* (2008) and *The New Religious Intolerance* (2012), she tackles the issue of accommodation and struggles to achieve it, both from an historical perspective but also using modern interpretations within the legal context, to illustrate how intolerance needs to be faced by offering a clear vision of how it needs to be overcome.

Roger Williams had an all-embracing accommodationist position extending religious liberty to all faiths and even non-believers, unlike Locke who proposed various exclusions to those entitled to tolerance. Nussbaum points out that the First Amendment of the US constitution protects religious liberty in a way that does not explicitly distinguish the wide accommodationist principle from the narrower Lockean position. It proposes that there should be a free exercise of religion, and that 'Congress shall make no law respecting an establishment of religion, or prohibiting the free exercise thereof.' The problem then was that non-religious forms of commitment are not specified and therefore may not in principle receive protection.[51]

Shortly after Independence, George Washington wrote an influential letter to the Quakers, in regard to their refusal to undertake military service, which became a byword for a broad interpretation of accommodation. He noted that he was familiar with how the Quakers were useful and exemplary citizens, and he wrote:

> I assure you very explicitly, that in my opinion the conscientious scruples of all men should be treated with great delicacy and tenderness; and it is my wish that the laws may always be as extensively accommodated to them as due regard to the protection and essential interests of the nation may justify and permit.[52]

This humane attitude to a minority contrasts with that of Locke,

> who would have told the Quakers that they had better obey their consciences, but that as a result they would have to pay a fine or go to jail. Washington treats the issue very differently. He adopts the principle that liberty should always be as extensive as is compatible with the nation's essential interests. All people's 'conscientious scruples' should be treated with 'great delicacy and tenderness,' and this he takes to entail that the law should be as 'extensively accommodated' to those scruples as is compatible with those weighty and urgent interests.[53]

After Independence and for a number of years the US Supreme Court applied an accommodationist standard, true to the spirit of Washington, holding that government may not impose a 'substantial burden' on a person's free exercise of religion without a 'compelling state interest'. For individuals to prove that their individual conscience qualified them for an exemption from, for example military service, was easier if they belonged to an established minority; if they argued on the basis of their own individual position, then the standard of proof was much higher, requiring them to give substantial evidence of their beliefs.

Two famous legal cases supported the accommodationist principle. In 1963 in the case of *Sherbert v. Verner*, a woman who was a Seventh-day Adventist won her case in the Supreme Court, overturning the judgment of the South Carolina court, when she was allowed to be exempt from working on a Saturday, due to her special religious needs. In the case of *Wisconsin v. Yoder*, in 1972, members of the Amish community were allowed to withdraw their children from the last two years of compulsory education in order to pursue community farming and other activities essential to the continuity of their religious tradition. Of course it could be argued that this infringed the rights of those children to have a modern education making them fit to be able to cope with a modern society. But that was not an argument that prevailed in the majority decision, with the view that there was no compelling evidence that the extra two years would make that much difference to the children, and that the argument for sustaining a valued community was a more powerful one.

Another famous case, *Employment v. Smith* in 1990 drew limits on the Supreme Court's view on accommodation. The judgment against a Native American Al Smith held that the state could deny unemployment benefits to a person fired for violating a state prohibition on the use of the hallucinatory drug peyote, even though the drug was used in his religious rituals. This judgment caused controversy, and eventually led to Congress passing a law to enable peyote to be used. However, it was argued with some force, for example by the conservative Justice Scalia, that a system based upon individual exemptions was difficult for judges to administer and would cause anarchy in the legal system. It also typically favoured religious rather than secular reasons for exemptions.

These tensions between fitting in, or assimilation, and accommodation remain both within the legal system but also within society a whole. The point once more is not that there is an ideal solution to such matters, but that there should be a structure for thinking about how to deal with them, and a tolerant way of thinking that can *imagine* the possibility of accommodation rather than a demand for all to fit in with a particular norm. As Nussbaum writes:

> Whatever intellectual position we favour ... we need to cultivate a spirit of curiosity, openness and sympathy, and a generosity to our neighbours that extends beyond our own self-concern ... In the world imagined by both Williams and Locke, the majority does not say, 'I'm the norm, now you fit in.' It says, 'I respect you as an equal, and I know that my own religious pursuits are not the only ones around. Even if I am more numerous and hence more powerful, I will try to make the world comfortable for you.'[54]

Of course it must be said that one of the failings of liberal thinking until now is that it had forgotten that being in the majority does not necessarily involve having much power to make anyone, including themselves, comfortable in the world. Resentment towards minorities who are misperceived as being privileged, or as taking away majority privileges and rights, such as work and access to services and adequate housing, has escalated, so much so that it may take years to rebuild trust in government. Intolerance to others becomes a reality when people, rightly or wrongly, feel that their needs are not being heard, encapsulated in the complaint 'Why should we care about *them*, when no one cares about *us*?'

Until now there has been a tendency to view such intolerant attitudes as a failing in empathy, or as a projection from the majority population onto minority groups of all kinds of failings of their own, finding a convenient target to blame for society not providing them with what they need. The larger the minority the more the majority group feel threatened. Many of these fears are irrational, some are based on prejudice and ignorance, but they have to be recognized if aggressive stand-offs within and between communities are to be avoided. Hence the need for a tolerance process to manage these emotionally highly charged assertions of identity.

Thinkers differ about how much the state should intervene to manage these kinds of problems. Thus some theorists, such as Chandran Kukathas, argue for tolerating minority groups by leaving them free from state interference, that a wide view of tolerance is the main way to manage these issues. He argues, there are no group rights, only individual rights. By granting cultural groups special protections and rights, the state oversteps its role, which is to secure civil peace, and risks undermining individual rights of association, thus ending up creating an increased risk of intolerance towards minorities. States should not pursue cultural integration or engineering, but rather a 'politics of indifference', or 'benign neglect' toward minority groups.[55]

Others argue that mere tolerance of group differences falls short of treating members of minority groups as equals; what is required is *recognition* and positive accommodation of minority group practices through what Will Kymlicka has called 'group-differentiated rights'.

Kymlicka[56] recognizes that liberal democracies can accommodate and embrace many forms of cultural diversity, but not all, and that there are limits to what can be tolerated. These limits consist of any internal restrictions whereby a minority culture aims to restrict the basic civil and political liberties of its members. Liberalism allows for individuals to have the freedom and opportunity to question and revise their traditional practices. External protections, guaranteeing the community's ongoing safety and identity are reasonable, provided that one group is not thereby enabled to oppress or exploit other groups. Therefore not all the demands made by minorities can be accommodated, for example if women's rights to vote are denied or girls refused opportunities to receive education.

One of the main issues in managing intergroup relations is how to accommodate non- or illiberal practices, and how far such accommodation should go. For example, where do arranged marriages become acceptable if agreed freely by the parties, and when are they unacceptable if imposed? There is no evidence that arranged marriages are less viable than others, and may even be more likely to last, given the likelihood of close family supports, but at what cost to the individuals concerned? Forcing an arranged marriage by threats of violence is clearly intolerable and anyway illegal if they take place under duress. But there is sometimes a fine line between threats and strong expectations, particularly when an individual wishes to remain an active member of their community, or does not wish to fall out with their family.

Kymlicka argues that, although the rights of national minorities should be protected by special legal status, there are difficult issues when some members of some minority cultures reject basic liberal views. Excluding obvious cases when the law is broken, liberals have no automatic right to simply impose their view on non-liberal minorities.

> But they do have the right, and indeed the responsibility, to identify what those views actually are. Relations between national groups should be determined by dialogue. But if liberal theory is to contribute anything to that dialogue, it is surely by spelling out the implications of the liberal principles of freedom and equality. That is not the first step down the path of interference. Rather it is the first step in starting a dialogue.[57]

Such a fruitful dialogue within a basically liberal society would not be possible if minorities had no protected rights, as the different parties would start from very different vantage points, with unequal sense of privilege and power. But at the same time, minorities cannot demand legal recognition if they do not simultaneously respect the basic rights of their members. For example if a community condones female genital mutilation, it cannot expect the wider community to stand by with indifference to the plight of the children being abused.

It is possible to manage minorities in different ways and still give them a measure of autonomy, such as took place under the Ottoman Empire with the millet system, as I referred to previously. While Islam remained the dominant religion in the Ottoman Empire, there was a relatively easy accommodation with other faiths, mainly Jews and Christians, through what one might call 'bureaucratic' tolerance, with the use of various rules to maintain the relations between communities. One could even argue that this would be a more satisfactory solution to ethnic tensions in many parts of the world, where a liberal democracy has little chance of being established.

Kukathas argues strongly that tolerance (or toleration) is at the heart of liberalism, and his arguments in favour of the central role that the virtue of tolerance should take when managing diversity, including relations between and within communities, provide a suitable place to end this overview of some key modern views on tolerance.

Kukathas sees tolerance as an independent value, checking moral certitude.[58] Underlying his argument is a vision of a society as an 'archipelago' of different communities operating in a sea of mutual tolerance. The liberal archipelago is 'a society of societies which is neither the creation nor the object of any single authority, though it is a form of order in which authorities function under laws which are themselves beyond the reach of any single power.'[59]

In this metaphor, communities live within the various islands of the archipelago, have dealings with one another, sail from one island to another, are free to leave their own island and go to other islands, with no overarching management. For Kukathas, this represents the essence of his libertarian view of liberalism, with minimum central interference, communities only abiding by the principles of freedom of association and mutual tolerance of different associations.

A fundamental problem with this approach is it is difficult to see how one can effectively manage conflict, hatred, and fear, an inevitable accompaniment of any human association; any approach to tolerance must take account of intolerant states of mind and practices. Just letting people get on with moving from island to island with no real attempt to understand or manage human frailties would seem doomed to remain an idealistic vision. And such a non-interventionist attitude, preferring persuasion rather than legal or strong political action, is also potentially irresponsible when it comes to managing strongly intolerant or dangerous practices, such as female genital mutilation or fascist movements.

The vision of human society as a series of interconnected islands is also telling in how Kukathas, consciously or not, sees human nature as essentially self-centred, each living in their own island of activities and desires. Although to be fair, he does see disputes being managed in the public realm where divergent practices converge in some way. He makes the important point that it is a fundamental feature of our nature to differ and disagree, and that rather than suppress this we need to work with it. He also rightly sees the dangers of attempts to *make* people agree by imposition from above. Very much in the tradition of Bayle and Voltaire, he recognizes that we are all fallible, and that tolerance is the prerogative of humanity, as we are all steeped in error and weakness. And Kukathas argues cogently against the holding of unitary views about how to live one's life in the face of human diversity, and that the pursuit of unity when people disagree is dangerous; tolerance of differing viewpoints is much less divisive, even if making tolerance work means people having to accept views and customs they find objectionable when they bring into the public realm their divergent beliefs and values.

But unless thought on tolerance takes full account of the nature of intolerance as an element of human nature that cannot merely be argued away by public reason, that in managing cultural diversity one needs to look at the tolerance/intolerance *dynamic*, there is a great danger of allowing the dark forces of intolerance to swamp those who offer reasonable arguments. As I have proposed, one of the most powerful reasons for people holding intolerant views, regardless of any amount of rational discussion, is a primal fear about loss of identity, which I have described as a fear of a loss of a psychic home. This primal fear can make individuals and groups have profound and irrational fears about being displaced by strangers and it can tear communities apart, as well as lead to discrimination against those who appear to be different. Managing intolerant attitudes and promoting tolerance is not then just a matter of providing reasonable arguments in the face of ignorance and prejudice, though that is important, but of confronting the human elements that make up intolerant thinking, such as anxieties around a loss of a psychic home; that is addressing the *emotional* context driving intolerance.

In the next chapter, I will address these sorts of human issues through looking at how the arts are essentially tolerant, and in particular how Shakespeare responded to his troubled society by creating a vision of how different and apparently alien cultures can be tolerated in a world of conflicting desires. Though this chapter may seem a deflection from the main arguments put forward so far, I would argue that by approaching the complexities of human dilemmas through artistic means, Shakespeare in particular offers us a glimpse of a hopeful vision for the future, with the human subject capable of opening up towards others, however strange and unfamiliar, though one where conflict and tragedy also have to be faced squarely if tolerance is to prevail. He thus continues to portray human situations whose exploration remains relevant to our intolerant times.

Notes

1 Canovan, 1988, p. 177 ff.
2 Villa, 2000, p. 9.
3 Arendt, 1958, p. 4.
4 Plato, 1930, Republic, 462C.
5 Honneth, 2000, p. 30.
6 Nisbet, 2005, p. 5.
7 Arendt, 1970, p. 25.
8 Canovan, 1988, p. 178.
9 Arendt, 1970, p. 27.
10 Canovan, 1988, p. 193.

11 Arendt, 1970, p. 31.
12 Arendt, 1982.
13 Kant, 1784, p. 18.
14 Beiner, 1982, p. 123.
15 O'Neill, 1989, p. 37.
16 Kant, 1790, p. 126, section 41.
17 Arendt, 1961, p. 221.
18 O'Neill, 2015, p. 4.
19 O'Neill, 2015, p. 7.
20 O'Neill, 2016, p. 208.
21 O'Neill, 2015, p. 33, fn. 16.
22 O'Neill, 1990, p. 166.
23 O'Neill, 1990, p. 167.
24 Rawls, 1971, p. 188.
25 Rawls, 1993, p. 133 ff.
26 Rawls, 1993, p. 12ff.
27 Rawls, 1999, p. 14
28 Rawls, 1999, p. 4.
29 Rawls, 1999, p. 15.
30 Rawls, 1993, p. 217.
31 Rawls, 1999, p. 16, fn.
32 Habermas, 2005, p. 258.
33 Habermas, 2005, pp. 14–17.
34 Habermas, 2005, p. 252.
35 Habermas, 2005, p. 265.
36 Habermas, 2005, pp. 266–7.
37 Habermas, 2005, p. 270.
38 Habermas, 2005, p. 270.
39 Forst, 2003, p. 146.
40 Forst, 2003, p. 241.
41 Forst, 2003, p. 246.
42 Brown and Forst, 2014, pp. 31–2.
43 Kennedy, 2007, p. 180ff.
44 Kristeva, 1991, p. 182.
45 Crepell, 2008, p. 316.
46 Crepell, 2008, p. 322.
47 Crepell, 2008, p. 330.
48 Crepell, 2008, p. 332.
49 Crepell, 2008, p. 332.
50 Piaget, 1947.
51 Nussbaum, 2012, p. 76.
52 Nussbaum, 2012, p. 77.
53 Nussbaum, 2012, p. 77.
54 Nussbaum, 2012, pp. 96–7.
55 Kukathas, 2003, p. 15.
56 Kymlicka, 1995, p. 152 ff.
57 Kymlicka, 1995, p. 171.
58 Kukathas, 2003, p. 126.
59 Kukathas, 2003, pp. 8–9.

9
TOLERANCE AND THE ARTS

It would be difficult to imagine an important and simultaneously intolerant work of art, whether that is in writing, the visual arts or music. Totalitarian art is usually just boring, as it tends to push one ideology, such as socialist realist portrayals of the benefits of cooperative labour, or the bland sculptures commemorating some heroic endeavour. Or it can be strangely fascinating if sinister, such as Leni Riefenstahl's 1936 film of the Berlin Olympics, with its beautifully filmed yet obvious promotion of the Nazi ideology. Intolerant art such as this film however promotes conflict, while lasting and successful art tries to resolve it. Cartoons and satire can push the boundaries of acceptable taste and even when successful may require a certain element of intolerance, but the accompanying humour usually provides some humanizing balance, and intolerance is usually aimed at satirizing some absurdity or even injustice. There are of course examples of intolerant cartoons such as those depicting racial stereotypes, but they hardly count as art. In general the arts are tolerant activities, their practice requires mutual understanding and communication on the part of artists, performers, and audiences in order for the artist's vision to be fully realized. They may evoke intolerant reactions, particularly when they push the boundaries of human understanding and perception, or challenge current values and beliefs, but their aim is to communicate not dominate; and if they sometimes challenge accepted values, it is to open up the world with a new vision.

Shakespeare's tolerant world

While there is no perfectly tolerant society, Shakespeare's texts, particularly his Comedies, offer a vision of how different and apparently alien cultures can be tolerated in a world of conflicting desires. His Tragedies, most obviously in *King Lear* and *Othello*, often reveal the damage and devastation brought about by intolerance, hatred, and jealousy.

The drama of *The Winter's Tale* shows how an intolerant figure such as Leontes can realize they have been unreasonable, though only after much suffering and the interval of years. His paranoid jealousy corrodes his relationships and leads to years of loneliness, followed by regret. The drama is resolved with a powerful image of the warmth of the human spirit—when Leontes touches the figure he believes to be a statue of his dead wife, Hermione, the one he accused unjustly of unfaithfulness, her hand is warm; it convinces him that the statue which came down from its plinth was no illusion or an effect of magic, but evidence of her human reality. It is one of the most powerful and moving moments in all Shakespeare.

In this scene, Hermione's once denigrated hand, defamed as lustful—'paddling palms and pinching fingers,' (I, II, 114–15)—is 'transformed into a hand that is for Leontes a proof of the miracle of human life in another person, for it is perceived to be miraculously warm.'[1] This is in contrast to a few moments before, when standing before what he believes to be a mere statue of Hermione, he recalls his past wooing of her.

> O, thus she stood,
> Even with such life of majesty, warm life,
> As now it coldly stands, when first I woo'd her!
> I am ashamed: does not the stone rebuke me
> For being more stone than it? O royal piece!
> There's magic in thy majesty, which has
> My evils conjur'd to remembrance, and
> From thy admiring daughter took the spirits,
> Standing like stone with thee.
> (The Winter's Tale, V, iii, 34–41)

His heart, once full of stone towards his wife, recognizing the loss of her warm life which had once captured him, is full of shame; he opens himself up to the image of Hermione, whom he now appreciates as a real person not the object of his hateful projections, a magical human spirit, and a real woman whom he thinks he has irretrievably lost. She comes to life, not only in reality but also as a human subject rather than a mere object of irrational hatred.

In *The Taming of the Shrew*, one sees two essentially intolerant characters, Petruchio and Katherina, come to learn to tolerate each other's characters and begin to make a companionable marriage. In *The Tempest*, there is a powerful movement towards tolerance through the play. By the end, Prospero gives up plans to take revenge on his usurping brother, despite the latter's betrayal, and even releases his servants Ariel and Caliban, allowing the latter the freedom of the island. In *Romeo and Juliet*, prejudice and hatred between the rival families abound, and there is only an attempt to make up and lay down hostilities after the death of the two lovers; a high price to pay for intolerance.

In *Twelfth Night*, the steward, Malvolio's hypocritical and sham puritanism, his excessive self-regard, and his basic intolerance of the comic spirit, make him both the butt of a cruel joke, when he is tricked into thinking his mistress, Countess Olivia, is in love with him, and the source of comedy. Shakespeare is relentless in his mocking of Malvolio, and by the end when he is released from his dungeon, he, who has learned nothing from his sufferings, continues his intolerant stand, swearing revenge on the whole pack of them. Yet the play does not end there. As throughout the proceedings, the clown Feste represents the spirit of non-judgmental tolerance. He sings of man's vulnerability and how resignation to the passing of time and to the realities of the 'wind and the rain', is all we can hope for. Yet by the art of the theatre, 'we'll strive to please you every day'.

Twelfth Night also explores the complexities of sexual identity, with the portrayal of shifting sexual identities, how love and desire drive us on but can confuse us. Viola disguises herself as a man, and has Olivia and Duke Orsino fall in love with him/her; Sebastian, Olivia's lost twin brother ends up loving Olivia; while Sebastian is befriended by a sea-captain, Antonio, who seems to fall in love with him. Olivia's relative, Sir Toby Belch, plays on Sir Andrew Aguecheek's self-regard, leading him to think that he could marry Olivia. And of course Malvolio, whom no one loves, loves his mistress Olivia and is deceived into thinking she loves him. Men can love men, women can love women, love can go wrong or right, and by the end some at least of the characters do end up with partners. Overall, Olivia strikes the general undertone of the play, promoting a generous tolerance, after Malvolio denigrates the humorous word-play of Feste.

> O, you are sick of self-love, Malvolio. And taste with a distempered appetite. To be generous, guiltless, and of free disposition, is to take these things for bird-bolts that you deem cannon-bullets.
>
> *(Twelfth Night, I, v, 89–93)*

The Merchant of Venice of course remains the most difficult play to fit under the theme of tolerance of otherness, with its harsh portrayal of Shylock and his embittered desire for a cruel payment of flesh for money owed. Even allowing for the fact that the play reveals other Jews who are less vengeful and more human, the play still has strong anti-Jewish elements. At the same time, it also reveals powerfully some of the origins of such prejudiced thinking, not only present in early modern England but to this day. Furthermore, it has been argued by James Shapiro, in his influential book *Shakespeare and the Jews*, that the play's vitality 'can be attributed to the ways in which it scrapes against a bedrock of beliefs about the racial, national, sexual, and religious difference of others,'[2] and it does so unrelentingly and honestly, thereby providing incomparable revelations about how people's dark and irrational attitudes come into play in dealing with otherness.

Shakespeare can thus still teach us much about tolerance; indeed, the literary critic Harold Bloom[3] famously asserted that he has 'invented the human as we continue to know it'. That is, Shakespeare has provided us with the vocabulary and complex and inwardly deep scenarios involving human characters, for what we still consider to be definitive aspects of the human condition.

Shakespeare's text itself is rich in ambiguity, antitheses, fundamental metaphors, and in-depth insight into human desires and motivation. The Shakespearean text itself is thus in a sense fundamentally tolerant, in the sense of being able to incorporate multiple viewpoints, while remaining free from moralistic judgments—which is not say that Shakespeare does not judge; evil is never tolerated in his works, though it may be well represented. His relationships are not often that happy, but through the driving forces of the drama, his characters often move on and learn from their confrontations with others. Conflicts can be robustly presented, but the end of the drama leaves one with an enlarged sense of human relations. Overall, as B.J. Sokol has put it in his classic text on *Shakespeare and Tolerance*: 'What we meet in Shakespeare's portrayals of tolerance is the celebration of those who can transcend rancor arising from human differences, and the tragic disasters of those who are misguidedly or pathetically unable to do so.'[4]

In terms of the historical and social background to the plays, Shakespeare's was an age of discovery and exploration. Around that time there may have been a 'veritable oasis of tolerance towards strangers'.[5] In addition, a large number of continental Protestants had fled to England between 1567 and 1590. A number of their workshops were located near Shakespeare's Globe Theatre, and are alluded to in *King Lear* and *The Winter's Tale*. At the same time, there were suspicions towards people like Shakespeare who was seen as a foreigner in London, coming as he did from outside—hence perhaps his particular sympathy for the outsider. Shakespeare's French contemporary Jean Bodin was arguing for significant religious tolerance,[6] though of course in the England of Queen Elizabeth and King James being Catholic was potentially dangerous to one's personal safety. Shakespeare never directly tackles issues of religious affiliations, tending to keep a point midway between Catholic and Protestant attitudes.

Perhaps rather like his near contemporary Montaigne,[7] whom Shakespeare very likely had read (and he almost certainly personally knew Montaigne's translator Florio), he managed to retain a fluidity and flexibility in the art of living and in his writings. Like Montaigne, Shakespeare was able to hold onto multiple perspectives on human situations, remaining open to the strangeness of people, while respecting their individuality, and to retain an essential scepticism about the human capacity to know reality.

Though *The Comedy of Errors* is an early play it is remarkably well constructed and, though in the form of a farce, touches upon a number of fundamental issues concerning identity and otherness, relevant for many of the themes I have been touching on in this and previous chapters.

Briefly, the play begins in Ephesus with a *stranger*, Egeon, from Syracuse being condemned to death unless he finds a fine of a thousand marks to give to the reigning Duke. This arrangement is due to the mutual antagonism of the two cities. It turns out that the stranger has a tale of trauma, which sets the scene for the farce. Death hangs over the play, although of course as we know it is a comedy, we also know that it will not have its way. The Duke and his wife had twin boys, both called Antipholus and also twin servants to the boys, both called Dromio, but after a storm at sea the children were separated—leaving one Antipholus and Dromio with the father Egeon and one pair of twins with the mother—though the latter twins are stolen and end up in Ephesus.

The play then turns to the Antipholus and Dromio from Syracuse, who come to Ephesus as part of their long-standing attempt to refind their lost family. They are apparently experienced travellers—in a personal voyage of discovery.

The comedy turns round a series of misunderstandings and misrecognitions, when for example the Antipholus from Syracuse meets the Dromio from Ephesus, each thinking the other is attached to them when they are not.

There is of course, on the one hand, simply a comedy at work, the various failed encounters are funny. But there is also a tragic underlying theme of loss, which comes to those exiled from their home, or in need of a place of asylum. As the Antipholus from Syracuse says at the beginning, thinking of his lost family:

> He that commends me to mine own content
> Commends me to the thing I cannot get.
> I to the world am like a drop of water
> That in the ocean seeks another drop,
> Who, falling there to find his fellow forth,
> Unseen, inquisitive, confounds himself.
> So I, to find a mother and a brother,
> In quest of them, unhappy, lose myself.
>
> *(Comedy of Errors, I, ii, 33–40)*

Adriana, the wife of the Antipholus of Ephesus (a very ill-tempered and possessive woman at first) becomes distraught when the person she takes for her husband falls in love with her sister; he becomes a *stranger* to her. Echoing the speech I have just quoted, she says with despair:

> Ay, ay, Antipholus, look strange and frown;
> Some other mistress hath thy sweet aspects.
> I am not Adriana, nor thy wife.
> The time was once when thou unurged wouldst vow
> That never words were music to thine ear,
> That never object pleasing in thine eye,
> That never touch well welcome to thy hand,
> That never sweet-savoured in thy taste,
> Unless I spake it or looked or touched or carved to thee.
> How comes it now, my husband, O how comes it,
> That thou art then estranged from thyself?
> Thyself I call it, being strange to me,
> That undivided, incorporate,
> Am better than thy dear self's better part.
> Ah, do not tear away thyself from me;

For know, my love, as easy mayst thou fall
A drop of water in the breaking gulf,
And take unmingled thence that drop again
Without addition or diminishing,
As take from me thyself, and not me too.

(II, ii, 111–130)

Presumably because the Antipholus and Dromio from Syracuse look identical to the other set of twins, they are not subject to the same harsh law that other strangers are subject to. But as the comedy unfolds and the misunderstandings accumulate, the Antipholus of Syracuse feels that he is in an uncanny place, where nothing can be taken for granted and that, 'There's none but witches do inhabit here' (III, ii, 155).

It is an added part of the comedy, and adds to the dreamlike nature of the events, that the twins from Syracuse never suspect that their brothers are in Ephesus, despite being in search of them for several years.

Eventually of course all is sort of resolved, with the twins and the father reunited, and even the mother being discovered to be living as an Abbess and the father and mother are reunited—in fact her Priory becomes a place of safety where the relationships can be re-established. Along the way, something fundamental about human identity and its relationship to place and home is revealed. For example, that identity can be a precarious entity, nothing about it can be taken for granted, and that perhaps we can rely too much on things being the same for reassurance about who we are. Yet we also need a firm base in order to know who we are; once we lose our home, we may end up in all kinds of strange states of mind, beset by confusion and helplessness.

Furthermore, as Sokol points out, 'The mistaken identification of separately raised twins in the play provides more than comic confusion; it also shows up the hollowness of legalistic nationality distinctions.'[8] Thus there is a radical undertone to the play, decentring not only our comfortable notions about identity, but also pointing to the fact that our identity cannot be confined to narrow nationalistic expectations.

Throughout the play there is a recurrent theme of a longing for home and the question of where is one's true home (one not to be confined to membership of one city)—the estranged wife longs for her husband's desire to be restored (actually she becomes more tolerant by the end as a result of her suffering), the true husband is locked out of his home and then incarcerated while his home is being completely disrupted by his long lost identical twin—that is by the stranger who is not really a stranger, but his other half. Shakespeare challenges comfortable notions of identity and difference, strangeness and familiarity, surface appearance as opposed to what lies beneath. If love is an emotion in which people come to understand their identity or mutual identities through the other person, this is brought out by Shakespeare in a painful way. There is a terrible trauma at the heart of the play, with the family being split apart. Then there is the great confusion about identities through misunderstanding, and then a resolution and reunification in which all are changed, identities are 'alter-ed'; the loves are rebalanced, with the wife no longer so possessive, and her sister finding a husband.

To underline the fact that Shakespeare's world is an essentially tolerant one, the Duke of Ephesus finally waves aside the proposed thousand ducats fine, even when it is offered to him (V, i, 390). While the two Dromios walk off hand in hand:

> We came into the world like brother and brother,
> And now let's go hand in hand, not one before the other.
>
> *(V, i, 425–6)*

Tolerance prevails!

Shakespeare demonstrates in this and other texts a remarkable ability to tolerate conflicting, strange, and ambiguous elements, which offer us a vision of a *respectful* and *human world*, where *otherness is to be wondered at*, not disavowed, a vision which still stands as a beacon of humanity in dark times.

Tolerance and music

Emotional connectedness and attunement to one another are essential elements in musical performance, perhaps owing something to the early musical foundations of intersubjectivity in mother/baby interactions, to which I shall refer below. In that sense, an openness towards others, essential to tolerance, is integral to the work of the musician. Of course the playing has to reach a certain level for this to be a successful process; shoddy playing is not tolerable.

A combination of cooperation and individual expression takes place, with the musicians mutually adjusting their actions and sounds, particularly in small ensembles, where close mutual and intersubjective and empathic listening is essential. This is a form of 'reflecting-in-action',[9] where one adjusts as one is performing. It is most clearly visible in the improvisations of jazz musicians, who reflect through a 'feel' for the music. But it is also clearly *visible* in any small ensemble; one can observe the human context, the intense communication between the players, which allows for an intense musical experience. I think the visual experience for the audience is part of the pleasure of experiencing the music. How a pianist for example comes on stage, engaging the audience with their eyes, hands, and gestures, is all part of the aesthetic experience.

Some orchestras such as the Berlin Philharmonic are able to organize for their players to be able to play a fair amount of chamber music outside of their orchestral duties. This makes for a special capacity to work together and therefore an especially rich sound.

A key notion in this context is that of the synchronization of the body with the environment or '*entrainment*', that is, the 'alignment or integration of bodily features with some recurrent features in the environment'.[10] Musical entrainment involves perceiving the regularity of beat and can be seen for example when dancing to music or marching in time to music. It seems hard-wired into the brain, since it is a skill that children can be seen to acquire naturally. There is even evidence that participating in musical activity such as synchronized singing and drumming can promote cooperation in four-year-olds.[11]

With musicians there is obviously a complex form of entrainment, where they 'regulate the temporal alignment of their musical behaviours by engaging in continual processes of mutual adjustment of the timing of actions and sounds'.[12] Ensemble performance involves acting in synchrony, an openness to each other's reactions and requires 'constant temporal negotiations, that are at once cognitive and embodied'.[13] This involves conscious and unconscious communications between the players, communication at both the bodily and emotional level, with the reading of gesture and eyes as well as the building up of trust and mutual understanding. Emotional focus, where the performers are enabled to be absorbed and focused *within* the music somehow seems to be a vital part of giving a good performance[14] and requires this sort of close common understanding and communication.

Because music occurs in time, it can under certain circumstances provide a powerful sense of *continuity*. Already with the early mother-baby relationship one can see how the maternal voice echoes and re-echoes to the baby's sounds, in a kind of musical manner, imitating and repeating what comes from the baby and providing, as Daniel Anzieu[15] describes as a sort of sound mirror, not a static mirror but a dynamic and responsive mirror providing a sense of continuity over time. In distorted mother-baby relationships, for example with a depressed or borderline mother, there may be a lack of responsiveness, and the maternal echo can become more like the plaintive echo in the myth of narcissus, and the sense of time can become deadened. Anzieu also describes how the sound mirror can become pathogenic when the mother's response is dissonant, contradicting what the baby feels or expects; or can be too abrupt, causing confusion and psychic damage to the baby's protective defences; or impersonal, when the mirror of sounds fails to provide emotional information for the baby. Otherwise, the mother's vocal responses normally provide a positive experience for the baby, enveloping or wrapping the baby in a comforting and enlivening sound world.

Based on years of mother-infant research, Gratier and Trevarthen describe how the 'behaviour of infants in their delicately negotiated engagements with sympathetic partners and playmates demonstrates that there is an *innate intersubjectivity* that enables synchrony of intentional rhythms, expressive gestural forms and qualities of voice with others from birth.'[16]

Indeed, there is good evidence that human infants are well equipped to learn the musical regularities of their environment. Thus at least by six months babies have the probably unique human ability to perceive relative pitch, the ability to recognise that a melody is the same when the pitches are transposed up or down. By one year, the child can show sensitivity to musical keys.[17] While the ability to move in synchrony to a musical beat requires complex motor skills and does not appear until about five years of age, babies do move rhythmically much more to music than to speech,[18] and not surprisingly singing is more effective than speech in calming infants.

Stephen Malloch[19] used computer-aided musical acoustic techniques to study vocal exchanges between infants and adults to clarify how the pulse and expressive and emotional qualities of voices are engaged in improvised musicality, or what he called 'Communicative Musicality'.

Gratier and Trevarthen propose that the expressive rhythm of human voices, or the communicative musicality of the mother–baby interchange has a vital role in promoting the well-being and comfort of the baby. Using Winnicott's notion of physical and mental holding, they propose that, 'the vocal rhythms of interpersonal engagement constitute a Holding environment for the infant that is in continuity and coherent with the physical holding involved in the caregiver's mothering techniques.'[20]

Overall, one can say that communicative musicality is a vital element of bonding and attuned attachment between mother and infant. Without musicality the internalization from the interaction between voices is distorted and emotions are disturbed.

In addition, a mother's voice is also the voice of her community; it carries the imprint of others' styles of speech. In that sense the baby is early on exposed to the conventional styles of their community, with all its particular speech rhythms and style, forming the basis for belonging; or what one could call a 'speech home', one of the dynamic elements of the psychic home.

Daniel Barenboim describes how in musical performance, 'two voices are in dialogue simultaneously, each one expressing itself to the fullest, whilst at the same time listening to the other'.[21] This kind of communication, obviously close to the kind of intersubjective communication I have already referred to, is not only about music but is a life-long process. For Barenboim this capacity of music for engaged conversation, its dialogic quality, can help in mutual understanding between people who might otherwise be deaf to what they have in common. His West-Eastern Divan orchestra, formed from Israelis, Palestinians, and other Arabs, is a concrete manifestation of this hopeful principle. One can see here the power of *music's ability to bring people together* in a mutually satisfying endeavour, breaking down barriers to understanding and facilitating and heightening mutual communication.

The processes of emotional and musical entrainment, with music's power to synchronize emotions and actions, seem to have their origins not only in early communicative musicality but go back some way in evolution.

I have already referred to Ian Cross'[22] account of music as capable of communicating ambiguity and of being a form of communication more adept than language at conveying shared and cooperative interactions. From this, follows his argument that the faculty for music is as a result likely to have had strong evolutionary advantages for humans in their interactions.

Gary Tomlinson[23] provides an overview of the gradual evolution in parallel of language and music through interpretation of data from tool making and settlements over a million years or so. Crucial to this evolutionary process was the increasing organization of hominin tool-making or 'taskscaping', the source of increasing cognitive and social complexity, which finally resulted in language and music production as separate but interconnected developments. My reading of this account is that the gradual building up of a home base through a process of what one could call 'homescaping' became one crucial element of this evolution. One can see in the data how tool-making became slowly but increasingly sophisticated as loose gatherings of hominins began to form settlements, where skills could be passed on rather than created ad hoc. Music may have evolved as a powerful means of enhancing early intersubjective communication as early humans began to gather into loose and then more organized communities and early homes. This in part accounts for how music reaches powerfully into the depths of our psychic rootedness, into the interior of our souls or the 'other world' of our unconscious. Unlike, for example Steven Pinker[24] who, controversially, sees music as a mere side-effect of language development, or 'cheesecake', music can thus be seen to be vitally linked to the very ground of our being as a direct result of its evolutionary origins.

Thus there is evidence that from the early days of our evolution, humans had a strong desire to communicate, to entertain but also to come together for mutual and open exchanges. There may also of course have been rivalries and competition, wars and conflicts of all sorts, but from the beginning there was also the possibility of human entrainment, close bodily and emotional togetherness, the basis I would maintain of subject tolerance, openness to others.

Notes

1 Sokol, 2008, p. 55.
2 Shapiro, 1996, p. 228.
3 Bloom, 1998, p. xviii.
4 Sokol, 2008, p. xiv.
5 Goose, 2005, p. 129.
6 Bodin, 1583.
7 Bakewell, 2010.
8 Sokol, 2008, p. 71.
9 Schön, 1983, p. 54.
10 De Nora, 2000, pp. 78–9.
11 Kirschner and Tomasello, 2010.
12 Cross, 2009, p. 189.
13 Cook, 2013, p. 411.
14 Bostridge, 2011, p. 111.
15 Anzieu, 1995, p. 174.
16 Gratier and Trevarthen, 2007, p. 170.
17 Trainor and Hannon, 2013.
18 Zentner and Eerola, 2010.
19 Stephen Malloch, 1999.
20 Gratier and Trevarthen, 2007, p. 174.
21 Barenboim, 2008, p. 20.
22 Cross, 2009.
23 Tomlinson 2015.
24 Pinker, 1997.

10

CONCLUSIONS

The tolerance process

Throughout the book, I have made the point that tolerance and intolerance inevitably go together; there is a dynamic between them; one needs to provide a framework and a willing atmosphere in which the conflict between them can be examined, with no necessary perfect resolution. The resolution in a sense is in the *processing* of the dynamic. It is hard work.

In order to provide some guide to the vast landscape of tolerance studies, I would suggest that one could summarize the different ways of conceptualizing tolerance as follows. It is worth noting that these categories are not rigid and that they usually involve interplay between different positions, and that, as I have noted, in a given situation there is usually a mixture of tolerance and intolerance:

1. One can divide the field into *Subject* and *Object Tolerance*. By Subject Tolerance I mean that one *respects* the other and others as subjects *of* their experience, with agency and capacity for independent judgment. This contrasts with Object Tolerance, when the other and others are seen as mere objects to be treated as subject *to* those in power. Those that are merely tolerated as objects may be confined in a ghetto or walled off from society in less visible ways, but their object status remains. The degree to which others are treated as subjects will of course vary, providing a complex interplay between subject and object tolerance.
2. One can divide the field, as does Forst, into the *Permission* or *Respect* conception of tolerance. The Permission conception is about those in power allowing others, usually a minority, to live in accordance with their own convictions. This would be to accept a minority's minimal demands for freedom of belief and practice, but may be better than nothing, at least for a while. It is a kind of '*vertical*' tolerance, from top down. With Respect Tolerance, the tolerating parties respect one another as *autonomous* persons, as

equally entitled members of a community under the rule of law. Clearly this is similar to Subject Tolerance and is more like a '*horizontal*' form of tolerance, involving more equal relationships.
3. There is *Negative Tolerance*, in which one just puts up with a person or persons, while *Positive Tolerance* involves a willingness to actively engage with and actively accept the other. This is similar to a position of putting up with the other for pragmatic reasons, such as it not being worthwhile to challenge different ideas, beliefs, and practices for reasons of, for example, state security or stability of an institution, as opposed to accepting positively that they have liberty of conscience to hold their beliefs, etc.
4. Finally, there is *Repressive Tolerance*. Herbert Marcuse argued that tolerance only masks and cements social exclusion. He urged for the suppression of objectionable views, not their toleration. Wendy Brown argues that tolerance can too easily hide and sometimes even legitimate violence and the misuse of power by those in authority. Too much emphasis on tolerance can become paternalistic, seeing strangers as 'other', as uncivilized, or needing civilization or needing to be 'taught' tolerance; there is an inevitable asymmetry between the tolerant power and the object of toleration.

While such latter views need to be taken account of as an antidote to paternalistic thinking, and it is true that an authority which tolerates could just as easily not tolerate, they would seem to run too much risk of losing something essential in the management of human relations; one has only to see the consequences of living in regimes where tolerance is not tolerated. Pure tolerance may never be achieved, but some tolerance is surely better than none. The point is that there needs to be a '*tolerance process*', in which critical thinking and respectful judgment can take place in an atmosphere of debate and reasonably open dialogue and communication, when issues around what can and cannot be tolerated about different beliefs, practices, and attitudes in people in our own and other cultures, are examined. There needs to be a 'facilitating environment' for such open debate to be available and possible. This implies, as I sketched out in Chapter 8, that public debate has an intrinsic value, that this has implications for the tolerance of different political differences, that diversity of views and opinions, provided one has access to the proper facts, is integral to politics, and that the political condition of *plurality* and freedom depends upon a commitment by all those concerned to maintain the common political world that guarantees rights to all citizens.

One could envisage such a *tolerance process* consisting of the following broad steps, which could provide the basis for a practical framework:

1. Tolerance is not just to be seen as an end-point but requires time to achieve. The very act of going through a process in itself potentially promotes tolerance. It goes without saying that for this process to even begin, there would need to be an atmosphere of respectful debate and a wish to examine uncomfortable realities, including a natural ambivalence towards the very

process itself. It requires tackling various *obstacles* to tolerance, including irrational states of mind. The tolerant public space needs to be open to all, while being guarded against the forces of intolerance. I have put forward *two basic limiting principles* to be applied on the part of both sides of a potential conflict; these limits may act in accord or be taken separately in any situation under consideration. The first limiting principle is the '*harm principle*', borrowed from J. S. Mill, my version of which states that one needs to tolerate people's practices, beliefs or values provided they do not significantly harm the current society and offend the basic rights of its citizens. The second principle limiting prejudice, based on the thinking of Rainer Forst and John Rawls, is the '*respect principle*', that is, that any actions towards others should be based on an assumption of mutual respect for different ways of life, based on a reasoned and empathic or at least sympathetic judgment of the other's behaviour, ideas, and values.

2. Tolerance requires a *movement* from 'object' to 'subject' tolerance. As I indicated, I am thinking here of the parallel with psychoanalytic treatment, where the analyst is part of a process of helping the patient 'become a subject'. As I have described, this form of tolerance requires a *tolerant imaginative internal space*, and it also implies that one *respects* the other and others as subjects *of* their experience, with agency and capacity for independent judgment.

3. Seeing the other as a subject, being open to otherness, requires some self-reflection, where otherness in oneself is seen as part and parcel of being human. In Kristeva's words: 'How could one tolerate a foreigner if one did not know one was a stranger to oneself?'

4. Tolerance also requires acts of reflective judgment, and a special kind of *enlarged mentality*, where one takes account of the views and judgment of others, putting oneself in the position of others in the hope of coming to an agreement. This is a form of common human understanding, requiring thought and imagination. As O'Neill maintains, there needs to be an *obligation* to protect free and open communication, both by enabling practices of tolerance, but also by paying attention to how intolerance can undermine free public communication. This involves a fundamental change in attitude of citizens towards their fellows, an act of *imagination*. One could characterize this shift as providing what I have described as a '*home for otherness*'. Tolerance, as Habermas maintains, is not indifference; it is a much more active process involving the burden for those who hold different world views to make the *effort to respect*, if not fully understand, other world views.

5. With regard to the specific issue of how such a process may apply to, for example, the current refugee and migrant crisis, I have suggested that there is a complex interaction between the psychic homes of refugee, or migrant, and host. The newcomer feels a stranger in a new environment, carrying within their own sense of psychic home (however ravaged by trauma) and the host may feel a fear of a loss of their secure sense of a psychic home as a result of being 'invaded' and 'enveloped' by all these strangers. The hope is that

naming these anxieties can provide a framework for *mutual adjustment and accommodation* on both sides, leading not to some perfect solution to the current crisis, but one that affords the hope of some positive way forward, where there is an increased and more respectful tolerance towards strangers.

6. It remains to be seen how these principles could be put into practice. There would need to be a structured programme of meetings between community representatives, a place where open discussion of issues takes place, and an agreed timeframe after which areas of agreement and disagreement could be outlined. But the first step is to change attitudes towards the issues at hand, and that requires an act of imagination, an enlarged internal tolerant space within individuals as well as between them.

REFERENCES

Adorno, T. and Horkheimer, M. (1947), *Dialectic of Enlightenment*. London and New York: Verso, 1997.
Anderson, B. (2006), *Imagined Communities* (Revised Edition). London and New York: Verso.
Anzieu, D. (1995), *The Skin-Ego* (trans.) N. Segal. London: Karnac, 2016.
Appiah, A. (2006), *Cosmopolitanism: Ethics in a World of Strangers*. London: Allen Lane.
Arendt, H. (1951), *The Origins of Totalitarianism*. San Diego, New York and London: Harcourt, Revised edition, 1967.
Arendt, H. (1958), *The Human Condition*. Chicago and London: University of Chicago Press.
Arendt, H. (1961), *Between Past and Future*. London: Faber and Faber, published in Penguin, 1977.
Arendt, H. (1963), *On Revolution*. London: Faber and Faber.
Arendt, H. (1970), *Men in Dark Times*. San Diego, New York and London: Harcourt.
Arendt, H.(1982), *Lectures on Kant's Political Philosophy*, ed. R. Beiner. Chicago: University of Chicago Press.
Bakewell, S. (2010), *How to Live. A Life of Montaigne*. London: Chatto and Windus.
Barenboim, D. (2003), in *Parallels and Paradoxes*, D. Barenboim and E. Said.London: Bloomsbury.
Barenboim, D. (2008), *Everything is Connected*. London: Weidenfeld and Nicolson.
Bauman, Z. (1993), *Postmodern Ethics*. Oxford: Blackwell.
Bauman, Z. (2004), *Identity*. Cambridge: Polity
Bauman, Z. (2016), *Strangers at our Door*. Cambridge: Polity.
Bayle, P. (1682), *Pensées Diverses sur l'Occasion de la Comète*, translated as *Various Thoughts on the Occasion of the Comet* (2000) by R. Bartlett. New York: SUNY Press.
Bayle, P. (1686), *A Philosophical Commentary*, ed. J. Kilcullen and C. Kukathas. Indianapolis: Liberty Fund.
Bayle, P. (1697), *Historical and Critical Dictionary*, selections, trans. by R. Popkin. Indianapolis and Cambridge: Hackett Publishing Company.
Benvenuto, B. and Kennedy, R. (1986), *The Works of Jacques Lacan: An Introduction*. London: Free Association Books.

Beiner, R. (1982), Interpretive essay, in *Lectures on Kant's Political Philosophy*, ed. R. Beiner. Chicago: University of Chicago Press.
Berlin, I. (1969), *Four Essays on Liberty*. Oxford: Oxford University Press.
Bloom, H. (1998), *Shakespeare, The Invention of the Human*. New York: Riverhead.
Bodin, J. (1583), *On Sovereignty*, ed. and trans. by J. Franklin. Cambridge: Cambridge University Press, 1992.
Bollas, C. (1992), The fascist state of mind, in *Being a Character*. London: Routledge.
Bostridge, I. (2011), *A Singer's Notebook*. London: Faber and Faber.
Bourdieu, P. (1990), Structures, habitus, practices, in *The Logic of Practice*. Cambridge: Polity.
Brown, P. (2000), *Augustine of Hippo* (Revised edition). Berkeley and Los Angeles: University of California Press.
Brown, W. (2008), *Regulating Aversion: Tolerance in the Age of Identity and Empire*. Princeton: Princeton University Press.
Brown, W. and Forst, R. (2014), *The Power of Tolerance. A debate*, ed. L. Di Blasi and C. Holzhey. New York: Columbia University Press.
Burleigh, M. (2006), *Sacred Causes*. London and New York: Harper.
Burleigh, M. (2010), *Moral Combat*. London and New York: Harper.
Canovan, M. (1988), Friendship, truth and politics: Hannah Arendt and toleration. In *Justifying Toleration*, ed. S. Mendus. Cambridge: Cambridge University Press.
Carens, J. (2013), *The Ethics of Immigration*. Oxford: Oxford University Press.
Cavell, S. (1979), *The Claim of Reason*. Oxford: Oxford University Press.
Cook, N. (2013), *Beyond the Score*. Oxford: Oxford University Press.
Crepell, I. (2008), Toleration, politics and the role of mutuality, in *Toleration and its Limits*, ed. M. Williams and J. Waldron, New York and London: New York University Press.
Cross, I. (2009), The evolutionary nature of musical meaning. *Musicae Scientiae*. 13(2): 179–200.
de M'Uzan, M. (2005), *Aux confins de l'identité*. Paris: Gallimard.
De Nora, T. (2000), *Music in Everyday Life*. Cambridge: Cambridge University Press.
Dent, N. (1988), Rousseau and respect for others. In *Justifying Toleration*, ed. S. Mendus. Cambridge: Cambridge University Press.
De Tocqueville, A. (1835), *Democracy in America*, trans. and abridged by H. Reeve.Oxford: Oxford University Press, 1946.
Dooley, B. (1999), *The Social History of Skepticism*, Baltimore and London: The Johns Hopkins University Press.
Durkheim, E. (1893), *The Division of Labour in Society*, trans. by W. Halls.London: Macmillan, 1984.
Edwards, E. (1988), Toleration and Mill's liberty of thought and discussion, in *Justifying Toleration*, ed. S. Mendus. Cambridge: Cambridge University Press.
Fenichel, O. (1940), Psychoanalysis of antisemitism. *American Imago*, 1B(2): 24–39.
Finley, M. (1954), *The World of Odysseus*. Harmondsworth: Penguin, 1979.
Forst, R. (2003), *Toleration in Conflict*, trans. by C. Cronin. Cambridge: Cambridge University Press, 2012.
Foucault, M. (2004), *Security, Territory, Population*, trans. by G. Burchell.London: Palgrave Macmillan, 2007.
Freud, S. (1919), The uncanny, in *The Standard Edition of the Complete Psychological Works of Sigmund Freud*, vol. 17, ed. J. Strachey. London: Hogarth, pp. 217–256.
Furedi, F. (2011), *On Tolerance*. New York and London: Continuum.
Goldie, M. (1984), The theory of religious intolerance in Restoration England, in *Persecution and Toleration*, ed. W. Sheils. Oxford: Oxford University Press, pp. 331–368.
Goody, J. (2006), *The Theft of History*. Cambridge: Cambridge University Press.

Goose, N. (2005), Xenophobia in Elizabethan and early Stuart England: an Epithet too far? In *Immigrants in Tudor and Early Stuart England*, ed. N. Goose and L. Lau. Eastbourne: Sussex Academic Press, pp. 110–135.

Gratier, M. and Trevarthen, C. (2007). Voice, vitality and meaning. *International Journal of Dialogical Science*, 2(1): 169–181.

Habermas, J. (1968), *Knowledge and Human Interests*, trans. by J. Shapiro.London: Heinemann, 1972.

Habermas, J. (2005), *Between Naturalism and Religion*, trans. by C. Cronin.Cambridge: Polity, 2008.

Hall, S. (1990), Cultural identity and diaspora, in *Identity and Difference*, ed. K. Woodward. London: Sage Publications, pp. 51–59.

Havel, V. (1986), *Living in the Truth*. London: Faber and Faber.

Hazard, P. (1935), *The Crisis of the European Mind*, trans. by J. Lewis May. New York: New York Review Books, 2013.

Heidegger, M. (1926), *Being and Time*, trans by J. Macquarie and E. Robinson.Oxford: Basil Blackwell, 1962.

Heidegger, M. (1971), *Poetry, Language, Thought*, trans. by A. Hofstadter. New York and London: Harper and Row.

Hobsbawm, E. (1990), *Nations and Nationalism since 1780*. Cambridge: Cambridge University Press.

Hollander, M. (2002), *An Entrance for the Eyes: Space and Meaning in Seventeenth-Century Dutch Art*. Berkeley: University of California Press.

Honneth, A. (2000), *Disrespect*. Cambridge: Polity, 2007.

Hughes, R. (1991), *The Shock of the New*. London: Thames and Hudson.

Israel, J. (1995), *The Dutch Republic: Its Rise, Greatness and Fall, 1447–1806*. Oxford: Oxford University Press.

Israel, J. (2001), *Radical Enlightenment: Philosophy and the Making of Modernity*. Oxford: Oxford University Press.

Israel, J. (2006), *Enlightenment Contested*. Oxford: Oxford University Press.

Israel, J. (2010), *A Revolution of the Mind*. Princeton and London: Princeton University Press.

Israel, J. (2011), *Democratic Enlightenment*. Oxford: Oxford University Press.

Jefferson, T. (1774), A summary of the rights of British America, in *Jefferson: Political Writings*, ed. J. Appleby and T. Ball.Cambridge: Cambridge University Press, 1999.

Jefferson, T. (1777), A bill for establishing religious freedom, in *Jefferson: Political Writings*, ed. J. Appleby and T. Ball.Cambridge: Cambridge University Press, 1999.

Jefferson, T. (1802), Letter to Messrs. Nehemia Dodge et al., in *Jefferson: Political Writings*, ed. J. Appleby and T. Ball.Cambridge: Cambridge University Press, 1999.

Judt, T. (2005), *Postwar. A history of Europe since 1945*. London: Heinemann.

Kant, I. (1784), What is enlightenment? In *Practical Philosophy*, trans. and ed. By M. Gregor. Cambridge: Cambridge University Press, 1996.

Kant, I. (1790), *Critique of Judgement*, trans, by J. Meredith. Oxford: Oxford University Press, 2007.

Katz, J. (1961), *Exclusiveness and Tolerance*. New Jersey: Berman House.

Kennedy, R. (1998), *The Elusive Human Subject*. London: Free Association Books.

Kennedy, R. (2007), *The Many Voices of Psychoanalysis*. London: Routledge and the Institute of Psychoanalysis.

Kennedy, R. (2014), *The Psychic Home, Psychoanalysis, Consciousness and the Human Soul*. London and New York: Routledge.

King, P. (1976), *Toleration*. London: George Allen and Unwin.

Kirschner, S. and Tomasello, M. (2010), Joint music making promotes prosocial behaviour in 4-year-old children. *Evolution and Human Behavior* 31(5): 354–364.
Kristeva, J. (1991), *Strangers to Ourselves*. New York: Columbia University Press.
Kukathas, C. (2003), *The Liberal Archipelago*. Oxford: Oxford University Press.
Kymlicka, W. (1995), *Multicultural Citizenship*. Oxford: Clarendon Press.
Lacorne, D. (2007), *Religion in America*, trans. G. Holoch. New York: Columbia University Press, 2011.
Lacorne (2016), *Les frontières de la tolerance*, Paris: Gallimard.
Lifton, B. (1994), *Journey of the Adopted Self*. New York: Basic Books.
Lifton, R.J. (1986), *The Nazi Doctors*. New York: Basic Books.
Lifton, R.J. (2003), *Superpower Syndrome*. New York: Nation Books.
Locke, J. (1689), *Letter on Toleration*, ed. R. Vernon.Cambridge: Cambridge University Press, 2010.
Locke, J. (1690), *An Essay concerning Human Understanding*, ed. P. Nidditch. Oxford: Clarendon Press, 1975.
Maalouf, A. (1996), *On Identity*, trans. By B. Bray.London: Harvill Press, 2000.
Makari, G. (2015), *Soul Machine*. New York and London: Norton.
Marcuse, H. (1969), Repressive tolerance, in *A Critique of Pure Tolerance*, R. P. Wolff, B. Moore, and H. Marcuse (eds.). Boston: Beacon Press, pp. 81–117.
Malloch, S. (1999), Mothers and infants and communicative musicality. *Musicae Scientiae*, Special Issue: 29–57.
Marshall, J. (2006), *John Locke, Toleration and Early Enlightenment Culture*. Cambridge: Cambridge University Press.
Mill, J. (1826), *The Principles of Toleration*. London: Hooper.
Mill, J.S. (1843), *The Logic of the Moral Sciences*. London: Duckworth, 1987.
Mill, J.S. (1859), *On Liberty*, in *Utilitarianism*, ed. G. Warnock.London: Fontana.
Mill, J.S. (1869), *The Subjection of Women*, in *On Liberty and The Subjection of Women*, ed. A. Ryan.Harmondsworth: Penguin, 2007.
Mill, J.S. (1873), *Autobiography*, ed. By J. Robson.Harmondsworth: Penguin, 1990.
Nisbet, H. (2005), Introduction to *Lessing: Philosophical and Theological Writings*. Cambridge: Cambridge University Press.
Nussbaum, M. (2008), *Liberty of Conscience*. New York: Basic Books.
Nussbaum, M. (2012), *The New Religious Intolerance*. Cambridge MA and London: Harvard University Press.
O'Neill, O. (1986), The public use of reason , in *Constructions of Reason*. Cambridge: Cambridge University Press, 1989.
O'Neill, O. (1990), Practices of toleration, in *Democracy and the Mass Media*, ed. J. Lichtenberg.Cambridge: Cambridge University Press.
O'Neill, O. (2015), *Constructing Authorities*. Cambridge: Cambridge University Press.
O'Neill, O. (2016), *Justice across Boundaries*. Cambridge: Cambridge University Press.
Orwell, G. (1946), Politics and the English language, in *Essays*, ed. J. Carey.London: Everyman Library, 2002.
Papadopoulos, R. (2002), Refugees, home and trauma, in *Therapeutic Care for Refugees*. Ed. R. Papadopoulos.London: Karnac.
Piaget, J. (1947), *The Psychology of Intelligence*, trans. by M. Piercey and D. Berlyne.London: Routledge, 2001.
Pinker, S. (1997), *How the Mind Works*. New York: Norton.
Plato (1930), *The Republic*, trans. by P. Shorey, Cambridge MA and London: Loeb Classical Library, Harvard University Press and Heinemann.
Parker, G. (2013), *Global Crisis*. New Haven and London: Yale University Press.

Popper, K. (1987), Toleration and intellectual responsibility, in *On Toleration*, ed. S. Mendus and D. Edwards. Oxford: Clarendon Press.
Rawls, J. (1971), *A Theory of Justice*. Oxford: Oxford University Press.
Rawls, J. (1993), *Political Liberalism*. New York: Columbia University Press.
Rawls, J. (1999), *The Law of Peoples*, Cambridge MA and London: Harvard University Press.
Rousseau, J.-J. (1755), *Discourse on Inequality*, in *The Social Contract and Discourses*, trans. by G. Cole.London: Everyman, 1973.
Rousseau, J.-J. (1762), *The Social Contract*, in *The Social Contract and Discourses*, trans. by G. Cole.London: Everyman, 1973.
Rybczynski, W. (1986), *Home: A Short History of an Idea*. New York: Viking Penguin.
Said, E. (1993), *Culture and Imperialism*. London: Chatto and Windus.
Schön, D. (1983), *The Reflective Practitioner*. New York: Basic Books.
Schutz, A. (1944), The stranger: an essay in social psychology. *American Journal of Sociology*, 49(6): 499–507.
Sebek, M. (1996), The fate of the totalitarian object. *International Forum of Psychoanalysis*, 5 (4): 289–294.
Sen, A. (2006), *Identity and Violence. The illusion of destiny*. Harmondsworth: Penguin Books.
Shapiro, J. (1996), *Shakespeare and the Jews*. New York: Columbia University Press.
Simmel, G. (1971), *On Individuality and Social Forms: Selected Writings*. Chicago and London: University of Chicago Press.
Smith, A. (1759), *The Theory of Moral Sentiments*, ed. R. Hanley.London: Penguin, 2009.
Sokol, B.J. (2008), *Shakespeare and Tolerance*. Cambridge: Cambridge University Press.
Solomon, R. (2007), *True to our Feelings*. Oxford and New York: Oxford University Press.
Spinoza, B. (1670), *A Theological-Political Treatise*, trans. R. Elwes.New York: Dover, 2004.
Spinoza, B. (1677), *The Ethics*, trans. by E. Elwes.New York: Dover, 1955.
Spinoza, B. (1678), Letter LXII, in *The Ethics*, trans. by E. Elwes. New York: Dover.
Steiner, J. (1993), *Psychic Retreats: Pathological Organizations in Psychotic, Neurotic and Borderline Patients*. London and New York: Routledge and Institute of Psychoanalysis.
Sylvester, D. (2000), *Looking Back at Francis Bacon*. London: Thames and Hudson.
Tomlinson, G. (2015), *A Million Years of Music*. New York: Zone Books.
Trainor, L. and Hannon, E. (2013), Musical development, in *The Psychology of Music*, 3rd edition, ed. D. Deutsch. London: Elsevier.
Vidler, A. (1992), *The Architectural Uncanny*. Cambridge, Mass. and London: MIT Press.
Villa, D. (2000), The development of Hannah Arendt's thought, in *The Cambridge Companion to Hannah Arendt*, ed. D. Villa. Cambridge: Cambridge University Press.
Von Humboldt, W. (1854), *The Spheres and Duties of Government*. On Line: oll.libertyfund.org/people/wilhelm-von-humboldt.
Voltaire (1734), *Lettres Philosophiques*, ed. F. Taylor. Oxford: Basil Blackwell, 1965.
Voltaire, (1763), *Treatise on Tolerance*, trans. S. Harvey.Cambridge: Cambridge University Press, 2000.
Voltaire, (1764), *A Philosophical Dictionary*, trans. J. Fletcher.Oxford: Oxford University Press, 2011.
Waldron, J. (1988), Locke, toleration and the rationality of persecution, in *Justifying Toleration*, ed. S. Mendus. Cambridge: Cambridge University Press.
Walzer, M. (1983), *Spheres of Justice*. New York: Basic Books.
Walzer, M. (1997), *On Toleration*. New Haven and London: Yale University Press.
Williams, B. (1999), Tolerating the intolerable, in *Philosophy as a Humanistic Discipline*. Princeton and Oxford: Princeton University Press.
Williams, R. (1664), *The Bloody Tenant of Persecution*, in Volume 3, *The Complete Writings of Roger Williams*. New York: Russell and Russell, 1963.

Winnicott, D. (1949), Mind and its relation to the Psyche-Soma, in *Through Paedatrics to Psychoanalysis*. London: Hogarth Press and Institute of Psychoanalysis, 1975.
Wolin, S. (2004), *Politics and Vision*. Princeton and Oxford: Princeton University Press, 2016.
Wood, M.M. (1934), *The Stranger, a Study in Social Relationships*. New York: Columbia University Press.
Zentner, M.R. and Eerola, T. (2010), Rhythmic engagement of infants with music. *Proceedings American Academy of Science* 107(13): 5768–5773.
Zizek, S. (2009), *Violence*. London: Profile Books.
Zizek, S. (2016), *Against the Double Blackmail*. London: Allen Lane.

INDEX

accommodation 53, 62, 117, 125–7, 128 ,129, 130, 145
Adams, J. 87
adoption 34–5
Adorno,T. 55
alienation 2, 26, 55, 84, 85, 87, 119
American Constitution 61, 68, 78, 88
American Revolution 88, 89, 92, 110
Anderson, B. 41
anti-Semitism 20, 51–4
Anzieu, D. 141
apocalyptic violence 27
Appiah, A. 25–6
Arendt, H. 29–30, 85, 88, 109–114
atheists 56, 72, 73, 75, 82, 90, 123
attachment 19, 24, 33, 35, 40, 42, 43, 140
Augustine, St. 50, 51, 67, 68, 72, 74, 81
Austen, J. 41
autonomy 4, 33, 40, 53, 62, 92, 130
Averroes, 51

Bacon, F. 38–9
banking 64
Baptists 64, 90, 93
Barenboim, D. 13, 38, 140
Bauman, Z. 1, 23, 39, 40
Bayle, P. 9, 51, 56, 66, 67, 72–6, 79, 101, 123, 131
Bentham, J. 99
Berlin, I. 105
Berlin Philharmonic 140
Bible 48, 49, 52, 59, 67, 81
Bill of Rights 89

blasphemy 75, 123
Bloom, H. 136
Bodin, J. 137
Bollas, C. 28
Bossuet, J-B 51
Braque, G. 25
brexit 30, 106
Brown, W. 12, 146
bureaucratic tolerance 53, 130
Burleigh, M. 28–9, 42

Calas, J. 77–81
Calvinism 66
Canovan, M. 111, 112
Carens, J. 23–4
Caribbean experience 42, 43, 88
Catholics 50, 55, 56, 66, 70, 72, 73, 76, 79, 80, 122
Cavell, S. 18
Charles II 63
China 10, 44, 55, 80, 81, 118
Christians 6, 20, 51, 52, 53, 61, 73, 81, 90, 93, 130
church 50, 54, 56, 61, 66, 68, 69, 70, 71, 72, 74, 79, 81, 89, 90, 91, 93, 94, 125
Cicero 49
citizenship 23, 24, 83, 117
civic religion 82, 83
Comedy of Errors 13, 18, 137–8
community 20, 22, 23, 24, 33, 42, 49, 52, 53, 59, 62, 66, 76, 84, 85, 86, 98, 99, 101, 107, 110, 111, 115, 119, 120, 121, 122, 123, 127, 129, 130, 140, 144, 145

Constantinople 53
conscience 47, 56, 61, 62, 64, 66, 68, 69, 70–6, 78, 89–93, 100–2, 116–7, 122–3, 126–7, 146
cosmopolitanism 25–6, 33
Cotton, J. 90, 91
Crepell, I. 124, 125
Cross, I. 14, 140

debate 9, 12, 61, 74, 83, 89, 103, 104, 106, 107, 109, 112, 113, 116, 118, 125, 144
Dent, I. 85–6
Descartes, R. 79, 87
dialogue 8, 13, 90, 110, 129, 140, 144
diaspora 42, 43, 53
Diderot, D. 83, 88
Dormont, R. 39
doubling of self 27
Dreyfus, A. 79
Durkheim, E. 84

Eastwood, C. 22
Edwards, J. 93
empathy 26, 27, 114, 128
Employment v Smith 127
Enlightenment 2, 3, 5, 10, 48, 51, 55, 56, 59, 80, 82, 83, 88, 92, 94, 100, 111, 113
entrainment 14, 138–9, 140, 141
Euripides 22
European Union (EU) 24
evil 6, 12, 22, 27. 49, 63, 73, 74, 75, 103, 104, 105, 133, 135
evolution 14, 19, 25, 86, 141

faith 3, 6, 49, 50–6, 58, 61, 62, 66–9, 72–5, 84, 91, 93, 94, 111, 123, 126, 130
fanaticism 74, 79, 81, 82
fascist state of mind 28
female genital mutilation 4, 123, 130
Fenichel, O. 20
Fideism 72, 76
First Amendment 89, 93
Forst, R. 5, 46, 51, 70, 72, 75, 91, 120, 121–4, 143, 145
foster care 16
freedom 4, 8, 18, 20, 22, 24, 37, 51, 54, 55, 56, 59, 61, 62, 64–6, 69, 72, 76, 78, 79, 89–93, 96, 100, 102, 103, 105, 106, 109, 111–3, 115–22, 129, 130, 133
freedom of movement 24
French Revolution 41, 78, 84, 88, 89
Freud, S. 17, 18, 85
fundamentalism 37, 69, 71

gay marriage 6,7, 122
Germany 20, 21, 29, 73, 83
ghetto 53–5, 124, 143
Glass, K. 107
God 1, 6, 20, 49, 50, 52, 58, 59, 60, 66, 68, 69, 70, 72, 73, 74, 78, 81, 82, 83, 90, 91, 92, 93, 126
Goody, J. 44
government 2, 5, 9, 47, 53, 56, 61, 62, 63, 68, 71, 76, 89, 92, 94, 96, 98, 101, 105, 128
Gratier, M. 139, 140

Habermas, J. 113, 119–21, 145
habitus 21
Habsburgs 53
Hall, S. 42–3
Hazard, P. 47, 64
harm principle 5, 6, 84, 96, 101–3, 118, 145
Havel, V. 30
Heidegger. M. 18
Henry IV (France) 51, 72, 121
heresy 47, 51, 64, 66, 75, 123
hijab 6, 73
Hindus 82
Hitler. A. 21, 27
Hobbes, T. 84, 87, 118
Hobsbawm, E. 41, 42
Holland 10, 56, 59, 60, 63, 64, 66, 67, 72, 73, 76
home 1, 9, 10, 13, 14, 16–26, 32–44, 48, 49, 54, 65, 73, 76, 85, 86, 115, 118, 121, 131, 136, 137, 140, 141, 145
home for otherness 19, 118, 143
homelessness 1, 17, 18
homescaping 14, 141
Homer 16–7, 38, 48
horizontal tolerance 67, 122, 143
Horkheimer, M. 55
hospitality 1, 17, 48, 49, 53
Huguenots 51, 66, 72, 73, 80, 122
Humboldt, W. 96, 97, 98
Hume, D. 87
Hutcheson, F. 87

Ibn Rushd (Averroes) 51
identification 33, 34, 35, 121
identity 1, 2, 7, 13, 16–8, 20, 21–4, 25, 26, 32–44, 62, 64, 85, 90, 94, 121, 123, 128, 129, 131, 134, 135, 137
imagination 6, 17, 42, 102, 114, 120, 124, 145
immigrants 2, 9, 10, 76
individuality 4, 33, 85, 86, 96, 99, 103, 104, 105, 135

infant 13, 19, 35, 62, 119, 120, 139, 140, 145
information 10, 11, 35, 47
intersubjectivity 14, 52, 119, 138, 139
intolerance 2, 3, 4, 5, 6, 7, 8, 9, 11, 20, 24, 25, 26, 28, 29, 33, 46, 47, 51, 55, 59, 62, 63, 64, 66, 67, 71, 72, 73, 74, 76, 78, 80, 81, 82, 83, 86, 90, 91, 100, 104, 111, 112, 116, 118, 126, 128, 131, 132, 133, 134, 143, 145
inwardness 62, 84
Iraq 23, 55
ISIS 27
Islam 25, 51, 53, 55, 64, 89, 130
Israel, J. 55, 56, 70, 88, 93

James II 63
Jesus 49, 50, 52, 74, 81, 84, 90
Jefferson. T. 88, 89, 92, 93
Jews 20, 42, 49, 50, 51–4, 64, 66, 70, 73, 81, 82, 90, 91, 92, 120, 130, 134
Judaism 48, 51, 54
judgment 8, 11, 26, 76, 87, 91, 103, 106, 112, 113, 114, 115, 118, 124, 127, 135, 143, 144, 146
Judt, T. 21
justice 22, 23, 58, 70, 78, 79, 84, 87, 91, 116, 118, 127

Kant, I. 112, 113, 114, 115
Katz, J. 51
King, P. 4
King Lear 134–5, 135
Koran 49
Kristeva, J. 18, 20, 124, 145
Kukathas, C. 128–31
Kymlicka, W. 129–30

Lacan, J. 33
laicity 6
Lacorne, D. 71, 90, 94
Lateran Council 5 2
Leone, S. 22
Lessing, G. 111–2
Levi-Strauss, C. 33
liberalism 3, 11, 12, 13, 63, 67, 76, 85, 96–107, 109, 114, 116, 117, 118, 120, 128, 129, 130
liberty 5, 9, 55, 56, 58, 59, 60–2, 69, 70, 73, 79, 90–2, 96, 99, 100–2, 103–6, 116, 117, 126, 127, 144
liberty of conscience 56, 62, 73, 91, 92, 116, 117, 126, 144
Lifton, B. 34–5
Lifton. R.J. 27, 28

limiting principles 5, 6, 13, 145
little ice age 10
Locke, J. 9, 56, 61–71, 72–6, 79, 80, 82, 83, 88–91, 100, 101, 124, 126, 127, 128
Louis XIV 72, 83
Luther. M. 50, 73, 122

Maalouf, A. 43
Madison, J. 88, 89
Maimonides, M. 51
Makari, G. 63
Malloch, S. 140
Marcuse, H. 12, 144
Marmontel, J-F. 99
McCarthyism 24–5, 76
Merchant of Venice 134
middle ages 20, 51
Mill, J. 97, 99, 144
Mill, J.S. 5, 47, 93, 96–108, 109, 111, 145
Miller, A. 91
millet system 53, 130
Mohammed 4
Montaigne, M. 74, 135
Mosques 53
mother 13, 35, 36, 140, 141, 142
mothers and babies 25, 37, 138, 141–2
multiculturalism 121
Muslims 6, 25, 53, 70, 73, 82, 120
mutual toleration 70, 72, 124
music 13, 14, 38, 54, 134, 138, 140–3
M'Uzan, M. 18, 37, 38

Nantes Edict 51, 72, 121
nationalism 42
nature 47, 60, 61, 62, 63, 70, 78, 82, 87, 92, 93, 94, 97, 105, 130, 131
naturalism 62, 86
nazis 26, 27, 28, 29, 42, 54, 119, 133
negative tolerance 146
Newton, I. 56, 63, 79, 88
North Korea 25, 27
Nussbaum, M. 25, 89, 91, 126, 128

object tolerance 5, 6, 124, 143
Odysseus, 16–7, 48
O'Neill, O. 113, 114, 115, 147
Orwell, G. 28, 115
Othello 133
otherness 1, 8, 13, 19, 25, 26, 39, 98, 118, 124, 134, 135, 138, 145
Ottomans 53, 55, 70, 130
overlapping consensus 13, 116, 117

Papadopoulos, R. 16, 17
Parker, G. 10

permission concept of tolerance 72, 120, 121, 122, 143
Picasso, P. 25
Pico della Mirandola 54
Piaget, J. 126
Pinker, S. 141
Plato 110
pluralism 13, 58, 61, 62, 93, 109, 111, 112, 114, 117, 121
polis 109–110
Pope Francis I 20
populism 9, 29, 44
positive tolerance 144
post truth 2, 47
power 5, 9, 12, 30, 36, 42, 59, 60, 62, 69, 72, 73, 76, 82, 84, 89, 92, 93, 99, 101, 102, 105, 106, 118, 120, 121, 122, 124, 128, 129, 130, 145, 146
prejudice 2, 3, 5, 8, 9, 20, 22, 58, 59, 61, 78, 100, 107, 114, 118, 128, 131, 135, 136, 147
psychic home 1, 17, 22, 32–7, 38, 42, 121, 131, 142, 147
psychic retreat 35
psychoanalysis 5, 12, 19, 20, 34, 49, 119
psychological tolerance 26, 46
public reason 115, 131
Puritans 90, 91

Quakers 64, 82, 90, 126, 127

racism 7, 12
Rawls, J. 2, 5, 113, 116–9, 145
reason 18, 55, 56, 59, 63, 69, 70, 72, 74, 75, 76, 78, 90, 81, 82, 83, 86, 87, 110, 113, 114, 115, 117, 118, 119, 120, 122, 123, 124, 131
refugees 16, 20
religious clothing 4, 13, 20, 21, 23, 64, 65
religious intolerance 3, 25, 60, 67, 72, 74, 78, 79, 104, 126
religious tolerance 2, 64, 65, 72, 88, 120, 121
Rembrandt 65
respect 4, 5, 6, 8, 13, 19, 24, 26, 27, 33, 35, 39, 41, 48, 64, 75, 76, 81, 85, 86, 87, 91, 93, 111, 116, 117, 118, 120–6, 128, 129, 133, 140, 145, 146, 147, 148
respect principle 5, 6, 13, 27, 118, 123, 147
revocation of Nantes Treaty 51, 72, 79, 122
Rhode Island 90, 91
Riefenstahl, L. 132
rights 5, 23, 24, 41, 53, 58, 59, 61, 62, 70, 71, 72, 89, 92, 93, 96, 100, 106, 112, 117, 120, 121, 122, 123, 127, 128, 129, 146, 147
Robespierre, J. 84, 85
Romeo and Juliet 133
Rousseau, J-J. 82, 83–7

Said, E. 40–1, 42
Samaritan 48, 81
Scalia, A. 126
Sebek, M. 29
self 1, 18, 25, 27, 28, 35, 38, 62, 76, 83, 85, 86, 101, 105, 119, 124, 128, 129, 136, 147
Sen. A. 43
Seneca 49
separation of church and state 68, 70, 89, 91, 93
sexuality 37, 39, 51, 66
Shakespeare, W. 13, 131, 134–40
Sherbert v Verner 126
Siegel. D. 24
Sikhs 120
Simmel. G. 22
skeptical tolerance 78
slavery 88, 92, 100
Smith, A. 87
social membership 24
social tolerance 101
Socrates 110
Sokol. B.J. 137, 139
soul 9, 14, 18, 49, 50, 51, 63, 68, 69, 70, 83, 91, 110, 143
Spinoza, B. 9, 56, 58–60, 62, 63, 75, 76, 83, 101
Stalin, J.21
State, the 4, 5, 6, 8, 9, 10, 23, 24, 30, 40, 41, 42, 53, 61, 62, 64, 68, 69, 70, 72, 73, 75, 82, 83, 84, 89, 91, 93, 96, 97, 101, 103, 105, 106, 109, 110, 115, 120, 121, 122, 127, 128, 146
state of society 86, 97–9
Steiner. J. 35
strangers 1, 8, 10, 17, 18, 19, 20, 22–6, 33, 34, 47, 48, 49, 64, 65, 66, 90, 131, 137, 146, 147, 148
stranger anxiety 19–20
subjectivity 34, 37, 115, 119, 140, 141
subject tolerance 5, 6, 8, 124, 143, 146, 147
Sunday Times 107
Supreme Court (US) 90, 94, 127
Sylvester, D. 39
symbolic order 33
sympathy 26, 80, 84, 88, 98, 128, 137
Syria 20, 21, 23, 53
Swift, J. 79

Taming of the Shrew 133
Taylor, H. 96
The Tempest 133
terrorism 8, 9, 27, 37, 72, 106
Thirty Years War 5, 53
Tocqueville, A. 99
tolerance (passim): acceptance component 5; bureaucratic 53, 130; framework 7; horizontal 67, 122, 143; and intolerance dynamic 2, 46, 63, 131; mutual 70, 72, 124; negative 146; object 5, 6, 124, 145; objection component 5; psychological 26, 46; permission 72, 120, 121, 122, 145; positive 146; process 12, 106, 145–8; religious 2, 64, 65, 72, 88, 120, 121; skeptical 78; social 101; subject 5, 6, 8, 124, 143, 146, 147; vertical 67, 122, 145
tolerant internal space 6, 12, 65
Tolerantia 49
Tomlinson, G. 14, 140
totalitarianism 8, 23, 25, 29–30, 42, 7 3, 84, 85, 109, 110, 111, 112, 115, 123, 134
totalitarian object 29
transference 35
trauma 17, 19, 20, 21, 22, 24, 29, 33, 42, 49, 135, 139, 145
Treaty of Westphalia 5
Trevarthen, C. 137. 139
Trump, D. 30, 106
tyranny 62, 99, 101, 104, 107
Twelfth Night 133

uncanny 17–8, 20, 21, 139
unconscious 14, 20, 33, 79, 105, 141, 143

veil 6
Venice 53–5, 134
vertical tolerance 67, 122, 145
Vidler, A. 18
violence 12, 27, 28, 43, 82, 87, 119, 129, 146
Voltaire 9, 62, 76, 78–88, 131

Waldensian Sect 64
Walzer. M. 2, 23
wars of religion 67, 72
Washington, G. 88, 126, 127
Wells, H.G. 25
West-Eastern Divan 14, 140
Whitfield, G. 93
William and Mary 63
Williams, B. 3
Williams, R. 89–91, 92
Winnicott, D. 35, 126, 142
Winter's Tale 133, 135
Wisconsin v Yoder 126
Wolin, S. 84–5
Wood, M.M. 23
work of the day 34

xenia 48

Zizek, S. 12, 26, 55
Zola, E. 79

TOLERATING STRANGERS IN INTOLERANT TIMES

In this interdisciplinary and wide-ranging study, Roger Kennedy looks at the roots of tolerance and intolerance as well as the role of the stranger and strangeness in provoking basic fears about our identity. He argues that a fear of a loss of attachment to one's home might account for many prejudiced and intolerant attitudes to refugees and migrants; that basic fears about being displaced by so-called 'strangers' from our precious and precarious sense of a psychic home can tear communities apart, as well as lead to discrimination against those who appear to be different.

Present day intolerance includes fears about the 'hordes' of immigrants confused with realistic fears about terrorist attacks, populist fears about loss of cultural integrity and with it a sense of powerlessness, and fearful debates about such basics as truth, including the so-called 'post truth' issue. Such fears, as explored in the book, mirror old arguments going back centuries to the early enlightenment thinkers and even before, when the parameters of discussion about tolerance were mainly around religious tolerance. There is urgency about addressing these kinds of issue once more at a time when the 'ground rules' of what makes for a civilized society seem to be under threat. Kennedy argues that society needs a 'tolerance process', in which critical thinking and respectful judgment can take place in an atmosphere of debate and reasonably open communication, when issues around what can and cannot be tolerated about different beliefs, practices, and attitudes in people in our own and other cultures, are examined and debated.

Tolerating Strangers in Intolerant Times, with the help of psychoanalytic, literary, social, and political thinking, looks at what such a tolerance process could look like in a world increasingly prone to intolerance and prejudice. It will appeal to psychoanalysts as well as scholars of politics and philosophy.

Roger Kennedy is a psychoanalyst in private practice in the UK and past president of the British Psychoanalytical Society. He was an NHS Consultant for 30 years at the Cassel Hospital and is now Chair of The Child and Family Practice. His previous Routledge books include *Psychoanalysis, History and Subjectivity*, (2002), *The Many Voices of Psychoanalysis* (2007), and *The Psychic Home* (2014).